Though sex workers can be among the most vulnerable in society, notions of tolerance and charity rarely extend to encompass them. In this timely book Sarah Kingston explores the tensions that exist between residents and sex workers, suggesting that stereotypes of stigma and deviance can combine to position sex workers and their clients as beyond the bounds of respectable society.

Though grounded in the context of contemporary prostitution policy in the UK, this book is sure to be of international import given the long-standing failure of governments to evolve regulations protecting the interests of landowners and residents without penalising sex workers.

Phil Hubbard, Professor of Urban Studies, University of Kent, UK

By examining prostitution from the vantage point of residents affected by the presence of prostitution in their neighborhoods, Sarah Kingston illuminates a dimension of struggles over sex work that has rarely been researched. A major, unique contribution to the literature on prostitution.

Ronald Weitzer, Professor of Sociology, George Washington University, USA

Policies restricting consensual adult prostitution are often justified in terms of the alleged negative effects on the communities that provide venues for 'the sex trade'. This book examines the empirical basis for this assumption by accessing and unpacking the complex attitudes to sex workers, their business partners, and clients, formed by those who live and work near them.

By drawing from her own ethnographic data and the work of other researchers, Kingston offers new ways of studying sex markets that will help public officials and concerned citizens rethink how societies suppress and regulate them.

Laurie Shrage, Professor of Philosophy and Women's and Gender Studies,
Florida International University, USA

Prostitution in the Community

Prostitution often causes significant anxiety for communities. These communities have been known to campaign against its presence in 'their' neighbourhoods, seeking the removal of street sex workers and their male clients.

Although research and literature has begun to explore prostitution from the standpoint of the community, there is no comprehensive text which brings together some of the current literature in this area. This book aspires to cast light on some of this work by exploring the nature, extent and visibility of prostitution in residential communities and business areas, considering the legal and social context in which it is situated, and the community responses of those who live and work in areas of sex work.

This book aims to examine current literature on the impacts of prostitution in residential areas and considers how different policy approaches employed by the police and local authorities have mediated and shaped the nature of sex work in different communities. It explores what communities think about prostitution and those involved, as well as studies the techniques and strategies communities have utilized to take action against prostitution in their neighbourhoods. This book will also demonstrate the diversity of public attitudes, action and reaction to prostitution in the community.

This book is a useful contribution for academics and researchers in the fields of Criminology and Sociology who wish to understand current policy initiatives surrounding the issue of prostitution in local, national and international community settings.

Sarah Kingston is Senior Lecturer in Criminology and Course Leader of the BA (Hons) Criminology degree at Leeds Metropolitan University. Her research interests focus on the sex industry, sexuality and prostitution policy. Her previous publications include *New Sociologies of Sex Work* (Ashgate, 2010) for which she was co-editor.

Routledge studies in crime and society

1 **Sex Work**
   Labour, mobility and sexual services
   Edited by JaneMaree Maher, Sharon Pickering and Alison Gerard

2 **State Crime and Resistance**
   Edited by Elizabeth Stanley and Jude McCulloch

3 **Collective Morality and Crime in the Americas**
   Christopher Birkbeck

4 **Talking Criminal Justice**
   Language and the just society
   Michael J. Coyle

5 **Women Exiting Prison**
   Critical essays on gender, post-release support and survival
   Bree Carlton and Marie Segrave

6 **Collective Violence, Democracy and Protest Policing**
   David R. Mansley

7 **Prostitution in the Community**
   Attitudes, action and resistance
   Sarah Kingston

Prostitution in the Community
Attitudes, action and resistance

Sarah Kingston

First published 2014
by Routledge
2 Park Square, Milton Park, Abingdon, Oxfordshire OX14 4RN

and by Routledge
711 Third Avenue, New York, NY 10017

First issued in paperback 2015

Routledge is an imprint of the Taylor & Francis Group, an informa business

© 2014 Sarah Kingston

The right of Sarah Kingston to be identified as author of this work has been asserted by her in accordance with sections 77 and 78 of the Copyright, Designs and Patents Act 1988.

All rights reserved. No part of this book may be reprinted or reproduced or utilized in any form or by any electronic, mechanical, or other means, now known or hereafter invented, including photocopying and recording, or in any information storage or retrieval system, without permission in writing from the publishers.

Trademark notice: Product or corporate names may be trademarks or registered trademarks, and are used only for identification and explanation without intent to infringe.

British Library Cataloguing in Publication Data
A catalogue record for this book is available from the British Library

Library of Congress Cataloging-in-Publication Data
Kingston, Sarah
Prostitution in the community: attitudes, action, and resistance / Sarah Kingston.
  pages cm. – (Routledge studies in crime and society)
  Includes bibliographical references.
  1. Prostitution--Social aspects. I. Title.
  HQ118.K56 2014
  306.74--dc23   2013015733

ISBN 13: 978-1-138-92240-2 (pbk)
ISBN 13: 978-0-415-68867-3 (hbk)

Typeset in Times New Roman
by Wearset Ltd, Boldon, Tyne and Wear

Contents

Preface		viii
Acknowledgements		ix
1	Introduction	1
2	Prostitution policy and the community	19
3	Researching the community	37
4	Community attitudes	54
5	The impact of prostitution on communities	78
6	Community action and resistance	97
7	Responding to community concerns: local authority and the police	124
8	Stigma management: the individual and the community	151
	Bibliography	167
	Index	197

Preface

This book has emerged from my masters and PhD research at the school of Sociology and Social Policy, University of Leeds, which was fully funded by the Economic Social Research Council 1+3 Competition Scholarship (PTA-030–2004–00805). This research sought to determine the concerns of communities affected by the presence of prostitution, primarily street prostitution, and perceptions of men who buy sex. I was particularly inspired by a critical appraisal of Pitcher *et al.*'s (2006) study of community views in five cities across England and Scotland. The study identified a comment made by a male resident regarding the safety of friends and family. This male resident said that he would often pick up female family members, rather than let them walk home late at night in areas of street sex work. These comments made me wonder what it was about men who buy sex on the street that prompted this man to act in such a manner. Were men who buy sex from women on the street perceived as dangerous?

From these initial questions, I began to consider how men who buy sex were perceived by the public and whether these constructions were mirrored by official discourse. The importance of the research became apparent from an examination of the *Coordinated Prostitution Strategy*, as the Home Office (2006) identified a key objective of challenging wider public attitudes. The political importance of achieving this objective was in the review on *Tackling Demand* in November 2008, as the government identified that changing public perceptions was key to tackling demand. Yet, despite these objectives, I questioned how the government knew what public perceptions were, given that no thorough review or survey was undertaken to determine public attitudes. It was with these critical questions that this research arose. From these foundations, this book has built upon this empirical research, as well as exploring further literature and research, which has unearthed the concerns, experiences, desires and distastes of 'communities' affected by the presence of prostitution in 'their' neighbourhoods.

Acknowledgements

This book would not have been made possible without the valuable input of the research participants and many others who have helped move this research forwards. The support and advice of Dr Teela Sanders, Moria Doolan and Dr Kirk Mann have guided and nurtured the research upon which this book was originally based. I would also like to give thanks to Professor Sylvia Walby, who, alongside Teela, offered me the opportunity to undertake my PhD at the University of Leeds. I would, furthermore, like to thank the many cited and unreferenced academics and writers who have contributed to my 'understanding' of this work, research and the field of prostitution research. My understanding must also be attributed to the many discussions and 'chin-wags' with fellow PhD students: Ana, Chris, Laura and Laura, Mark, Carole, Tom and Rachel, to name but a few. Thanks, guys! In the transitional period, I would like to say thank you to Professor Phil Hubbard, who helped me to develop the thesis into a book proposal. Further thanks go to Dr Natalie Hammond, Professor Colin Webster, Professor Terry Thomas and Professor Nick Frost for reading many chapters of the book and talking about my work. Last, but by no means least, I would like to thank my loving family: Mum, Dad, Christian, Leon, Steve and Andrea, my many aunties and uncles, cousins and grandparents, and friends Claire and Pam. Thank-you for accepting me for me. Your love, support and nurturing has coloured this book no end. This book is dedicated to the loving memory of Bettie Kingston and Ralph Armstrong Gardner. This is for you, Grandma and Grandad.

1 Introduction

Traditionally, United Kingdom (UK) research on prostitution has focused on female sex workers and not the managers of sex businesses or those who live near the spaces where sex is bought and sold. This 'fundamental flaw in sex work research' has resulted in the marginalization of the experiences and perceptions of those who live and work in areas of street sex work (Sanders 2008b: vii). This has occurred despite the safety and well-being of the local community frequently being cited as a justification for changes to the laws surrounding prostitution (Home Office 2006), with often punitive forms of policing being deployed in response to community complaints about sex work in their neighbourhoods (Matthews 2008).

In redressing this absence, research has sought to engage the wider community in determining which approaches are effective in reducing the level of street prostitution (Carter *et al.* 2003; Hester and Westmarland 2004). Further research has endeavoured to determine whether residential streets could exist as shared spaces for sex workers and residents (Pitcher *et al.* 2006) and has identified attempts by communities to tackle street prostitution through community activism (Hubbard 1998; Sagar 2005; Williams 2005). This research has highlighted a number of issues from people who live and work in areas of street sex work, such as concerns over environmental debris, the visibility of street sex workers and increases in traffic.

Although research and literature has begun to explore prostitution from the standpoint of the community, there is no comprehensive text that brings together the current literature in this area. This book aspires to cast light on some of this literature by exploring the nature, extent and visibility of sex work in residential communities and business areas, considering the legal and social context in which it is situated and the community responses of those who live and work in areas of prostitution. It will explore how sex work is managed by local stakeholders, both in national and international contexts, drawing on literature that considers the existence of prostitution in the community. The book aims to examine the current literature on the impacts of prostitution in residential areas and consider how different policy approaches have mediated and shaped the impacts of sex work in different communities and across a variety of national contexts. Finally, this book will utilize my Doctor of Philosophy (PhD) research, which explored community perceptions of prostitution and highlighted a number of important issues that have significant implications for criminal justice and policing. By doing so, this book will demonstrate the diversity of public attitudes, actions and reactions to prostitution in the community.

This book will, hence, be a useful resource for policymakers who wish to understand current policy initiatives in other local, national and international community settings, consider what communities think about the sex industry, how they have responded to it and what strategies they believe are best to deal with local concerns. This book will also be a useful resource for academics, students and researchers and will be a useful addition to existing knowledge on the impact of prostitution on local communities.

Why explore 'the community'?

Traditionally, the focus of prostitution research has centred on the figure of the female sex worker (Sanders 2008b). Academic literature has explored the experiences and practices of sex workers (Sanders 2005), their clients (Hammond 2010; Sanders 2008b) and, more recently, male and transgender sex workers (Whowell 2010), lap dancers (Hubbard 2012; Sanders and Hardy 2010; Billie 2012), transsexuals and transgendered individuals, fetish work and dominatrix services in the UK (Bloor *et al.* 1992; Brents and Hausbeck 2007; Elifson *et al.* 1993a; Elifson *et al.* 1993b; Harcourt *et al.* 2001; Kulick 1998; Valleroy *et al.* 2000). Yet, there has been an absence in UK research on prostitution, in that it has largely ignored the experiences and perceptions of those who live and work in areas of street sex work (Sanders 2008b).

This lack of research has occurred, despite 'the community' often being cited as a key factor in international policy approaches to prostitution, which, in the UK, has sought to criminalize activities associated with prostitution. As Crawford explains:

> 'Community' has become a policy buzz word. In the field of crime and criminal justice this emphasis upon 'community' has been particularly acute, as witnessed by the various initiatives in 'community policing', 'community based crime prevention', 'community mediation' and 'punishments in the community'. The attraction of the notion of 'community' transcends the established British political parties.
>
> (Crawford 1997: 44)

This focus on 'the community' is evident in recent UK policy documents. For instance, the political party in office at the time that the most recent UK prostitution policy documents were created, New Labour, emphasized the need to involve the community in developing local responses to prostitution. The Home Office consultation paper *Paying the Price* included a chapter, 'Protecting Communities', in which it explored the impact of prostitution on communities, community engagement and community solutions to tackling street prostitution

(Home Office 2004). Within the *Coordinated Prostitution Strategy* document, which, at the time of writing, was the UK strategy for dealing with prostitution, the Home Office identifies that:

> The community has a significant role to play in the development of an effective local response to prostitution. It will be important to ensure that residents are involved at a consultative stage so that their concerns are articulated and properly understood, and community representatives are involved in the development of the different strands of the strategy.
>
> (Home Office 2006: 15)

The problems identified by the Home Office included communities' serious concerns 'about the existence of local street-based prostitution.... Prostitute users will often mistakenly focus their attention on other women passing by' (Home Office 2004: 62). As a result, the government classified that 'the focus of enforcement will be on kerb-crawling to respond to community concerns and to reduce the demand for a sex market' (Home Office 2006: 9). Although the impact of street prostitution on local communities has been the main focus of political concern, the impact of indoor sex markets will also be considered in this book, due to an increase in indoor sex establishments throughout the UK and increasing legislative interventions in indoor sex markets (Sanders 2006a). Furthermore, research has identified community resistance and outrage towards the indoor sex industry (Hubbard 1998; Sanders 2005c), as well as more recent research that has explored people's attitudes to lap-dance and striptease clubs in towns and cities throughout England and Wales, which found that most people are only concerned by them if they are situated too near their own homes or local schools (Hubbard 2012).

Political focus on local communities is considered to be a core constituent of attempts to forge a new political agenda (Calder 2005). As Imrie and Raco (2003: 5) explain: 'discourses of community are pivotal in framing the policy agenda for cities, and at the core of New Labour's approach to the revitalization of cities is the revival of citizenship and the activation of communities to spearhead urban change'. Consulting communities is seen as 'vital in terms of identifying problems and finding solutions' (Home Office 2004: 63). The appeal to community partnerships, community policing and community consultations are nothing new and have evolved over the past few decades. As Crawford describes, when he explores the work of Beck (1992), Rose (1999) and Rhodes (1996), there has been:

> A pattern of shifting relations which involve: the fusion of, and changing relations between, the state, the market, and civil society; a move from 'the social' to 'community'; greater individual and group responsibility for the management of local risks and security; and the emergence of new forms of management of public services and structures for policy formation and implementation.... In contemporary appeals to 'community' and

4 *Introduction*

> 'partnerships', crime control is no longer conceived as the sole duty of the professional police officer or other criminal justice agents. Rather, it is becoming more fragmented and dispersed through state institutions, private organizations, and the public. Responsibility for the crime problem, according to current governmental strategies, is now everyone's. It is shared property.
>
> (Crawford 1997: 25)

The UK Government has been keen to encourage shared responsibility to prevent crime such as prostitution, in order to provide assistance to local police. The engagement in partnerships between the police and the community and the encouragement of 'multi-agency approaches' is supported within legislation and prostitution policy (Home Office 1998, 2004). In particular, the *Coordinated Prostitution Strategy* argues that 'strong partnerships' are needed to eradicate street prostitution from residential neighbourhoods (Home Office 2006). Such partnerships can be observed in Sagar (2005) and Williams' (2005) research, both of which explored how members of the community voluntarily patrolled their streets in small groups and reported their findings to the local police. The Street Watch schemes that they observed in Cardiff and a large city in the north of England were identified as being 'very much in line with current ideologies with regard to the future of policing ... particularly ... in the form of "active citizenship"' (Williams 2005: 527).

In this sense, 'the community' are sometimes able to shape local politics and inform how local police deal with prostitution in the community. As a result, 'the community' can often influence and inform how, when and where the sex industry operates, by shaping governmental policy through consultations, protest and activism. This book will explore how attitudes can inform policy and how community protests and activism can displace prostitution to other areas. Yet, it is important that this new emphasis on encouraging the community to take action in terms of crime prevention considers the implications that this may have in terms of legitimacy, accountability and justice, as Crawford describes:

> New patterns of local governance ... evoke key questions about the legitimate responsibilities of individuals, organizations and the state; the regulation of social conflicts; the nature of organizational and democratic accountability; and notions of social justice.
>
> (Crawford 1997: 6)

Key questions, therefore, need to be asked about those individuals and groups who take to the streets to protest against prostitution. For instance, how are these protests being monitored? Who are involved and why? And what will be done to those who go beyond protest and commit acts of violence or act in a threatening way? Furthermore, these strong partnerships are generally only locally based and often do not extend beyond the geographical boundaries of a 'community'.

Therefore, only certain individuals are considered to be part of 'the community', and it is often assumed that sex workers and their clients are not part of this group.

Locating the 'community'

With an increased emphasis on community engagement and collaboration, an understanding of what constitutes a community is needed, in order to direct services and intervention where appropriate (MacQueen *et al.* 2001). The lack of an accepted definition can result in 'different collaborators forming contradictory or incompatible assumptions about community and can undermine our ability to evaluate the contribution of community collaborations' (MacQueen *et al.* 2001: 1929).

The notion of what constitutes a 'community' is arguably 'somewhat of a chameleon concept', due to the diversity of explanations (Fielding 2005: 460). As a concept or ideological assumption, determining what constitutes a community is problematic, due to the difficulty in specifying its definition precisely (Cohen 1985; Young 1995). Its use 'has become so pervasive in our everyday language that its meaning is overlaid with a host of associations and emotions' (Hawtin *et al.* 1994: 38). Despite this diversity, the term has been widely utilized as a tool of social policy (Bentley *et al.* 2003; Rose 1999) and linked to notions of active citizenship, mutual obligation, self-discipline and individual responsibilities (McLaughlin *et al.* 2001; Worley 2005). Yet, use of the term has often been undertaken without asking: 'what do we mean by our community?' (Partington 2005: 241).

Bellah *et al.* define community as:

> A group of people who are socially interdependent, who participate together in discussion and decision making, and who share certain practices that both define the community and are nurtured by it. Such a community is not quickly formed. It almost always has a history and so is also a community of memory, defined in part by its past and its memory of the past.
> (Bellah *et al.* 1985: 333)

A common definition of community is a group, section of the population or participants, who have a constituted set of social relationships based on something they have in common (Hawtin *et al.* 1994; MacQueen *et al.* 2001; Marshall 1994). Additionally, McMillan and Chavis (1986: 9) define community as 'a feeling that members have of belonging, a feeling that members matter to one another and to the group, and a shared faith that members' needs will be met through their commitment to be together'. Social responsibility, personal development and shared experience have all also been identified as characteristics of a community (Abu-Lughob 1995). Others have defined community as the result of interaction between people that are brought together by similar interests and common goals (Westheimer 1998). According to Rovai (2002), definitions such as these suggest that the most essential elements of community include mutual interdependence among members, a sense of belonging, connectedness, spirit, trust, interactivity, common expectations, shared values and goals, and overlapping histories among members.

Common characteristics may also form the basis of a sense of community, such as gender, age, ethnicity, nationality or religious beliefs. These characteristics may be seen as part of the collective identity of the community members and create a sense of belonging from common bonds, such as the sharing of a social problem (Hawtin *et al.* 1994). Communities may, therefore, be based upon a collective gain to remove street prostitution from a specific area. This has been observed in parts of the UK where community activists and vigilante groups have been united in their desire to remove street sex workers from residential streets, with campaigns hailing: 'prostitutes out' (Haslam 2004: 1); 'No hookers here please' (Asian News 2005: 1). However, sex workers often live in the areas in which they work, and previous research has engaged with sex workers in light of their criticism of Home Office recommendations for community conferencing (Hubbard *et al.* 2007).[1]

Yet, when a community is considered to be what people do together, rather than the means in which they come together, the notion of what constitutes a community is separated from geography and the physical environment (Wellman 1999). As Friedman argues, however:

> It must also be remembered that nonvoluntary communities of place are not without value. Most lives contain mixtures of relationships and communities, some given/found/discovered and some chosen/created. Most people probably are ineradicably constituted, to some extent, by their communities of place, their original families, neighborhoods, schools, churches and nations.
>
> (Friedman 1995: 203)

This sense of commonality may be based on geographical locations that range in size, such as a single street, villages, districts, parishes, counties and nations (Hawtin *et al.* 1994; Mullan *et al.* 2004). Those who work in the community, but do not necessarily live in the area, may also be seen to be part of a community; for example, doctors, nurses and teachers that work in the locality of the community, but do not live in the area. Therefore, under this definition of a community, street sex workers may be seen as part of a community, as often sex workers operate within a specific geographical location. However, the notions of community implied by the Home Office (2004, 2006), and the characteristics that determine what a community constitutes, do not appear to involve street sex workers, their clients, pimps or drug dealers.

For the purposes of this book, when I discuss my empirical research, 'the community' is defined as including residents, businesses, local authority officials and the police from two separate geographical sites in Leeds, West Yorkshire, UK. My research sought to identify key stakeholder groups, who were seen to represent 'the community'. Although their social position and status may change – i.e. the police or business employees may be identified as residents in different contexts – people were identified as being from one particular group, according to the location of the research and their role/status within the geographical boundaries of the research location: Area 1 or Area 2. This, as will be shown, has important implications for our understanding of attitudes, action and impact, because geography and its relationship to identity influences how people perceive and respond to prostitution.

Social obligations of 'the community'

Concerns about the community must be situated within a context of the rise and popularity of communitarianism, as it is widely accepted that political thinking has been somewhat underpinned by communitarian ideas (Calder 2005; Fremeaux 2005; Prideaux 2005).[2] Much discussion around communitarian values has highlighted the work of Amatai Etzioni, whose definition of a community emphasizes social interaction as a means of social control:

> Communities are social webs of people who know one another as persons and have a moral voice. Communities draw on interpersonal bonds to encourage members to abide by certain values.... Communities gently chastise those who violate shared moral norms and express approbation for those who abide by them.
>
> (Etzioni 1995: ix)

Communitarianism is said to represent 'a tradition concerned with the revival of social structures that will enable strong bonds to be forged between individuals and broader collectives' (Imrie and Raco 2003: 7).[3] The community is seen to be key to meaningful social interaction and the basis for the distribution of social obligations and responsibilities (Imrie and Raco 2003). Through active citizens in the context of the community, citizens are transformed 'from passive recipients of state assistance into active self-sustaining individuals' (Clarke 2004: 448). Such activation within communities is encouraged within the prostitution policy consultation document, *Paying the Price*, in the form of community engagement and Crime Reduction Partnerships.

Coupled with this empowerment and community activism, members are considered to be responsible citizens. Members of communities within areas where street prostitution persists are encouraged to take responsibility for 'reclaiming their streets' (Home Office 2004: 63). In reclaiming their streets, any action taken or choices made must, however, be exercised responsibly. Such choices are moralized and framed in the context of reasonable behaviour and reasonable choices (Clarke 2004), an illustration of which can be seen by the Home Office in *Paying the Price*, where it is stated that 'it is important that such community action should not slide into vigilantism or the aggressive persecution of already vulnerable women' (Home Office 2004: 63).

Critiques of this focus on the community argue that community engagement is limited, as it is unlikely to engage with disengaged and disaffected people. Others argue that decisions are likely to be made by powerful groups behind closed doors (Miller 2001). This raises questions about who the community is made safe for and why. Furthermore, communities often create social boundaries and a sense of 'us and them', which can lead to social segregation and exclusion (Young 1995). Sex workers are often not considered to be part of these communities and are often cast as outsiders – those to be displaced and removed. Therefore, 'community' is not just 'a word to describe our understanding of connected human relationships, but of power, of control and of change' (Robson 2000: 1). Therefore, the existence of this power and control suggests that, within communities, there exists a balance between coercion and consent (Robson 2000). At different times, this balance may slide either way and provide some explanation for diverse community responses to street prostitution in the UK. This reinforces Michel Walzer's (2002) claim that civil society creates unequal power relationships and, thus, behind the appearance of a cohesive community, there may be great inequality and dissent.

The notion of a 'community' is, therefore, not without criticism. The belief that communities are cohesive and share common values is questionable. Furthermore, who makes a community and what a community constitutes is known to shift and change over time. For instance, the dramatic changes with people moving from traditional communities, such as those characterized by agriculture and farming, to cities where many diverse individuals and groups lived and worked together demonstrate the degree of social change and the impact that it can have on individuals and groups. In traditional communities, people lived their lives within small social circles, in which most shared values and were known to each other, whereas, in cities, people could remain anonymous and often held different belief systems (Simmel 2000).

Durkheim's (1893) seminal work explored the scale and rapidity of social change and made a distinction between what he termed mechanical and organic solidarity within society. In mechanical societies, typically found in traditional communities, cohesiveness depends on a collective conscience, underpinned by a common core of values and moral rules, allowing little scope for individuality or dissent. In contrast, within organic societies, found particularly in socially diverse areas of modern cities, solidarity is maintained by both a collective conscience and economic interdependence and does not depend in the same way on homogeneity of belief, rituals and intolerance of those who do not conform to social norms.

Clearly, this change to organic solidarity could lead to social conflict and disagreement as diverse subcultures and individuals attempt to live together (Durkheim 1893). More recent work further supports these suggestions, as people are increasingly becoming more self-reliant and see themselves more as individuals than as part of a group. Tonnies (1955) classic work, *Community and Association*, described and analysed a shift from agrarian – feudal to capitalist – urban societies; the movement from Gemeinschaft (Community) to Gesellschaft

(Society of Individuals and Association). His work describes the consequent alleged decline in 'community'. This idea is also evident in Bauman's (2000) work, where he has described contemporary society as a period of 'liquid modernity', in which traditional forms of solidarity are being eroded, and people are less embedded in local networks.

Therefore, how we define 'community' is important, as when we talk about communities, we are often not always talking about communal solidarity, but more about individuals who come together and reproduce or modify social and structural patterns. Symbolic Interactionists, such as Mead (1967), suggest that individuals are very much involved in their own socialization. As Charon further explains:

> Human action not only is caused by social interaction but also results from interaction *within* the individual. Our ideas or attitudes or values do not influence what we do as much as the active process of thinking does. We act according to how we think; we act according to the way we *define the situation* we are in, and although that definition may be influenced by others with whom we interact, it is also the result of our own definition.
> (Charon 2009: 41 [emphasis added])

Thus, although individuals and the sense of 'the self' are created through social interaction, so, too, is society created through social interaction. Those who come together to form 'the community' can thereby influence the social world, while, at the same time, being influenced by it. Therefore, this does not suggest that commonalities do not occur; rather, that assumptions should not be made about the cohesiveness of communities, as they are continuously subject to modification and change.

Attitudes, action and resistance

This book explores the issue of prostitution from the standpoint of 'the community'; namely, those who live and work in areas of sex work. Based upon my PhD research, which explored community attitudes towards men who buy sex, in addition to a review of internet newspaper articles and reflections on research and literature in this area, it documents community responses to prostitution in local communities, both nationally and internationally, their attitudes to prostitution and the impact it can have.

Attitudes

Determining the attitudes of local and national communities has had significant implications for policy and law surrounding prostitution, in terms of shaping law and how the state seeks to change these views. In the UK, the Policing and Crime Bill 2009, which included a new strict liability offence of paying for sex with someone who has been subjected to force, deception or threats, was introduced in the context of concerns over public attitudes towards prostitution (Home Office 2009). Identifying the reasons why the UK Government would not follow the Swedish model, where it is a criminal offence to buy sex, the Home Office concluded in its review on tackling demand that 'it would be a step too far at this time, given the relative size of the UK sex industry compared to that in Sweden and current public attitudes in the UK' (Home Office 2008: 13). The aim of the Swedish Prohibiting the Purchase of Sexual Services Act 1999 was to reduce levels of prostitution and trafficking in women through tackling demand (Home Office 2008).

In the UK, it was suggested that 'public attitudes are currently much more divided' than in Sweden, but that 'over time the Swedish public grew to support the proposed legislation' (Home Office 2008: 13). The findings of the *Sex and Exploitation Survey* conducted in January 2008 for the government indicated that attitudes towards making paying for sex a criminal offence were divided (Wintour 2008). As a result, the government argues that 'it needs to work to challenge the attitudes of the sex buyers and the public as a whole before criminalizing the purchase of sex' (Home Office 2008: 13). In particular, a key objective of the Home Office's (2006: 13) *Coordinated Prostitution Strategy* was to challenge 'a general perception that prostitution is the "oldest profession" and has to be accepted'.

Previous research on public attitudes towards the sex industry has shown a division, although this research was not considered in the context of the 2009 law change. For example, Pitcher *et al.*'s (2006) study across five major cities in the UK has demonstrated communities' increasing intolerance of visible forms of prostitution, but also, in some instances, toleration of the industry is apparent. Community intolerance was observed in Williams (2005) and Sagar's (2005) research, where communities protested against street prostitution in their local areas. Yet, tolerance of visible forms of prostitution has also been identified in Liverpool, where local people were consulted about implementing a tolerance zone in the city (Bellis *et al.* 2007).

A division in attitudes can also be observed in feminist thought. Debates about sex work have predominantly revolved around a polarized argument that 'constructs sex work as either exploitive or liberating and, sex workers as coerced victims or empowered whores' (Wahab 2002: 51). Although there are many grounds upon which feminists respond to prostitution, the most divisive distinction in feminist thinking is between those who seek the abolition of prostitution in any form and pro-sex worker's rights' feminists, who wish to improve prostitution as it is currently practiced – i.e. the abolitionist sex-as-work debate.[4]

The abolitionist approach is argued most forcefully by radical feminists, such as Kathleen Barry (1984), Sheila Jeffreys (1997), Carole Pateman (1989) and Katherine MacKinnon (1989). They reject the notion that women freely choose to sell sex, as prostitution is considered as the institutionalization of women's dependence on men and is therefore exploitative and inherently violent and oppressive. In contrast, the sex-as-work stance advocated by pro-sex workers' rights or liberal feminists, such as Valerie Jenness (1993), believe that most women engaged in prostitution have made a conscious decision to sell sex.

According to Outshoorn (2005), the difference between the two positions stems from their conflicting views of male and female sexuality. In the 'sex work discourse', male sexuality is unquestioned and deemed as a given (Outshoorn 2005). In contrast, male sexuality is considered as the problem from the radical perspective, as it is seen to be predicated on the domination of women (Outshoorn 2005; Sanders 2008b). Thus, men who buy sex are considered a 'prostitution user' (Jeffreys 1997: 4) – an analysis that, according to O'Connell Davidson (2003), likens men who buy sex with rapists.

From the abolitionist perspective, prostitution is seen as 'the absolute embodiment of patriarchal male privilege, clearly disallowing feminist support or participation' (Kesler 2002: 219). Radical feminists, by denying women's agency, see prostitution as an institution that serves to underpin and reinforce women's subordination under a system of male supremacy. The notion that women choose to sell sex is thus rejected, as radical feminists suggest that the gendered nature of the sex industry is the result of the institutionalization of a gendered hierarchy, which seeks to privilege and normalize male sexual desire. Apparently, men buy sex and women sell access to their bodies, because they have been socialized into a specific gender order, which reduces women to sexual commodities. Therefore, for radical feminists, prostitution epitomizes men's domination over women. Men who buy sex are, therefore, sexual exploiters.

Such an analysis has, however, been criticized for reducing prostitution to gender, as often female clients and sex tourists are ignored (Sánchez-Taylor 2001). These gendered assumptions about who buys and sells sex have permeated throughout UK culture, as well as throughout political discussion, policy and law. Sánchez-Taylor (2001) suggests that the theoretical privileging of gendered power ignores radicalized and economic power, which may explain the existence of female sex tourism. The privileged economic status of Western women enables them to 'exercise' their economic power over impoverished men – a position traditionally absent from Western societies. Furthermore, scholars have identified that the sex worker–client interaction is not one-dimensional and that men who buy sex may also be exploited. Moving away from the assumption that the act of paying for sex is exploitative, some have suggested that the act of paying for sex acts may be viewed as submissive. By paying for sex, men are conceding that they are unable to engage in non-commercial sex (Earle and Sharp 2008). Furthermore, male power and sexual privilege is questioned by research that demonstrates that, for some men who buy sex, sex workers' mutual sexual pleasure is a priority (Sanders 2008b). Thus, as O'Connell Davidson (1998: 16) points out: 'power relations involved in prostitution are far more complicated than those argued by abolitionist feminists, wherein the view of power is uni-dimensional'.

As with any form of work, there are many reasons why women sell sex. Economic reasons are, however, often the most commonly cited reasons for women's entry into prostitution (Matthews 2008; O'Neill 1997; Phoenix 2008;

12 Introduction

Weitzer 2007). Although women enjoy greater access to education and employment than in the past, women are 'still circumscribed by the same dynamics of inequality that have existed for centuries. These dynamics continue to structure women's poverty and their economic dependency on men' (Phoenix 2006: 78). Thus, as Phoenix argues:

> It should come as no surprise, therefore, that adult and young women report that involvement in prostitution provides them with a means to get money to buy things that they cannot otherwise afford (such as consumables), to fund drug and alcohol problems (both their own and their partner's) and as a means of supporting themselves and their dependents.
> (Phoenix 2006: 79)

From this standpont, structural inequalities are seen to shape women's entry into prostitution, but, ultimately, they deemed to have some agency.

Although it is suggested that feminist thinking has been deeply divided on the issue, there are some who sympathize with both sides of the debate. O'Connell Davidson (1998), for example, finds the sex work and abolitionist lobbies bitter and hindering, as someone who agrees with elements of each argument. Thus, attitudes towards prostitution are not always 'straightforward'; instead, as will be shown, they are complex and often contradictory. They are informed by multiple factors, and, thus, sometimes a person's attitudes seem confused. This book seeks to explore some of these complex views and examine some of the factors that may inform them.

Action and resistance

Often people's attitudes can lead to action, both by those 'officially' permitted to take action to deal with prostitution, such as the police and local authority officials, but also by residents and businesses. Such action has included policing crackdowns and increased law enforcement, creating gated communities and designing public spaces in ways that exclude certain individuals and groups, making complaints and reporting incidents to the local police to take action and mobilizing in groups to deter prostitution from local streets. The types of action taken by the community will be explored in this book, as well as considering the reasons why action is taken and why sometimes it is not.

Community action can have a direct impact on policy and law, as well as how local police and officials respond to community concerns. For example, concerns over forced marriages in the UK led to activism from groups such as Southall Black Sisters, Newham Asian Women and Bradford Freedom Charity, who protested local councillors to take action, eventually leading to the Forced Marriage (Civil Protection) Act 2007 (Home Office 2007b). Clearly, then, community action can have a direct effect on policy and law.

'Community' action has been encouraged by the UK Government through partnership working, encouraging citizens to take greater control over communities. Appeals to community and partnerships were observed in the 1990s, alongside increasing governmental interest in crime prevention. Policing the community is seen to involve a broad range of activities undertaken by individuals and groups other than the police (Bayley and Shearing 1996; Jones and Newburn 1998). This 'pluralization' of regulation and law-enforcement activities can be observed in commercial security (Jones 2009), new forms of public sector policing, such as local authority patrol forces and neighbourhood wards (Crawford 2003; Loader 2000), increases in 'informal' policing in the form of vigilantism and pressure groups (Johnston 1996) and the emergence of new policing forms that exist over and above the state (Sheptycki 2000). Yet, with this pluralization of policing and encouragement of greater community involvement in partnership working and by taking action, questions need to be raised about how such actions can be made accountable. Policing can only be effective when it is made accountable to the local community, through public consultation, democratic accountability and public cooperation (Kinsey *et al.* 1986).

Furthermore, community action can also impact on the health, safety and well-being of those involved in prostitution, as action to remove street prostitution from an area may lead to prostitutes and their clients taking greater risks to avoid police prosecution or steer clear of potential violence from vigilante groups. Previous research has demonstrated how the criminalization and policing of sex work has led sex workers and their clients to move to unknown locations or take less time screening clients, which can increase the risk of violence and abuse (Sanders 2005c).

Exploring the action taken by local communities therefore raises issues around citizenship, belonging and identity, as well as concerns around legitimacy, accountability and justice. In taking action, 'you get the sense that by participating you are part of something larger, engaged in efforts bigger than yourself, defining your own identity by your participations in the construction of a larger community through collective action' (Meher 2002: 10). Through this participation, those involved often self-identify as a collective group and those whom participation is aimed against are considered 'outsiders'. Therefore, the action and its outcome are driven by the needs and desires of the group, and those who do not belong are ignored. As such, the action taken in areas known for prostitution has important implications, as the action often determines who the area is made safe for.

Cultural context and the social order

The cultural context in which prostitution is situated is crucial to understanding how it is perceived and responded to within society. As members of a community, people acquire culturally specific knowledge about codes of conduct, such as the expectations and norms of good behaviour, through socialization. These social rules are not universal and are mediated by a specific cultural context, which includes everyday social interactions, as well as public discussions and debates, the media and policy. Community members therefore learn what appropriate and inappropriate behaviour is, often acting in ways that conform to these social rules.

Prostitution is one activity that, in the UK, often disrupts social order, as it goes against what is deemed acceptable moral and legal behaviour. Sex workers and their clients are seen to deviate from accepted norms around sexual behaviour. Female sex workers are, consequently, subject to the 'whore stigma' (Pheterson 1993: 39) and often associated with disease, dirt and pollution, which can fuel hostile attitudes and acts of violence (Kinnell 2008). As Sanders and Campbell (2007: 3) explain: 'There is a historical, cultural endurance of intolerance and hostility towards street workers fostered by a general culture of distaste and disrespect towards women who sell sex.' Thus, prostitution is often stigmatized, and those who are involved are considered 'others' or 'outsiders' to 'the community'.

This stigma is perpetuated in everyday interactions and is also enshrined in law. In the UK, prostitution is not illegal per se, but the activities that surround it are illegal. In this context, those who are involved in prostitution are considered 'offenders' and become stigmatized, effectively taking on a 'spoiled identity' (Goffman 1963: 11). The law, by identifying deviance and illegality, separates 'criminal' from 'non-criminal' individuals and groups, thereby casting them as different. As Meher argues:

> The process of turning physical features or social practices into 'identities' is forged from the interaction between people and that state. By forcing some people to sit in the back of the bus, wear a yellow star, or hide their sexual orientations, states create the conditions in which particular identities develop. States can create identities be enforcing or prohibiting religious or sexual practices, by regulating access to social goods, and by setting rules of interaction between individuals and groups. Within these parameters, activists choose how to define themselves, by alliances, claims and tactics.
> (Meher 2002: 5)

Yet, in others countries around the world, prostitution is not always stigmatized in the same way, and, in some instances, the practice of paying for sex and being a prostitute is considered to be part of that society. The cultural context of places such as Pattaya (Thailand), Las Vegas (Nevada, US), Amsterdam (Netherlands) and New South Wales (Australia) being places commonly associated with prostitution, because of the visible and extravagant sexual landscapes, can often be crucial in terms of how people perceive prostitution and those involved. Because these locations are saturated with sexual images and the offer of sexual transactions for money is openly displayed and discussed, it has been suggested that this atmosphere leads to the normalization of prostitution. People who live and visit these locations thus consider prostitution to be a normal aspect of everyday life in these areas.

The legal context can also inform how prostitution is responded to within society. Jakobsson and Kotsadam (2011) argue that different policy regimes may influence attitudes towards prostitution. Their research suggests that:

Norwegians are more positive than Swedes ... possibly due to, their different legal histories, and we propose that Swedes are more negative toward buying sex than Norwegians. One possible explanation would suggest that Sweden might have made buying sex illegal earlier than Norway as a result of being more negative toward buying sex. Alternatively, living under this law for several years may have made Swedes more negative toward buying sex. Norwegians think it is more morally justifiable to buy sex, as hypothesized.

(Jakobsson and Kotsadam 2011: 37)

Brehman's (2010) research also explored whether legality and proximity to legal prostitution contributes to attitudes towards prostitution – in particular, whether living near Las Vegas, where prostitution is legal and regulated, led to a positive perception of prostitution. He conducted a survey with 315 male undergraduate students from the University of Nevada, Las Vegas, and 260 male undergraduate students from the University of British Columbia. Brehman (2010) found that over 50 per cent of male students from the University of Nevada would accept their son visiting a prostitute, whereas 82 per cent of students from the University of British Columbia would disagree. However, the fact that both groups of students from these universities would equally disapprove of their daughter choosing to become a prostitute demonstrates that legality is not the sole reason for these attitudes. Rather, it is often the cultural norms and values attributed to the types of engagement involved in prostitution. In line with the historical vilification of prostitutes, which will be explored later in detail, women's engagement in prostitution is stigmatized, whereas men's engagement has been normalized and accepted for many years. Overall (1992) has argued that sexuality and gender are socially constructed and based upon patriarchal, heterosexual notions of male sexual desires. It is clear from a close examination of the attitudes expressed in Brehman's survey that they reflect many stereotypes and myths that surround prostitution and those involved. Both questions and answers given reflect many assumptions made about prostitutes; namely, that they are immoral, disreputable, drug addicts and have psychological problems.

It is through these comparisons that the importance of the cultural context in which prostitution takes place can be more visible. Although places where prostitution is more 'normalized' are not without controversy, concern and debate, which tells us more generally about the place of prostitution within society, it is apparent that there are significant differences in how prostitution is responded to and perceived in different locations, contexts and spaces. The cultural context in which prostitution takes places also plays a fundamental role in shaping the nature of sex work and how sex markets operate (Sanders *et al.* 2009). It is also a significant lens through which the sex industry should be viewed and analysed. In particular, work that has explored various contexts in which prostitution operates, such as vehicle artillery routes or rural villages, demonstrate that it is important to attempt to understand, not only the actions and behaviours of those involved in sexual transactions, but also the much wider social and cultural context (Agustín 2005).

16 *Introduction*

Why prostitution and not sex work?

Given my previous work in this area, such as *New Sociologies of Sex Work* (Kingston and Sanders 2010), and belief that, for some people, 'sex' can be a form of work, some may question why I have chosen to use the term prostitution and not sex work in the title of this book. The reason why I have used the term prostitution is to represent the research upon which this book is based. The term prostitution was used by my participants. Although I prefer the term sex work, because it is used by many sex workers themselves – i.e. those who make an uncoerced choice to sell – this book is about the attitudes, impact and action taken by 'the community'. Furthermore, this book focuses on the direct sale of sexual services and does not, unless explicitly stated, focus on indirect sex work. Direct sex refers to the purchase of sex acts that involve genital stimulation, whereas indirect sex can be referred to as lap dancing or internet sex (Harcourt and Donovan 2005; Rehle *et al.* 1992). Although indirect sex may be included in the category of sex work, respondents did not consider indirect sex as 'sex' or as a form of prostitution. Therefore, unless explicitly stated, prostitution is defined as involving the purchase of sex acts.

The book also focuses upon the female sex worker – the male client market. As this relationship is most commonly associated with the sex industry, this book focuses upon this 'traditional' interaction. The book is also limited specifically to a focus on voluntary prostitution, which takes place between apparently consenting adults. Although using the term prostitution does not differentiate between forced and unforced prostitution – which is not the focus of this book – only unforced prostitution will be discussed in this book, unless stated otherwise.

In addition, this book focuses upon 'traditional' forms of prostitution. There are many groups of clients and sex workers with a range of sexualities and sexual orientations, such as men who buy sex from men, men and women who are bisexual and clients who buy sex from transsexuals and transgendered individuals, fetish work and dominatrix services (Bloor *et al.* 1992; Elifson *et al.* 1993a; Elifson *et al.* 1993; Harcourt *et al.* 2001; Kulick 1998; Valleroy *et al.* 2000). These diversities in sexuality and sexual consumption patterns will not be covered in this book, as space is not available to give each diverse sexual practice the consideration it deserves.

Sex work also takes place in a range of different settings, from the street to brothels, lap-dancing clubs, flats, massage parlours and from escorts (Monto 2000; Sanders 2008a, 2008b; Weitzer 2005). Although, predominantly, the focus of research and political debate has been centred on street-based prostitution, there has been an increase in interest and concern over indoor sex markets. This book will discuss both street-based and indoor sex work, making explicit reference to the location in which the sex act is purchased, in order to situate attitudes, impact and action. As will be shown, the 'place' of prostitution can have significant implications for how it is seen and dealt with.

Chapter outline

The following chapter (Chapter 2) will examine the policy that surrounds the community, in terms of how the community is seen as crucial in dealing with social problems, as well as the legal context that surrounds prostitution. This chapter reviews the reasons why the community has been increasingly conceived of as a focal point of local crime prevention interventions and the ways in which this has risen up political agendas. In this sense, it considers the developing role that the community is believed to play in challenging crime and criminality, therefore highlighting the need to gain a greater understanding of what communities think about prostitution and the forms of action that they sometimes take, as these views and actions are often fully supported politically. The chapter also places the community in a specific cultural context, as previous research has demonstrated its significance. As the research upon which this book was originally based is UK-specific, this chapter explores the UK prostitution policy context. In particular, this chapter examines key legislation and social changes that identify prostitution and those involved in specific ways. As I have highlighted above, the law, the state and wider society are able to cast certain individuals and groups as different.

Chapter 3 will document how I researched community attitudes of prostitution – in particular, men who buy sex. This chapter will look at the methods that I employed to determine what community members thought about men who buy sex from women and the factors that may have informed them. It also considers some of the methodological challenges I faced, in order to identify some of the boundaries of the research, as well as the socio-demographic characteristics of my participants.

Chapter 4 explores attitudes towards prostitution and those involved. This chapter considers how prostitution is viewed as 'the oldest profession' and the evidential basis of this commonly held belief. This assumption, in particular, is one that the UK Government has sought to challenge, in order to support further legal changes to criminalize sex buyers. In addition, this chapter identifies perceptions of prostitutes and their clients – in particular, their gender, motivations and backgrounds, which, in some instances, mirrored academic research findings and the current literature. Furthermore, this chapter also explores concerning beliefs about the responsibility of violence perpetrated towards sex workers and the influence of cultural myths and stereotypes on these attitudes.

The impact that prostitution and those involved is deemed to have on residential and business neighbourhoods is considered in Chapter 5. In doing so, this chapter will explore both the positive and negative consequences that prostitution can have for residents and business employees. Negative consequences/issues examined include noise and nuisance, environmental waste, women being propositioned by kerb-crawlers, men being mistaken for male clients, fear and insecurity. The positive influences that prostitution can bring to an area, such as economic and in terms of crime prevention and detection, will also be considered.

The actions taken by local communities will be examined in Chapter 6. The types of activism that are taken, the reasons why techniques for action are employed and the consequences of such actions will be dealt with. This chapter will show that communities often employ a variety of methods to, in the main, remove street prostitution from their neighbourhoods. Yet, of concern are methods that lead to acts of vigilantism and violence. Thus, this chapter will consider some of the consequences of such actions, in terms of accountability and legitimacy.

Chapter 7 charts how the police and local authorities have dealt with prostitution in the areas that they govern. Differing proprieties and the impact that this can have is discussed, as well as how they are often torn between police priorities, legislation and community needs. In addition, this chapter documents acceptance and tolerance of prostitution, both on the street and indoors, as the police and local authorities see the benefits in spatial containment and regulation.

The final chapter of this book will critically evaluate many of the nuances apparent in participants' narratives – in particular, focusing on the intolerance expressed towards street prostitution. What will be argued is that, because of the stigma that surrounds street sex work, distance is sought, both socially and geographically, between the community and those with a 'spoiled identity'. Utilizing the work of Goffman (1963) and others, this chapter demonstrates how the stigma associated with prostitution is perceived to 'spread out in waves' through living and working in areas of street prostitution. As a result, the community seeks to create distance, both symbolically, through speech and language, as well as geographically, through 'designing out' prostitution or, for those who buy sex, travelling to other countries to escape the cultural context that stigmatizes sex work.

Notes

1 Hubbard *et al.* (2007) have criticised the Home Office's (2006) advocating of community conferencing, which hints at increasing sex worker's engagement in community life, yet, within the same document, argues for increased and stricter enforcement of kerb-crawling and soliciting legislation.
2 For a critique of this belief, see Hale, S. (2006). *Blair's Community: Communitarian Thought and New Labour*. Manchester: Manchester University Press.
3 For an examination of the Communitarian theoretical movement, see Calder (2005).
4 For a more detailed examination of feminist theoretical contributions, see Kesler (2002), O'Connell Davidson (1998) and Scoular (2004).

2 Prostitution policy and the community

The previous chapter examined how an approach, which seeks to put 'the community' at the heart of crime prevention, has been favoured in UK prostitution policy and how politically involving communities is seen as a key strategy in dealing with social disorder. Involving the community in local decision making and engaging community members in partnership with local agencies and bodies has risen up the political agenda, as it has been recognized that 'community' may be a site through which social problems can be tackled. The policy rhetoric of this approach is that various relevant agencies, organizations and the public are summoned to become active co-producers of crime prevention and public safety. By becoming active citizens, community members take a more proactive role in local decision making. This chapter will explore the increasing importance of including communities in policy decision making and local political decisions on how to deal with prostitution. The importance of community attitudes, and how they can challenge and change how social problems such as prostitution are dealt with, will therefore be considered.

The chapter will then move on to consider the socio-legal context of the UK, which helps us to understand the wider social context in which 'the community' is based. Academic research has illustrated the importance of cultural context in our understandings of the conceptual construction of sex and prostitution (Brown 2007). Furthermore, research has demonstrated how the legal context – i.e. whether prostitution is legal or not – can influence people's perspective and attitude towards prostitution and the sex industry (Brehman 2010; Jakobsson and Kotsadam 2011). This exploration is, therefore, important, as although communities may influence local and national decision making, legal and social norms and values can equally influence community views.

Community engagement and policy

Community engagement in dealing with social problems, such as prostitution, has risen up the political agenda since the 1990s. As Crawford describes:

> In Britain, a consensus has developed among policy-makers and many academics as to the desired reorientation of the criminal justice system away

from the over-reliance upon detection, apprehension and sentencing towards the prevention of offending before it occurs.... [A] 'multi agency' approach has successfully secured a prominent place in the rhetoric of all the major British political parties. Since then the proliferation of crime prevention 'partnerships' and 'multi-agency forums' has been stimulated by various financial incentives at the central and local levels.

(Crawford 1994: 498)

Consulting and engaging the community is one aspect of this 'multi-agency' approach, as politicians have recognized the possibilities of a 'bottom-up' social movement-based strategy of community empowerment against crime. From this perspective, the view is that community 'breakdown' is a key contributing factor in patterns of rising crime, social disorder and delinquency. If various forms of disturbances and petty crimes are ignored, then over time, communities become fearful, demoralized and fragmented. Therefore, it was believed that the spiral of blighted communities must be tackled.

The growing appeals of community based strategies emerged in part during the aftermath of the *Scarman Report* of 1981, regarding the policing of problematic inner-city communities, such as Brixton. As Edwards and Hughes describe, following:

increases in recorded crime, further instances of major urban disorder throughout the 1980s and Treasury resistance to further public expenditure on policing and criminal justice, the Thatcher administrations switched tack by arguing, in the Home Office Circular 8/84, that crime prevention cannot be left to the police alone but, 'it is a task for the whole community' (Home Office, 1984).

(Edwards and Hughes 2002: 6)

Legislative changes, with the introduction of the Police and Criminal Evidence Act 1984 (PACE), incorporated some of these ideas (Home Office 1984). This law placed responsibilities on police authorities to consult the local community as partners, in order to find out their views about local crime problems and develop crime prevention measures. Community based crime prevention strategies increasingly sought to involve local communities in devising local solutions to local crimes – a strategy further endorsed by the successive New Labour government, which came into power in 1997. Following the introduction of the Safer Cities programme by the conservative government, Labour party groups began developing strategies that focused on the social and economic causes of crime and redefined crime control in terms of community safety. The landmark Home Office report, *Safer Communities: The Local Delivery of Crime Prevention through the Partnership Approach*, commonly known as the *Morgan Report*, because it was led by independent consultant James Morgan, is identified as 'marking the start of a rapid expansion in local community safety strategies' (Edwards and Hughes 2002: 7).

Prostitution policy and the community 21

The perceived benefits of engaging in these types of partnerships allows for the possibility of 'active citizens' to shape and influence these new spaces, in which, in the past, they had often been excluded (Taylor 2007). The New Labour government encouraged public authorities to involve citizens and service users in policy formulation. Their argument has been that social problems need 'joined-up' solutions to national and local policy. The Labour government has argued that what is needed is a multi-agency partnership response, which harnesses the strengths and expertise of a variety of partners to tackle social problems (Milbourne *et al.* 2003). In 1998, the New Labour government indicated its plans to develop more effective links to tackle social exclusion and strengthen local communities. As part of this, the Home Office launched a crime reduction strategy to include 'increasing informal social control and social cohesion in communities and institutions that are vulnerable to crime, criminality, drug use and disorder' (Hancock 2001: 10).

This shift, in what has been described as a move from government to governance across the globe, has been identified as the result of growing recognition that 'it is no longer possible in the context of globalization, or given the complexity of today's society, for the state to govern without the co-operation of other actors' (Taylor 2007: 297). With increasing recognition that governments are no longer able to effectively deal with social problems, a more devolved community led approach is said to allow governments to control at a distance. Community members thereby take on greater responsibility to deal with local problems and produce local solutions, as this responsibility is devolved from central government to individuals, local bodies and groups (Rhodes 1996; Stoker 2000). Garland (2001) has suggested that, increasingly, citizens and commercial firms have been encouraged to take on greater responsibility for their security and well-being.

Despite this move towards involving local communities, 'a substantial body of research suggests that the scope for communities to exercise real influence in these spaces has been limited' (Taylor 2007: 297). Often disadvantaged communities remain on the margins in partnerships and other initiatives, which may reinforce feelings of insecurity and undermine people's desire for a sense of belonging. A material factor, such as poverty, which may prevent some people from engaging in consultations or meetings, has not always been considered. These concerns were realized in 2001, following riots in the northern cities of Oldham, Burnley and Bradford. Ted Cantle's subsequent review, the *Cantle Report*, criticized government policy for forcing communities to compete against each other for limited grant aid for regeneration initiatives (Home Office 2001). This led, in the case of Bradford, to the view that 'black' communities were being privileged over disadvantaged white communities – a perception utilized for the political benefit of the Right-wing British National party (Edwards and Hughes 2002). Therefore, in dealing with different community groups, such approaches may not be able to control the competing or counteracting policies and actions of different agencies. Community crime prevention programmes can themselves inadvertently create the very problems that they are attempting to solve – social division and potentially an increase in crime.

Furthermore, involving local communities in local decision making and crime prevention strategies demonstrates an assumption that towns and cities are populated with vigilant, morally engaged and 'active citizens', who are successfully involved in the fight against crime and disorder in their neighbourhoods. In increasingly diverse inner-city areas, the likelihood that all 'citizens' will hold similar views is unlikely. Moreover, there also appears to be a failure to recognize the nature of inter-organizational conflict and different power relations between the parties (Crawford 1997).

Yet, despite these criticisms, others have seen the move towards involving local people and communities in developing locally based solutions to social problems as beneficial, as it has allowed communities to take a more tailor-made approach to specific local problems. Rather than a 'one size fits all' approach, community governance gives a voice to local people to 'regulate the affairs of their own members according to the values shared by those members' (Edwards and Hughes 2002: 4). As Hirst (2000: 142) suggests: 'for that core of common offences, agreed by all, the police would enjoy greater cooperation and respect'.

Leaving debates aside, communities remain at the forefront of policy making, both in the UK and internationally. For instance, the Coalition government, who, at the time of writing, were still in office, has shown a commitment to the promotion of community based social action (Alcock 2010). David Cameron's 'Big Society' very much continues to perpetuate ideas of collective accountability and responsibility of UK citizens. Therefore, understanding what communities think about prostitution and how they deal with it collectively can have important implications for prostitution policy and policing strategies.

The socio-legal context of the UK

With the community increasingly seen as crucial in the fight against crime, how they view specific crimes will often be fundamental to how they respond to, and deal with, these issues. Therefore, how the community tackles prostitution is often informed by their attitudes and views, which are also mediated by a specific social background. This section will explore the cultural context of the UK, thereby situating views of prostitution within a particular historical and cultural setting. Key social changes, cultural norms and practices, shifts in legislation and approaches to prostitution will all be examined. Although this is in no way an attempt to chart the social history of the UK, as this would be a huge task in itself, my attempt here is to explore some of the important issues, both past and present, which have informed how society responds to, and deals with, prostitution and, in particular, men who buy sex, because of the focus of my research. As this book will show, these much wider UK societal issues can shape public attitudes and inform how communities react to prostitution, as they may be influenced by changing forms of social and legal regulation. The aim is to demonstrate that UK societal views and reactions to prostitution, prostitutes and their clients have a particular social history. As will be argued, community attitudes, action and resistance are mediated by a specific cultural and historical context.

Pre-1950s

An examination of the UK socio-historical context illustrates that specific shifts in social attitudes and the law have occurred in recent decades (Brooks-Gordon and Gelthorpe 2003a). Through examining attitudes towards men who buy sex from early civilizations through to the Victorian period, Brooks-Gordon and Gelthrope (2003a) demonstrated that the whole of this period was characterized by the acceptance and even encouragement of the purchase of commercial sex. This tolerance and acceptance is evident from the increase of indoor sex markets, as Sanders (2006a) has argued. While indoor sex workers were punished and sometimes publicly executed during the sixteenth and seventeenth centuries, brothels and bathhouses flourished.

The privileging of male sexual desire and the belief that men who buy sex are weak and powerless to the allurement of women was apparent in the Victorian period (Brooks-Gordon and Gelthorpe 2003a; Carroll 2003; Walkowitz 1980). This belief reinforced a double standard of sexual morality, which justified male sexual access to a class of fallen women and yet punished women for engaging in the same sexual act (Walkowitz 1980). The belief that a strong sex drive was inherent to male behaviour 'produced an enduring double standard that has tolerated, and even encouraged, the solicitation of prostitutes as a natural male activity' (Carroll 2003: 379). Thus, it was sex workers, rather than their clients, who were deemed to be the source of 'the problem' of prostitution within this period.

In dealing with prostitution, Hubbard (2011) explored how the nineteenth century witnessed a period of regulation, which did not seek to eradicate prostitution, but instead recognized its inevitability and, in some instances, desirability in cities. Its presence was deemed to provide unmarried men with the opportunity to release their sexual energies. As a result:

> [U]rban governors and politicians thus sought not to eradicate prostitution but to intervene in economies of sex at the local scale to direct prostitution into spaces where it could be surveyed and controlled away from the eyes of those who were most vexed about its existence.
>
> (Hubbard 2011: 57)

Indeed, as he further argues, it was the presence of prostitutes in public spaces that created the most hostility, and, as a result, indoor establishments were recognized as a means through which these anxieties could be dealt with.

Shifts in social norms and values following the Second World War, however, saw the previous encouragement and acceptance of the purchase of commercial sex questioned, as the 'sexual revolution' and increasing importance of sexual reciprocity emerged. It is the period from the 1950s onwards that we will now focus on.

Reports, regulation and legislation in the 1950s

The socio-historical examination is limited to the past fifty years, in light of criticisms that contemporary debates about prostitution have been deemed as 'guilty of selective historical amnesia, cherry-picking the past for convenient contrast and continuities, whilst ignoring complexities and ambiguities' (Howell *et al.* 2008: 235).[1] Taking this criticism into account, this examination will begin with the publication of the *Wolfendon Report* in 1957. The period in which this report was commissioned has been identified as a key decade of legal regulation (Phoenix and Oerton 2005).

The 1950s have been pinpointed as an important period, in respect to the legal regulation of sexuality in general and, in particular, commercial sexual interactions (Brooks-Gordon and Gelthorpe 2003a). Street prostitution was implicated in a wider process of postwar moral decline that lead to societal decay and family breakdown (Hubbard 2006c). In this period, the family was reaffirmed as the privileged site of sexual normality, and marriage was seen as key to respectable adulthood (Weeks 2007). Thus, it was feared that men who visited prostitutes may never learn the values of sex within marriage (Weeks 1981). Within this environment, legislation emerged to control and constrain prostitution, as, prior to this period, laws governing prostitution were fragmented and rarely enforced (Phoenix and Oerton 2005).

In 1954, a departmental committee was appointed by the then-Conservative Home Secretary, Sir David Maxwell Fyle, to investigate street offences, in response to public concerns over the number of women involved in prostitution (Linnane 2003; Phoenix and Oerton 2005). The report, chaired by John Wolfenden, focused its enquiry on homosexual offences and prostitution, making recommendations for legal reform (Wolfenden 1957). The findings of this report and its recommendations have come to be known as the *Wolfendon Report*.

The report identified the problem of street prostitution as the visibility of women soliciting in public places, as such visibility was considered to offend 'public decency'. Consequently, the report recommended that criminal law:

> Should confine itself to those activities which offend against public order and decency or expose the ordinary citizen to what is offensive and injurious, and the fact is that prostitutes do parade themselves more habitually and openly than their prospective clients, and do by their continual presence affront the sense of decency of the ordinary citizen.
> (Wolfenden 1957: 14)

This focus on sex workers and not their clients was incorporated into the Street Offences Act 1959, which made it an offence for a woman to loiter or solicit for prostitution in a street or public place (Home Office 1959: S.1.1). The Street Offences Act was a direct result of Wolfenden and drove women off the streets by increasing fines and imprisonment (Linnane 2003). Yet, rather than suppressing the sex industry, sex workers simply moved indoors (Self 2003).

The exclusion of men who buy sex from the focus of the *Wolfendon Report* was coupled with an exclusion of criminal law from private sexuality. The report made a crucial distinction between private actions and public order, proposing that it should not be the function of the law to regulate private behaviour, regardless of how distasteful it may seem to others (Weeks 2007). According to the report, only the public realm was considered as an appropriate site of legal control:

> We clearly recognise that the laws of any society must be acceptable to the general moral sense of the community. But we are not charged to enter matters of private moral conduct, except in so far as they directly affect the public good.... It is not in our view, the function of the law to intervene in the private lives of citizens.
>
> (Wolfenden 1957: 9–10)

Within the report, prostitution 'is seen as a matter of private morality, except when it creates a public nuisance' (Kantola and Squires 2004: 78–79).

Hall (1980) argues that the *Wolfendon Report* was forged on a campaign to encourage family values and marriage and return women to the home (cited in Matthews 2008). Furthermore, it is suggested that the visibility of prostitution undermined ideologies of femininity and sexuality, as well as women's traditional domestic role in the family (Matthews 2008). The basic policy agenda that was set by the *Wolfendon Report* was characterized by an attempt to control and constrain female sexuality that was considered a public nuisance. Men, in contrast, were not penalized by law and were thereby able to engage in the sex industry with relative freedom.

This lack of legislative intervention to deal with male clients was similarly evident in legislation that preceded the 1959 Street Offences Act. According to Sanders (2006a), it is commonly accepted that the Sexual Offences Act 1956 focused on criminalizing relationships between those who organize the sale of sex and their workers, but not clients. The Sexual Offences Act 1956 made it an offence to procure a woman into prostitution, for a man to live off the immoral earnings of a woman or a woman to control another woman's activities. Men who buy sex were absent from this legislation.

Wider social attitudes mirrored this legislative gender bias, as the Lord Archbishop of Canterbury (1957: 1) stated that: '*men*, have every right to a reasonable supply of prostitutes, and should not in any way be restrained from resorting to them.... The customers, even if they are kerb crawlers, are innocent and untouchable.' Men who buy sex from women were perceived to have every right to buy sex, because it was believed that 'both in marriage and prostitution, sex is the bait which woman offers to man' (Scott, cited in Brown and Barratt 2002: 134).

Reconstructing the client as a threat in the 1960s

The importance of family values continued into the 1960s, as public emphasis on compassionate love and mutual sexual gratification began to emerge. The socially desirable state of romantic love sustained through the sexual liberation movement of the 1960s changed expectations of relationships that idealized sexual exclusivity (Beck 1992; Giddens 1992). This model of the ideal relationship based on mutuality, monogamy and trust has 'had a hegemonic influence on social attitudes and the law. To go outside a monogamous "relationship" and purchase intimacy or sexual practices violates these contemporary ideals and cultural customs' (Brooks-Gordon and Gelthorpe 2003a: 442).

This emphasis has been attributed to a change in attitude towards male clients in the 1960s (Sullivan 1997). Social scientists began to question what kinds of men would purchase sexual services, arguing that such men failed to find sexual satisfaction elsewhere (Mancini 1963, cited in Brooks-Gordon and Gelthorpe 2003b). The idea that such men cannot forge normal relationships with women informed the perception that male sex buyers were sexual deviants and 'abnormal'. By the late 1960s, men who bought sex began to be perceived as posing a threat to non-prostitute women.

Public attitudes towards prostitution became complicated in the 1960s. In one sense, liberalized ideas around sexuality were evident in the growing acceptance of sexual permissiveness and popularity of pornographic material, which encouraged 'an association of masculinity with freewheeling sexuality' (Carroll 2003: 379). Debates around free love and sexual freedom for all women emerged (Seidler 1989). In addition to this, birth control and the erosion of chastity as a feminine value gave women greater sexual equality (Kaminer 1990).

On the other hand, a growing critique of male sexuality and masculinity gained pace with the influence of radical feminism, which questioned the sexual double standard. Polarized perceptions of male clients began to arise and, thus, perceptions of men who buy sex diverged. Second-wave feminist debates emerged in the 1960s and 1970s, commonly referred to as the 'sex wars' (Outshoorn 2005; Wahab 2002). Weitzer (2005) suggests that the radical feminist perspective remains the most popular perspective within contemporary debates. It is this perspective that, Sanders (2008b) argues, has contributed to the cultural production of the image of men who buy sex as dangerous abusers of women. This construction of male punters as a sexual danger to women was fuelled throughout the 1980s by the emergence of the 'Yorkshire Ripper' murders.

The construction of the offence of kerb-crawling

Concerns over the potential sexual threat posed by men who buy sex on the street spiralled in the 1970s and 1980s in the wake of the 'Yorkshire Ripper' murders. The notorious case of the 'Yorkshire Ripper' fuelled women's fear and anger towards victimization, strengthening existing negatives associated with kerb-crawlers. The media frenzy throughout the 1980s of a single male client who posed a serious threat to the safety of all women exaggerated the threat posed by men who buy sex on the street (Segal 1994; Smith 1989). Public perceptions of violence in the sex industry have been profoundly influenced by the serial murders of sex workers by Peter Sutcliffe – an acclaimed 'typical' punter in the 1980s (Kinnell 2008). His crimes have greatly influenced and provided credibility for radical feminist ideology, which suggests that sex work is intrinsically violent, because it reduces women to sexual commodities (Kinnell 2008).[2]

Continued media coverage of the Ripper case publicized the vulnerability of women working as prostitutes, which – it may be argued – was subsequently incorporated into legalization (Brooks-Gordon and Gelthorpe 2003a). The first piece of legislation to criminalize the purchase of sex was introduced with the Sexual Offences Act 1985, which specifically created an offence for any man who:

> Solicits a women for the purposes of prostitution from or near a motor vehicle, persistently ... or in such a manner likely to cause annoyance to the woman solicited, or nuisance to other persons in the neighbourhood (s.1); or, in a street or public place persistently solicits a woman for the purpose of prostitution (s.2).
>
> (Home Office 1985)

This legislative change shifted the focus of who was perceived as the problem of prostitution during the 1980s and 1990s (Matthews 1986; Matthews 2005). Up until this point, the application of the law and discriminatory law enforcement had penalized sex workers, not their clients. Provisions to prohibit kerb-crawlers from continual kerb-crawling behaviour and exclude them from specific areas were previously available in the form of civil injunctions, which were obtained by local authorities under s222 of the Local Government Act 1972 (Home Office 1972). Yet, these powers were rarely, if at all, enforced (Brooks-Gordon and Gelthorpe 2003a).

The 1985 Act constructed the kerb-crawler as someone very different to the decent, ordinary man in the street, emphasizing the nuisance that his behaviour causes to communities. Yet, the construction and creation of an offence of 'persistent kerb-crawling' occurred, despite previous advice, which highlighted the need for research to be conducted on the role and needs of the prostitute client (Trott 1979, cited in Brooks-Gordon and Gelthorpe 2003a).

The strip-club boom in the 1990s

While men who buy sex on the street became reconceptualized as a social problem, indoor sex venues began to flourish. Since the 1990s, there has been significant growth in what Farley (2001: 881) calls 'legitimized pimping'. Strip clubs, nude dancing, massage parlours, phone sex, escort agencies and computer sex have rapidly expanded since this period (Farley 2001). The first lap-dance club, For Your Eyes Only, opened in Park Royal, west London, in

1995. Imitators spread rapidly across the UK, offering dances of varying levels of nudity at tables, in private booths and VIP areas. 'VIP' rooms were introduced, which included private cubicles or curtained-off areas, where, for a fixed fee, services were offered, which could include champagne and fully-nude intimate dancing, with 'bed dances' also available. In the UK, it was estimated that there were 200 lap-dancing clubs in 2002, with an estimated annual turnover of £300 million (Jones et al. 2003). Thus, the expansion has been attributed to the profit levels of the strip-club industry.

High-profile clubs Spearmint Rhino and Stringfellows demonstrate the popularity of such venues, with Spearmint Rhino UK taking £2.3 million in profits in 2003, and Stringfellows' annual profits reaching £7.32 million in 2007 (Spanier 2008; Walsh 2003). Leading figures, such as Margaret Thatcher, Price Harry, Jade Goody's widowed husband, Jack Tweed, and Tony Blair's son, Euan Blair, have all been reported to have visited Spearmint Rhino, increasing the clubs respectability and, arguably, demonstrating its 'normalization'.

The rise in lap dancing and strip clubs has, Jeffreys (2009) argues, gradually decensored the practice, and, increasingly, nudity and touching have been permitted. According to Farley (2001), although stripping has changed greatly over the years, the general public have not recognized the business transformation and escalation of physical contact. With an alleged increase in physical contact and the sale of sexual acts, Farley suggests that the lines between prostitution and non-prostitution are being increasingly blurred.

Although evidence suggests that not all strippers or lap dancers sell sexual acts (Barton 2006), the expansion of strip clubs and lap dancing demonstrates an increasing social acceptance and 'normalization of the erotic' (Sanders 2005b: 11). Alongside these non-contact sexual services, Sanders (2005b) suggests that direct sexual services are also becoming increasingly tolerated and, therefore, visible. The availability of guides to local brothels and massage parlours and increasing proximity of such venues to the centre of the city, she argues, is testament to the extent of supply and demand. Adding to this, Hubbard (2011) argues how the city, through lighting, billboards and advertising, may remind viewers that it is a site where bodies can be consumed and are on display. As he describes it: 'the city is not simply the context for sex but needs to be highlighted as playing an active role in the constitution of our sexualities' (Hubbard 2011: 10).

The sexualisation of popular culture from the 1990s onwards

The consumption of pornography as an acceptable sexual expression, the 'normalization' of the sex industry in the media, through *Pretty Women* (1990), *Band of Gold* (1995) and the *Secret Diary of a Call Girl* (2007) television series, and the social acceptance of lap-dancing clubs may be considered as attracting and encouraging people to engage in the sex industry and normalizing its existence within society from the 1990s onwards. Sanders (2008b: 45) describes 'the nature of the sex industry, what it offers and the glitzy or gritty images and promises that emanate from adverts, websites, stereotypes, pictures and the allurement of fantasy' as the 'pull' factor that attracts men into the sex industry. Noting the work of Brents and Hausbeck, Sanders (2008b) suggests that strategies that aim to mainstream the sex industry are apparent in brothels and gentlemen's clubs in the West. These strategies include up-scaling venues, specializing in specific markets and expanding existing services. As such, lap-dancing clubs are 'marketed as being a glamorous and socially acceptable night out, accompanied by professional advertising and in many cases an up-market ambiance' (Barlow 2008: 1).

According to Bernstein (2001: 392), the past thirty years has witnessed the demand for commercially available services not only soar, but become 'more specialized, diversifying along technological, spatial and social lines'. She considers how the scope of sexual commence has grown to encompass lap dancing, live sex shows, pornographic texts, images and videos, cyber-sex and organized sex tours to developing countries. This expansion, she argues, has produced an increased acceptance of the erotic and a tolerance towards men who pursue their sexual desires. Yet, despite this increasing acceptance, normalization and tolerance of certain aspects of the sex industry, the late 1990s and a change in the UK government office led to a shift in how prostitution, in particular, was to be responded to in the future.

New Labour and prostitution policy: the review

Shifting forms of legal regulation in the UK emerged from the late 1990s with a change in government. UK prostitution laws were reviewed for the first time in over fifty years by the New Labour government. This review of prostitution laws and strategies has been significant in terms of how prostitution has been dealt with by the police, as well as potentially impacting on public attitudes towards the issue. For example, by referring to the implementation of sexual predator laws in the United States (US), Websdale (1999) argues that the creation and implementation of these new laws has created a 'moral panic' around violence against women and children by persons identified as predators. Thus, the new laws introduced by the New Labour government could have influenced how the general public respond to prostitution.

In May 1997, New Labour won the general election. One year later, the Home Office's intention to review sex offences was announced by Alun Michael, then Deputy Home Secretary (Lord Williams of Mostyn 1999). Initially, the Home Office (1998b: 1) published a leaflet, *A Review of Sex Offences*, informing the public of its forthcoming review, stating that:

> A review of the criminal law on sex offences is long overdue. The structure of the law is complex and made more difficult by changes and amendments over time. Much of the law dates from a hundred years ago and more, when society was very different.
>
> (Home Office 1998b: 1)

This report emphasized the need to ascertain the views of the general public, as these views are deemed crucial for sex laws to mirror societal attitudes. Any resulting legislation should, therefore, mirror wider public attitudes towards prostitution. The review of prostitution policy was initiated in 2000, when the Home Office published *Setting the Boundaries* (Home Office 2000). This document recommended that there should be a further review of the law on prostitution.

Paying the price

In July 2004, the Home Office published a consultation paper, *Paying the Price*, 'intended as the starting point for the development of a realistic and coherent strategy to deal with prostitution and its serious detrimental consequences for individuals and communities' (Blunkett 2004: 5). The consultation process was informed by an evaluation of eleven crime-reduction programme projects and responses from members of the public, individuals directly involved in prostitution and those working in the public and voluntary sector. This consultation paper formed the first review of prostitution legislation since the *Wolfenden Report* over fifty years previously. As the then Home Secretary, David Blunkett, stated, the review was initiated because it was believed that 'many of the laws relating to prostitution are outdated, confusing and ineffective' (2004: 5). This process led to the government's proposals for *A Coordinated Prostitution Strategy* (Home Office 2006).

Within *Paying the Price*, a shift in official discourse can be observed, from perceiving sex workers as a problem to perceiving sex workers as more of a victim, and perceiving men who buy sex – particularly, at this stage, on the street – as the problem. As the Home Office (2004b: 67) explains: 'while women on the street soliciting for trade is acceptable to most communities, it is the nuisance caused by kerb-crawlers that is usually the first concern'. Clients on the street are identified as 'prostitute users', who 'harass women' and 'fuel exploitation and problematic drug use' (Home Office 2004b: 1–97). Kerb-crawlers were deemed 'victimizers' of sex workers and communities that lived in areas of street sex work. Yet, as I have argued elsewhere, no literature or research has been identified to support this suggestion, and the consultation process has appeared biased and lacks an evidence base (Kingston 2010).

Interestingly, according to Kantola and Squires' analysis of the debate on kerb-crawling, 'the problems associated with kerb-crawling are personified, not by male customers and kerb-crawlers, but by female prostitutes' (2004: 81). Furthermore, although kerb-crawlers have been deemed more of a problem, sex workers who choose not to exit prostitution are not considered to be 'victims'. Within the document, very limited notions of victimhood is evident, as the material and social conditions, such as poverty, and lack of choices, all of which often condition involvement in prostitution, are neglected (Phoenix and Oerton 2005). Furthermore, despite considering managed zones, the registration of sex workers and licensed brothels in *Paying the Price*, a policy of zero tolerance against sex workers and, in particular, their clients was announced in December 2005 (Travis 2005). According to the Home Office minister, Fiona MacTaggart:

> Prostitution blights communities. We will take a zero tolerance approach to kerb crawling. Men who choose to use prostitutes are indirectly supporting drug dealers and abusers. The power to confiscate driving licenses already exists. We want the police to use that power.
>
> (Cited in Travis 2005)

This, therefore, signalled that the forthcoming prostitution policy would be taking a hard-line approach to prostitution.

Negative societal attitudes towards male clients were evident during this period. For example, in November 2004, revelations emerged that Hugh Grant had been charged with indecent conduct with a prostitute in a public place in the US. The story spread across national newspapers and damaged his image as an actor (Helmore 1995; Hiscock 1995; Mail Online 2005). However, despite his misdemeanour, Hugh Grant remains a well-known and high-profile actor. Similarly, Wayne Rooney remains a popular footballer, even after revelations that he visited massage parlours and engaged with sex workers (*Telegraph* 2004). Therefore, in spite of initial negative responses to their sexual behaviour, over time, their reputations were not completely damaged.

A coordinated prostitution strategy: 'disrupting sex markets'

In January 2006, the Home Office published *A Coordinated Prostitution Strategy*, which was devised as guidance for dealing with street prostitution in England and Wales. The prostitution strategy included five key aims. The first aim, prevention, focuses on awareness-raising strategies aimed at prevention and early intervention measures to stop individuals, particularly children and young people, from becoming involved in prostitution. The second aim, tackling demand, includes responding to community concerns, by deterring those who create the demand and removing the opportunity for street prostitution to take place. Developing routes out is the third aim, which focuses on providing a range of support and advocacy services to help those involved leave prostitution. The fourth aim, ensuring justice, focuses on bringing those who exploit individuals through prostitution and commit violent and sexual offences against those involved in prostitution to justice. The fifth aim of the strategy, tackling off-street prostitution, aims to target commercial sexual exploitation – in particular, where victims are young or have been trafficked.

This strategy laid out the government's proposals, which took 'a new focus on the enforcement of the law on kerb-crawling' and 'a new staged approach to enforcement against loitering or soliciting' (Home Office 2006: 33). Tackling kerb-crawling, according to the Home Office (2006: 33), 'must be at the heart of local enforcement strategies ... in order to respond to legitimate concerns of local communities'. These concerns include unwanted propositioning of young people and increased traffic and noise.

At this stage, it was the kerb-crawler who was the focus of New Labour's attempt to 'tackle demand', as the kerb-crawler was deemed a problem for the community. Links between kerb-crawlers and their impact upon local communities is highlighted throughout the document, as tackling demand would respond to community concerns about men who buy sex on the street. Therefore, the public nature of street prostitution continued to be the focus of official concerns.

Although new legislation was not introduced by the strategy, support for the Swedish model, which criminalized the purchase of sex in 1999, was explicit. The Home Office (Home Office 2006: 7) suggested that 'many' respondents supported a shift in the focus of enforcement upon kerb-crawlers and stated that 'this would be an effective way to disrupt the market'. This support may be questioned, considering that conviction rates of kerb-crawlers has fallen year on year, following its highest levels in 2004 – the year that the consultation paper, *Paying the Price*, was published. Data from the number of kerb-crawling convictions during 1996 and 2007 illustrates that conviction rates have fluctuated from the highest – 1185 in 2004 – to the lowest – 599 in 1999 (Home Office 2004b, 2008a, 2009a). Interestingly, however, since 2004, convictions for kerb-crawling have steadily decreased, from a peak in 2004 down to 1079 in 2005, 927 in 2006 and fewer still in 2007 with 859. This decline in the number of convictions of kerb-crawlers goes against the policy approach advocated by New Labour, both in its consultation paper, *Paying the Price*, and the *Coordinated Prostitution Strategy*. Furthermore, Matthews (2005) has identified that, rather than convicting and criminalizing kerb-crawlers, alternative measures have been employed by police forces across the UK.

Almost twelve months after the strategy was published, concerns over the safety of street sex workers were highlighted in another high-profile case. In December 2006, the murders of five street sex workers in Ipswich brought the issue of UK prostitution policy 'to the forefront of policy debates once more' (O'Neill *et al.* 2008: 89). This case may seem to validate the Home Office suggestion that clients on the street are a danger and threat to sex workers and, therefore, in need of increased social and legal regulation. If we take O'Neill *et al.*'s (2008: 89) suggestion that 'noisy periods of intense regulation are connected to the emergence of media stories implicating prostitutes on specific outbreaks of deviance', it may seem unsurprising that a legislative change to further criminalize the purchasers of commercial sex would occur.

'Kerb-crawling costs more than you think' campaign

In line with the government's focus on 'tackling demand', the Home Office launched a marketing campaign to deter kerb-crawlers on 9 May 2007 (Home Office 2007a). The kerb-crawler campaign was piloted in seven areas, which included London, Middleborough, Peterborough, Southampton, Bristol,

Bournemouth and Leeds. The seven areas were selected 'because they had shown a real commitment to carry out kerb-crawling enforcement activity coupled with strong support services for women' (Government News Network 2007: 2). Marketing campaign posters and local radio advertising were deployed over a six-week period to warn kerb-crawlers that 'kerb-crawling costs more than you think' (Home Office 2007a: 1).

The kerb-crawler marketing campaign attempted to tackle demand and challenge the continued existence of street-based sex markets, along with the commonly held view that prostitution is inevitable and here to stay (Home Office 2007a). This government-led campaign addresses the first action point to be taken by the government, as identified in the *Coordinated Prostitution Strategy* document. The action to be taken by the government is to 'devise key messages to challenge attitudes and to ensure a clear understanding of the implication of buying and selling sex' (Home Office 2006: 3). What was highlighted as crucial was the need to move away from the general perception that prostitution is the 'oldest profession' and has to be accepted.

In an attempt to challenge the attitude that prostitution has to be accepted, the kerb-crawler campaign advertisements provided the details of arrested and convicted kerb-crawlers from a range of social backgrounds. Through utilizing radio and poster advertisements, which highlighted the lack of acceptance of street prostitution and the potential implications, the aim was that the message reached the general public, rather than just the immediate relations of an arrested and/or convicted kerb-crawler and those communities already apparently fed up with street prostitution (Government News Network 2007). It is not clear what impact, if any, this campaign had on the general public.

In keeping with the action point of the *Coordinated Prostitution Strategy*, the legal consequences of being arrested or convicted of kerb-crawling and the potential social consequences were emphasized (Home Office 2007a). The radio advertisements and posters suggested that being arrested or convicted of kerb-crawling could affect employment, family life and social relationships, as well as costing money and, potentially, loss of their car and driving license. Such media representations 'serve as one of the primary sites of social inclusion and exclusion in late modernity' (Greer and Jewkes 2004: 110). Such representations 'are constructed and consumed to allow readers/viewers/listeners to sidestep reality and establish the Otherness of those who deviate from their own "reality"' (O'Neill *et al.* 2008: 82). Therefore, the kerb-crawler campaign encouraged its listeners, readers and viewers to see kerb-crawlers as the deviant 'other'.

The motives behind the campaign follow on from those identified in the *Coordinated Prostitution Strategy*, which aimed to shine the spotlight on those creating the demand for street-based prostitution (Government News Network 2007). This focus stemmed from residents' concerns of the presence of kerb-crawlers in local communities (Home Office 2006). The concern appeared to arise out of unwanted propositioning of local residents – in particular, as Vernon Coaker states, 'innocent women mistakenly targeted and abused by men on the prowl' (cited in Government News Network 2007).

Criticisms of the kerb-crawler campaign have come from the English Collective of Prostitutes, who have suggested that such methods were 'draconian crackdowns', in which the women engaged in prostitution would be driven further underground, where they would be more vulnerable to attack (*Evening Star* 2007). Furthermore, the English Collective of Prostitutes asked how the police could have justified a policy that said nothing about women's safety – a focus identified by public opinion, time and time again, as an absolute priority (Press Association 2007). However, I would argue that recognition was paid to women's safety – the safety of local female residents, for whom it has been recognized that encounters can be 'intimidating, unpleasant and unsafe' (Vernon Coaker, cited in Home Office 2007a: 1), thus reinforcing notions of 'deserving' and 'undeserving' victims.

The review on 'tackling demand'

A further six-month review commenced on 14 January 2008, the *Tackling Demand For Prostitution: A Review* was commissioned by the then Home Secretary, Jacqui Smith, to assess what further measures could be taken to reduce the demand for prostitution. This review began with a visit to Sweden, followed by a visit to the Netherlands, which operates a licensing scheme for brothels, meaning that the organization of sex work by consenting adults is not considered a criminal offence (Home Office 2008b).

Although a visit to the Netherlands was undertaken by the government as part of the review, indications that the government was considering following the Swedish model were confirmed by Home Office ministers in December 2007, despite the official review beginning in January 2008. The shift towards viewing male punters as the 'fuellers' of human trafficking for the purposes of prostitution emerged in December 2007, when the Commons Leader, Solicitor General Harriet Harman QC, held that a Swedish-style law against the purchase of sex was necessary to tackle the demand for sex workers trafficked into Britain (Woodward 2007). According to Harman: 'unless you tackle the demand side of human trafficking which is fuelling this trade, we will not be able to protect women from it' (Harman 2007). In an attempt to deal with 'the vile new slave trade of trafficking people' (Baird, cited in Home Office 2008b: 1), the government was keen to tackle the demand side of the sex trade. This, they argued, is one of the areas that Vernon Coaker and his colleagues believe that they 'can have the greatest impact and this is why we are looking at what more we can do in this area' (Coaker, cited in Home Office 2008b: 1). This perspective became incorporated into the kerb-crawler campaign, launched in May 2008, which aimed to raise awareness of the exploitation and trafficking of some women among men who buy sex (Crime Stoppers 2008). Critics of this focus on clients have suggested that, 'in place of serious debate based on independent evidence, we are offered hyperbole and emotive rhetoric about sex slaves' (O'Connell Davidson 2007: 1). Criminalizing sex buyers arguably ignores the profound divergence of experiences of many migrant and trafficked women. What may be suggested is that the government have been engaging in a 'moral crusade' (Weitzer 2007b: 447).

The need for prostitution policy to intervene in indoor sex markets was pushed onto the UK political agenda by international concerns over sex trafficking. Kantola and Squires (2004) document how debates that focused upon trafficking for sexual exploitation began in the late 1990s, but emerged, within the UK public sphere, in 2001, alongside growing concerns over immigration. One year later in 2002, the Nationality, Immigration and Asylum Act became law, which made the trafficking of people for prostitution illegal (Home Office 2002). This legislation was then strengthened in 2003 with the Sexual Offences Act and again, one year later, with the Asylum and Immigration Act 2004 (Home Office 2003, 2004a). Following this, in 2007, the *UK Action Plan on Tackling Human Trafficking* clearly stated that tackling demand was a key element in its anti-trafficking strategy, through greater enforcement and awareness-raising (Home Office 2007c: 31).

The review on tackling demand ended in September and was then published in November 2008 (Home Office 2008c). Six recommendations were made, which included the introduction of a strict liability offence for paying for sex with someone who is controlled for another person's gain; a specific marketing campaign to raise awareness amongst sex buyers about sex trafficking; an amendment to the offence of kerb-crawling and soliciting to remove the requirements of persistence, thereby allowing prosecution for a first offence; a re-run of a national anti-kerb-crawling campaign; giving powers to police for closing premises linked to sexual exploitation and the encouragement of further multi-agency partnerships. These recommendations were then incorporated into the Policing and Crime Act 2009. This law made it an offence to buy sex from someone who has been subjected to force, deception or threats through s53A (Home Office 2009b). However, the government decided against completely adopting the Swedish model by fully criminalizing the purchase of sex, on the basis that wider public attitudes are much more divided in the UK than is the case in Sweden. As such, the government wishes to challenge wider public attitudes and, therefore, the historical tolerance of prostitution.

In addition, the Policing and Crime Act 2009 made a number of amendments to existing prostitution law. Schedule 8 of the Policing and Crime Act 2009 repealed the Sexual Offences Act 1985. This repealed the offences of kerb-crawling and persistent soliciting in that Act, replacing it with the single offence of soliciting (new section 51A of the Sexual Offences Act 2003). In effect, people looking to buy sex on the street can be arrested for their first offence. Police no longer need to show that kerb-crawlers are persistent to arrest them. In addition, Section 16 of the Policing and Crime Act 2009 amended Section 1 of the Street Offences Act 1959 to remove the term 'common prostitute' and insert the word 'persistently' and 'person' into the offence of loitering or soliciting for the purposes of prostitution. These changes were made in response to a widespread consensus that the term 'common prostitute' is outdated and offensive and should be removed. These legal changes also mean that the offence would only be committed by a person involved in prostitution 'who persistently loiters or solicits in a street or public place for the purpose of prostitution'. Persistence is defined as conduct that takes place on two or more occasions in any three-month period. Evidently, there are clear differences, even in the legislation, in terms of how sex workers and their clients are dealt with by the law.

Chapter summary

This chapter has attempted to situate 'the community' in the context of policy, both in terms of how the community is considered to be at the forefront of crime prevention strategies and in the context of prostitution policy. In doing so, it has examined how and why greater emphasis has been placed on involving and engaging local communities in tackling social problems such as prostitution through crime prevention initiatives and partnership working. With the growing recognition that nation states are unable to deal with crime and criminality alone, encouraging citizens to take action to alleviate social ills has crept up the political agenda. Community attitudes and action is therefore important in how sex work is managed and responded to. Yet, as this chapter has also alluded to, the community does not live in a vacuum, and it is equally influenced by the socio-cultural environment in which it is situated. In recognizing this, the chapter has considered the wider legal and social context and how prostitution and those involved have been responded to by prostitution policy and wider society. As the following chapters will show, the cultural context is important for understanding community attitudes, action and resistance.

Notes

1 For a more detailed historical examination, see Brooks-Gordon (2006), Phoenix and Oerton (2005) and Weeks (1981).
2 Although there is no exact definition of ideology, an ideology is understood as a body of ideas, which are characteristic of a social group, whose forms of thought are motivated by particular social interests (Eagleton 1994).

3 Researching the community

Researching the sex industry has often been fraught by many challenges, because of the secretive nature of sex work and prostitution, the stigma attached to its subject matter, the perceived dangerousness of participants and the ethical implications, in terms of the health and safety of the researchers and the potential threat to already stigmatized groups. These methodological challenges are exacerbated because prostitution is a 'sensitive topic', which, as Lees (1993: 4) argues, 'present problems because research into them involves a potential cost to those involved in the research including, on occasion, the researcher'. Consequently, there are common problems with ethical approval, access, recruitment, employing appropriate data collection methods, prevailing stereotypes and researcher safety during research encounters in the field (Melrose 2002; O'Neill 1996; Sanders 2005b, 2006b, 2008b; Shaver 2005).

Research on communities does not arguably pose the same methodological problems, as community members are not stigmatized in the same way, nor are they considered to be a danger to researchers. Yet, my research does highlight the difficulties that researchers can sometimes face when conducting research with communities affected by the presence of prostitution, both in terms of access, but also in terms of being a sex work researcher. This chapter will consider some of the methodological challenges that I encountered when researching community attitudes and the ways in which I overcame these problems.

Previous research conducted on communities has employed a range of methodological approaches and techniques. For instance, Pitcher *et al.* (2006) conducted interviews with a range of 'partners', in order to explore how residential areas in five UK cities, which were characterized as being used by female street sex workers, were shared by different sections of the community. Partners included project staff and volunteers working with street sex workers; staff in public services, including the police, local authorities and drug treatment agencies; interviews with thirty-six sex-working women and sixty-nine residents. In addition, they attended local meetings, such as local prostitution forums, police liaison meetings and community meetings, as well as undertaking observation of sex-work project activities, including outreach sessions. Similarly, Tracy Sagar's (2005) UK research, which sought to determine residents', sex workers' and local agencies' views of Street Watch (a local community crime prevention initiative), involved interviewing members of these key groups through face-to-face and telephone interviews. Kate Williams (2005b) employed similar methods to research Street Watch schemes utilized to deal with prostitution in the UK by conducting interviews with local police, protestors and local residents concerning their views and experiences of Street Watch schemes in their area.

Somewhat different methods were employed by Bellis *et al.* (2007), who, following meetings with local government agencies and businesses in Liverpool, surveyed sex workers and residents' attitudes towards the existence of a tolerance zone in the city using an online and paper questionnaire. Likewise, Jakobsson and Kotsadam (2011) employed an Internet survey to explore public attitudes towards various aspects of prostitution. Furthermore, Brehman (2010) also used survey methods to compare the attitudes of male undergraduate students from the University of Nevada, Las Vegas, and the University of British Colombia. By using questionnaires, Brehman sought to determine whether the 'hypersexuality' of Las Vegas affected attitudes towards prostitution among students at the University of Las Vegas.

The methods employed in my research were qualitative in focus, involving semi-structured interviews with members of 'the community', which included residents, business employees, local authority officials and police, as well as observations and focus groups with residents. This chapter will examine the methodological issues considered in the study, in order to contextualize the data explored in later chapters. This context is needed to enable an understanding of the data gained, as although I suggest that many of the issues emerging from the research can apply to many communities in the UK and beyond, no two people can be said to hold the exact same views or have the same experiences, and neither are two cities, towns or streets the same. However, despite this appreciation, 'even when those we study seem as distant as citizens of a foreign country, there is enough in our common humanity to create countless border-crossings' (Bruce 1999: 18).

The research project and aims

The research upon which this booked is based attempted to explore 'community' attitudes towards men who buy sex from women and the factors that informed these views. I was particularly interested in public attitudes towards the sex industry in general and saw the policy relevance of research in this area, given recent changes in law and the move towards criminalizing clients, as well as suggestions made by the government at the time – New Labour – that public attitudes towards prostitution needed to change. Yet, despite suggestions made by New Labour that public attitudes towards prostitution are deeply divided, there appears to have been very little research or reviews undertaken to ascertain what the public think about prostitution. This study sought to determine what the members of two communities in Leeds thought about men who buy sex and what factors may have influenced their views.

The research site

The research was conducted in Leeds, West Yorkshire. Leeds is a large city in West Yorkshire, located within the north of England. Formerly a city associated with the manufacturing of textiles, Leeds is now an important financial centre, second only to London, with a vibrant nightlife, tourism scene and extensive shops, bars and restaurants. The city has extensive transport links to many major cities, such as Manchester, Sheffield and London, making accessibility easy via rail or road. Two areas of Leeds were identified as potential research sites, due to their notoriety for being associated with prostitution (The Evening Press 2005). Both Area 1 and Area 2 have been historically associated with prostitution, with distinct sites being known for street prostitution and the presence of brothels and massage parlours.

The sex industry in Leeds has historical roots that are most famous for its links with the Yorkshire Ripper murders. During the 1970s and early 1980s, Peter Sutcliffe was known to have murdered thirteen women in Bradford, Manchester and Leeds. Although at the time that this research was undertaken it is almost thirty years after his conviction in 1981, the case has had a profound effect upon the ways in which society and the government have viewed and responded to street sex work ever since (Kinnell 2008). Kinnell (2008) argues that viewing Peter Sutcliffe as a client is part of the problem, and this is used to tar all clients as abusers and potential murderers. She rightly distinguishes killers like Sutcliffe from 'genuine clients' – the majority of whom understand the contract that they enter and the conventions that surround it.

Area 1 of Leeds has some historical connections with the Yorkshire Ripper murders, as two of his victims were killed in the area. Therefore, this connection may have impacted upon community perceptions in Area 1 and was considered during analysis. Parts of Area 1 have been well-known for its street sex scene in particular residential streets for many decades. In the late 1990s, a residents and communities association was established, in order to combat prostitution in the area. According to a Member of Parliament speaking for Area 1 in 2000:

> One of the biggest problems that my constituents face is the constant stream of vehicles carrying kerb crawlers and visitors to houses that are, in effect, brothels – usually houses in multiple occupation, interspersed with family homes in which children and young people live. Those families are trying to live a decent, ordinary life, but they are constantly plagued by the noise, detritus and disruption that are caused not only by the women who ply their trade, but by vehicles, pimps and drug dealers who make their deals in nearby phone boxes. They cannot get a decent night's sleep because of the goings-on around them.
> (Hamilton 2000a: 47WH)

One means of dealing with the perceived problem was the establishment of the first UK kerb-crawler re-education programme, which was set up in 1998. This programme only ran for one year, following a withdrawal of funding by West Yorkshire Police, and will be discussed further in Chapter 7.

Area 1 was a mainly white (83.15 per cent), working-class suburb of Leeds, with a distinct Afro-Caribbean (1.13 per cent) community (Leeds City Council 2004: 1). Known for gun crimes, hard drugs and race riots, Area 1 was considered to be one of the worst hit by drug-related crime in the UK (Home Office 2004c). It has also been considered as an area with a longstanding prostitution problem and is a concern to local residents (Nicholson 2007). However, street prostitution was almost eradicated from local streets, following several community campaigns which led to its displacement from Area 1 (Leeds City Council 2007; Hare 2006). Resident-led marches protested against street sex workers and their clients, who were using the district to meet and undertake their business. Community residents employed a variety of techniques, including lobbying politicians and local police, in order to displace street prostitution from the area. In addition, residents campaigned with posters and placards, which targeted sex workers and their clients with messages such as 'prostitutes out' and 'kerb-crawlers, we have your number'.

Following these marches, street prostitution was displaced from Area 1 into Area 2, which already had its own street sex scene. Area 2 was a mainly white (94.91 per cent), working-class community, situated on the outskirts of Leeds city centre, very close to the main arterial routes into Leeds (Leeds City Council 2004: 2). Historically, it is a site of industry; however, Area 2 has suffered significant decline since the nineteenth century, with industrial buildings and warehouses falling into disrepair. In the years prior to the research being undertaken, however, a regeneration initiative had attracted investment into a particular site in the area. The street sex scene had been tolerated for a number of years, until this regeneration of a previously run-down industrial site took place and pushed the street sex scene into the residential streets of Area 2. Residents living nearby then became concerned about the impact that the presence of prostitution may have on their property value. Another clampdown ensued, and, finally, the problem ended up in an older part of Area 1 – a poor, white, working-class area. In response to the perceived problem, a community action group was set up to deal with the issue in the local neighbourhood. As Councillor Angela Gabriel, who sat on the Area 2 Action Group on Prostitution, explained: 'There should be a city-wide approach. Everyone is just shoving the problem around the city' (cited in Hare 2006: 1). It was with this particular community group that I began the research, as I knew that local people were vocal about their concerns and would be more likely to engage with the study. I then moved on to research community perceptions in Area 1.

The decision to undertake the research in these particular geographical locations was made on the basis of my local knowledge of the city, familiarity with some local concerns and accessibility to the city. The fieldwork was conducted in my university town and based in areas where prostitution is known to exist. This 'knowing' was determined by media reporting of prostitution in Leeds (Edwards 2005, 2006; Heslett 2006; Robinson 2005) and discussions with peers and supervisors. Also, 'knowledge' of prostitution and response to its existence minimized difficulties in accessing the community. As was sometimes the case with some research groups and individuals, being unable to provide any 'useful information' was a common response for non-participation in the research. Furthermore, the proactive nature of some communities towards the issue illustrated consideration of prostitution and the suggestion that they would be more willing to participate.

It is recognized that these groups did not fully represent the diversity of the community in all areas of Leeds. Neither Area 1 nor Area 2 could have been characterized as a unified community, as they were fractured along class, ethnic and religious lines. For example, parts of Area 2 had undergone significant regeneration in the years prior to the research, with an influx of investors and developers, while sections of Area 1, further away from the city centre, remain deprived, with large areas of social housing. In light of the difficulties in terms of its precise definition and lack of representativeness, it may be suggested that the notion of community should be discounted. Yet, it is recognized that the community 'continues to be both a practical and an ideological significant to most people, and is thus an important area of study for the social sciences' (Hamilton 1985: 8). For whatever reason, people had chosen to live and work in these areas and, collectively, are taken to represent the community in Area 1 and Area 2 (Mullan *et al.* 2004).[1] Furthermore, the political significance of the notion of community and the belief that localized solutions to local problems should be sought is recognized here. The Home Office (2004a, 2006), for example, refers to geographically based notions of community, from which local solutions to prostitution should be based.

The fieldwork phase of the research project was conducted over a ten-month period between November 2006 and August 2007. Over this ten-month period, seven focus groups were undertaken with forty-four residents, as well as thirty-three interviews with local businesses, police officers and local authority officials and forty-five hours of observations.

Accessing residents

Residents were accessed through pre-existing groups based at local community centres. Because the research design sought to gain an in-depth understanding of the views of the community, I took a qualitative approach, with the intention of conducting interviews and focus groups with members of the centres in both areas. Once I had identified the research sites, I began by making contact with community centre managers and staff. In both areas, I met with the centre managers before attending any group meetings, in order validate myself as a bona fide researcher and begin gaining access to groups. Throughout the study, I maintained regular contact with centre managers, in order to build trust and rapport with staff. There were times when I felt that it was necessary to engage in idle chit-chat. Finding 'common ground' between myself and the centre manager – and, later, with most of the research participants – I felt, enhanced the researcher-researched relationship and enabled me to express my interest in them as people, remembering our discussions and personal details in future encounters.

Community group leaders were gatekeepers to the community groups in both areas. Preliminary access to the groups was therefore negotiated with group leaders, before the research could be undertaken. It was at this stage of the fieldwork that I began to encounter a number of difficulties in Area 2. The details of groups, numbers and focus, which were provided to me by the centre manager, did not exactly mirror what I found. A number of the groups were deemed to be inappropriate, due to the type of group and activities involved (sports activities, youth groups). More pronounced difficulties emerged when I tried to access a parent and toddler group, as group leaders expressed concern over child protection, despite the research being met with interest from the mothers that attended. Further difficulties with an over-55s group arose, when the formal arrangements to conduct the research were made. Despite giving consent in the preceding weeks, members retracted their consent and interest in participating in the research on the formal date agreed. In light of these difficulties, I spoke to members individually in an attempt to gain some feedback on their reasons for withdrawal and to ask whether they would consider taking part in a one-to-one interview. I managed to record a ten-minute discussion with a small group of members, which constituted pilot focus group three.

Following the difficulties with Area 2, I reflected upon the experiences with community groups and gatekeepers and the predominant success in conducting interviews with local authority officials and local police. The success experienced with interviews appeared to suggest that, in some instances, over-familiarization impacted on my ability to gain and maintain access. In reflecting on this, I decided to take a more detached approach to residents in Area 1. Rather than spending time at the centre prior to conducting focus groups, information was posted to managers of community centres in Area 1. This information provided details of the study, the potential involvement of research participants and the offer of a monetary incentive. A monetary incentive of ten pounds was offered to each participant, due to the difficulties experienced in Area 1. Response to this cold-calling technique came from a caretaker of an Afro-Caribbean community centre. Through discussions with the caretaker, four focus group workshops were arranged, with twenty-two residents from the Afro-Caribbean community, based at the community centre in Area 1. This process, in comparison to the initial difficulties encountered in Area 2, was undertaken with greater ease. From initial discussions via telephone through to the four focus groups, a two-week period had elapsed.

Community residents' socio-demographics

People's experiences and perceptions of crime have consistently been shown, by the *British Crime Survey*, to vary, according to their socio-demographic characteristics and attitudes (Jansson 2006; Jansson *et al.* 2007). Therefore, the socio-demographics of research participants may be important, as their views may be reflective of these characteristics. For example, Jakobsson and Kotsadam's (2011) research demonstrated that men were more likely to see prostitution as less of a problem, whereas women were more likely to take a negative view of prostitution and see it as a problem (Jakobsson and Kotsadam 2011). Cotton et al. (2000: 1793) argue that: 'men might support prostitution because men are more likely to believe that male sexual urges are an imperative'. Furthermore, research conducted by both Brehman (2010) and Jakobsson and Kotsadam (2011) demonstrated that younger people are more likely to be more tolerant of prostitution than older people.

Religion was another factor identified in previous research, although not fully considered in this study. Brehman's (2010) research demonstrated that religion had a significant influence on attitudes towards prostitution. The more religious an individual is, he claims, the more likely they are to disapprove of prostitution. In the UK, Matthews (2008) identified a change in moral and religious attitudes as informing a change in attitudes during the 1980s and 1990s. In some communities, he explains, the visibility of street sex workers and the sale of sexual services was deemed unacceptable.

These factors were considered in the analysis. Table 3.1 is a chart of resident participants, who are identified under a pseudonym, along with their age, gender, ethnicity and role.

As Table 3.1 and 3.2 demonstrate, thirty-five of the participants were female and the remaining nine were male. Their ages ranged from 18 to 68, with a mean age of 43. Twenty of the participants identified as white, British, and twenty-four participants identified as Afro-Caribbean, British. All Afro-Caribbean research participants were residents of Area 2 in Leeds. These socio-demographic characteristics were considered during the analysis of the data, as the ethnicity of the residents sample is different to the ethnicity of the remaining participants.

Focus groups

The main method through which data was gained from residents was through four focus groups with Afro-Caribbean residents from Area 2 and three pilot focus groups. Focus groups involve an organized discussion with a selected group of individuals to gain information about their views and experiences. Focus groups are useful for obtaining several perspectives on the same topic

Table 3.1 Interviews with residents

	Name	Age	Gender	Ethnicity	Role
One-to-One Interviews					
1 (pilot)	Vicky	31	Female	White, British	Researcher, Area 2
2 (pilot)	Patrick	53	Male	White, British	Resident, Area 2
3	Craig	46	Male	Afro-Caribbean	Community worker, Area 2
4	Terry	27	Male	Afro-Caribbean	Resident, Area 1

Table 3.2 Focus groups

Focus groups	Name	Age	Gender	Ethnicity	Role
Pilot Focus Group	Kate	26	Female	White, British	Residents
	Gina	27			
	Diane	22			
	Pamela	19			
	Joanne	25			
	Stacey	20			
	Tara	20			
	Ruby	23			
	Fiona	27			
	Wanda	41			
	Kylie	54			
Pilot Focus Group Two	Jane	28	Female	White, British	Residents
	Sian	26			
	Tanya	31			
	Phillipa	29			
Focus Group One Area 2	Doreen	67	Female	White, British	Residents
	Carol	68			
	Anne	64			
Focus Group Two Area 1	Angela	27	Female	Afro-Caribbean	Residents
	Claire	57	Female		
	Debbie	26	Female		
	Emma	27	Female		
	Brian	47	Male		
	Frank	55	Male		
Focus Group Three Area 1	Gemma	46	Female	Afro-Caribbean	Residents
	Helen	50	Female		
	Karen	32	Female		
	Debbie	18	Female		
	Ian	62	Male		
	James	60	Male		
Focus Group Four Area 1	Liam	54	Male	Afro-Caribbean	Residents
	Mary	44	Female		
	Naomi	32	Female		
	Paula	42	Female		
Focus Group Five Area 1	Tina	31	Female	Afro-Caribbean	Residents
	Rachel	43	Female		
	Susan	30	Female		
	Wilma	66	Female		
	Linda	62	Female		
	Vernon	57	Male		

(Gibbs 1997). This was particularly useful in this study, as it enabled me to speak to a number of people at the same time. They also allow the researcher to identify group norms; gain an insight into the shared understandings of everyday life and the negotiation of group processes; allow for an examination of the questions that respondents ask each other to identify factors that influence individual assumptions and the influence of moral values and models of thinking (Brooks-Gordon 2006b; Gibbs 1997). Observing group norms and shared values was crucial to this study, as focus groups allowed me to observe similar and divergent views of the same issue. Furthermore, the discussions raised often prompted detailed discussions, as participants would often challenge each other's views, seeking clarification and often questioning the meaning of what participants had said.

In order to facilitate discussions in the focus groups, vignettes were used (Hughes 1998). Vignettes refer to stimuli, which may include text and images, to which research participants are invited to respond (Hazel 1995; Hill 1997; Hughes and Huby 2004). They are generally short descriptions of a person or social situation, which contain precise references to what are believed to be the most important factors in the decision or judgement-making process (Cheryl and Henry Jay 1978). The decision to use vignettes in conjunction with interview questions was made with the potential participants and research aims in mind. When thinking about the potential participants, I reflected upon my experience as a youth and community worker and university teaching assistant. My experience of conducting group workshops suggested the need to structure the focus group around specific tasks, in order to maintain interest in the topic when group discussion subsided (Flick 2002). Providing participants with concrete examples, alongside abstract questions, facilitated more detailed discussions. Furthermore, vignettes can help contextualize participants' attitudes and perceptions in a more relaxed and less personal way (Barter and Renold 1999). They are useful when the topic of discussion is sensitive, as it was in this case, as they allow participants to distance themselves from the topic. Creating distance by discussing sensitive issues in relation to a third party can allow participants to talk more freely.

Guided by these considerations, five vignettes were developed, based upon five themes, which were explored in focus groups. These themes included the impact of media on public attitudes; the perception of tolerance zones; comparative perceptions of the indoor and street sex scene; perceptions of an approach made by a kerb-crawler on someone mistaken for a prostitute and perceptions of stag parties. These themes aimed to contextualize community perceptions, in order to examine the influence of factors such as gender relations, sexuality, visibility, distance, risk, age, ethnicity and religion.

The vignettes designed were hypothetical (Leahey 2004; Leahey et al. 2003), rather than actual scenarios (Spratt 2001). They were developed from real-life experiences of people involved in the sex industry (Edelstein 1988; Johnston 1988; Morgan 1988); news reports that identified the experiences of men who buy sex and women who sell sex (BBC News 2006; Crime Stoppers 2006;

O'Kane 2002; *Daily Mail* 2006); research that has identified the experiences of those who live in areas of sex work, men who buy and women who sell sex (Koskela and Tani 2005; McKeganey and Barnard 1996; Pitcher *et al.* 2006) and my own personal experiences (Hughes and Huby 2004).

The vignettes were developed from a written format into an audio monologue. While written narratives are the most commonly used format (Abreu *et al.* 2003; Boxer and Tisak 2003; Lee and Craig-Henderson 2005; Rayburn *et al.* 2003; Schumacher *et al.* 2003), vignettes have also been presented through music and music videos (Peterson and Pfost 1989), caricatured images (Chambers and Craig 1998), on videotapes (Cohen and Strayer 1996; McKinstry 2000) and on computers (Stolte 1994). The use of pictures or images of specific scenes that depict men who buy sex in different contexts was considered during the pilot phase of the research (Kitzinger 1994). However, the aims of the research were to tap into residents' perceptions of men who buy sex from women. Providing images of stereotypical or atypical men who buy sex could have impacted upon perceptions. Using an audio format, I believed, allowed participants to visualize an image of the person speaking in the audio vignette through their own frame of thinking.

The audio research method was chosen for the purposes of prompting discussions in focus groups. As with visual methods, the audio 'can become the basis for a discussion of broader abstractions and generalities; conversely, vague memories can be given sharpness and focus, unleashing a flood of detail' (Banks 2001: 88). The scenarios depicted may have caused the research participants to recall something that they may have previously forgotten or something that they may not normally intend to discuss during an interview (Mason 2002). Furthermore, the use of the audio method can minimize the awkwardness that an interviewee may feel from being placed on the spot and 'grilled' by the interviewer. As with the use of photographs, this awkwardness can be lessened by the use of audio, as direct eye contact need not be maintained. Instead, the interviewee and interviewer can both turn to the audio as a kind of third party (Collier and Collier 1986).

Non-participant observation of community meetings

Alongside conducting interviews and focus groups with forty resident participants, I spoke to a further thirty-three residents during my attendance at a number of community events and meetings. Attendance at these meetings allowed me to gain initial access to community groups, meet potential research participants, gain an understanding of local issues and collect further data. Attendance at these meetings provided me with a 'springboard', from which to base my initial contact with local police and councillors. Furthermore, I believe that attendance at these meetings illustrated my interest in local people and verified me as a bona fide researcher. It was during these meetings that I made contact with many Area 1 residents, as well as meeting local police officers, councillors and business employees. These meetings enabled me to make contact with many participants, as well as demonstrating my interest in local concerns.

Interviews

The interview method was used as an additional research tool, in order to gain an understanding of participants' views, as it has been identified as a key method of attitude research, which yields rich insights into people's perceptions, attitudes and feelings (May 1997). This methodological tool was chosen because of the potential difficulties involved in organizing focus group workshops with particular research participants. The semi-structured interview approach was employed, in order to elicit in-depth information, rather than limit perceptions to categories or boundaries contained within a structured interview (May 1997). Therefore, this tool allows for the interviewer to probe beyond the answers to the original question, in order to clarify or elaborate on points raised (Blaikie 2000). All interviews were conducted at either a place chosen by participants or the person's place of work, such as local police stations, business premises or council offices.

Local authority officials

Local authority officials were interviewed to gain an overview of community concerns in both Area 1 and Area 2. Local authority officials included local councillors, members of Leeds Community Safety and members of the Development and Planning department, all of whom could be said to represent and serve the local community in their official capacities. The names of specific local authority officials had been gained through an examination of Leeds Community Safety Partnership Board meetings, which were accessible online, conference proceedings (Leeds Community Safety Partnership Board 2004; Safer Leeds 2005; The Leeds Initiative 2006), newspaper articles (Heslett 2006; Waugh 2006) and Leeds Net online articles (Leeds Net 2004). Confirmation of their post, roles and responsibilities and contact details was gained through the pilot. Confirmation of these details allowed me to reassess the sampling frame, from which to select a sample of the research group. During the pilot, the two local authority officials that were interviewed left their posts shortly after the interviews took place. Therefore, the importance of confirming potential research participants' details became evident at this stage of the research.

The 'cold-calling' technique that I employed was relatively successful. I received many replies; some did not want to participate, suggesting that I speak with more experienced colleagues, but a high percentage were interested in taking part. Those interested suggested meetings either days or a couple of weeks or two after the initial contact. The interview date, time and location were generally agreed on through email. I found that this 'striking while the iron's hot approach' worked very successfully. Following the employment of a purposive sampling technique, a number of research participants were gained using snowball sampling (Kurtz et al. 2004; Raphael and Shapiro 2004; Wesley 2002). These individuals were either unknown to me or were contacted via a pre-existing research participant.

48 Researching the community

Local authority officials' socio-demographics

Ten local authority officials were interviewed about their own and their constituents' perceptions of men who buy sex from women. The sample consisted of four councillors, two youth and community workers, two members of a Leeds community safety partnership, a member of the drugs intervention team and a member of the Leeds development team. Three of the four councillors were Labour politicians, who represented or had previously represented Area 1 or Area 2, and the fourth Conservative councillor spoke about Leeds as a whole. The two youth and community workers were employed in Area 2, whereas the Community safety officers and Leeds development officer were employed in Area 1. The final participant from this sample was employed as a drugs intervention worker across the city of Leeds. This variety of employment backgrounds and areas were specifically chosen, in order to present local authority officials in each area.

As Table 3.3 demonstrates, all but one local authority official identified as white, British. Their ages ranged from 32 to 61. Three of the officials in the sample were female, with the majority of the sample being male. All of the data cited in Table 3.3 was obtained at the time of the interview. As with the residents sample, the ethnicity, gender and age of local authority officials was considered during analysis.

Police officers

Ten police officers were interviewed, in order to gain an understanding of the police's perceptions of men who buy sex from women. Details of police officers were accessed from the minutes of meetings and West Yorkshire Police online news reports (West Yorkshire Police 2005, 2006). Initially, an email was sent to the West Yorkshire Police's 'online front desk team', who forwarded the email on to the officers that I had identified. Once I had established a number of

Table 3.3 Interviews with local authority officials

Name	Age	Gender	Ethnicity	Role
One-to-One Interviews				
1 Alarna	32	Female	White, Other	Community safety, Area 2
2 Georgina	unknown	Female	White, British	Community safety, Area 2
3 Ivor	40	Male	White, British	Leeds development worker, Area 2
4 Daniel	62	Male	White, British	Labour Councillor, Area 2
5 Peter	35	Male	White, British	Labour Councillor, Area 2
6 Bernard	58	Male	White, British	Conservative Councillor, Area 1
7 Kevin	unknown	Male	White, British	Drug intervention, Leeds
8 Ronald	54	Male	White, British	Labour Councillor, Area 1
9 Eli	55	Male	Afro-Caribbean	Youth service, Area 1
10 Michelle	61	Female	White, British	Youth service, Area 1

contacts in one particular police force division, a number of emails were forwarded to potential research participants. The majority of those officers interviewed were officers that I had originally selected in my purposive sampling frame. Only two officers interviewed were suggested as potential contacts.

Police officers' socio-demographics

Of the ten police officers interviewed, three officers policed Area 1, and the remaining seven officers policed Area 2. Police officers' ranks ranged from police community support officer (PCSO) to Chief Superintendent. All participants identified as white, British, and only one police officer was female. Their ages ranged from 29 to 63. All such information is provided in Table 3.4.

The socio-demographic characteristics identified in Table 4.6 were considered during analysis.

Local business representatives

Local business employees were the final group of participants, identified through purposive and snowball sampling. In identifying business premises in both Area 1 and Area 2, I undertook internet searches of local street names and business websites, which identified the contact details of employees and owners. I also walked around Area 1 and 2 to familiarize myself with each location and identify local businesses. In addition, a contact from the Chambers of Commerce and an Area 1 development project team provided me with the details of businesses that had voiced concerns regarding prostitution in the locality. In this sense, I employed both a purposive and snowball sampling framework. Once I had identified local businesses in Area 1 and 2, letters were sent to managers and proprietors of numerous local businesses with information about the study. Approximately one-third of those contacted responded and agreed to be interviewed. Accessing this group proved to be the most difficult of all participants,

Table 3.4 Interviews with police officers

Name	Age	Gender	Ethnicity	Role
One-to-One Interviews				
1 Sian	29	Female	White, British	Police community support officer (PCSO), Area 2
2 Darren	36	Male	White, British	PCSO, Area 2
3 Dean	30	Male	White, British	Police constable (PC), Area 2
4 Edward	33	Male	White, British	Sergeant, Area 2
5 Clive	42	Male	White, British	Chief inspector, Area 1
6 Herbert	53	Male	White, British	Chief superintendent, Area 1
7 Simon	33	Male	White, British	Sergeant, Area 2
8 Terry	63	Male	White, British	PC, Area 1
9 Malcolm	36	Male	White, British	Detective inspector, Area 2
10 Paul	56	Male	White, British	Chief superintendent, Area 2

Researching the community

potentially because local businesses did not want to be identified, as one participant explained, or because businesses employees may have felt that they did not have the time or interest to engage in research.

Local business representatives' socio-demographics

All nine business representatives came from Area 1. The research focused on this sample, because of access difficulties in Area 2. The comments made about local business representatives may therefore not be applicable to Area 2. Furthermore, the businesses identified are located in a specific site of Area 1 that had strong associations with the sex industry. This previously industrial area has undergone 'regeneration' in recent years, and, subsequently, many businesses moved into the vicinity. Following the relocation of these businesses into Area 1, many employees and proprietors became aware that the area was notorious for street prostitution.

Table 4.7 provides further details about the business representatives. As is shown, seven of the nine research participants were male and two were female. Their ages ranged from 30 to 58 and all identified as white, British. Their employment backgrounds varied, from shop proprietor to property developer.

Transcription of interviews and focus groups

Interviews and focus groups were transcribed to provide the main source of qualitative data. Although it is commonplace for academics to hire individuals to transcribe tapes recorded for the purposes of data collection (Tilley 2003), I transcribed all of the interviews myself. At times, this felt like a laborious process – a feeling echoed by other academics (Agar 1980; Lapadat and Lindsay 1999). However, this process refreshed my memory of what particular individuals had said and enabled preliminary analysis of the data.

Audiotapes were transcribed word-for-word in an attempt to minimize researcher bias in the transcription process. Referred to as naturalism (Oliver *et al.* 2005), the transcriptions included repetitions, 'erms' and laughter, in order to

Table 3.5 Interviews with local business representatives

Name	Age	Gender	Ethnicity	Role
One-to-One Interviews				
1 Desmond	45	Male	White, British	Marketing director, local developer
2 Anthony	34	Male	White, British	Manager, business park
3 Roger	57	Male	White, British	Director, local developer
4 John	55	Male	White, British	Manager
5 Ian	30	Male	White, British	Proprietor, delicatessen
6 Judith	37	Female	White, British	Proprietor, delicatessen
7 Roland	50	Male	White, British	Director, estate agent
8 Roxanne	50	Female	White, British	Director, local solicitors
9 Alan	58	Male	White, British	Caretaker, business park

represent the event as fully as possible. Word-for-word transcription also ensured that inadequate transcription did not affect the analysis process (McLella et al. 2003).

Research participants were not offered the opportunity to comment on or amend the interview transcription. Allowing research participants to check interview transcripts is not generally considered a reliable way to validate the generated data (Mason 2002). Rather, it is considered to be a civil act to those research participants that have given their time and access to their lives (Schwandt 1997). Before the interviews and focus groups took place, I decided that I would not give participants the opportunity to check the interview transcripts. This decision was made with the belief that the vast majority of participants would want to amend the transcriptions, in order to have their perceptions represented in a 'politically correct' manner.

Research difficulties

A number of difficulties arose while researching local business representatives' perceptions of men who buy sex from women. The first difficulty was one of access. During the fieldwork, I contacted three times as many business representatives than I had police officers and local authority officials. I wrote numerous letters and made numerous telephone calls to local businesses, visited local cafes, bars, restaurants and shops to make contact with employees and proprietors, but did not gain the same level of interest in participating in the research as I had with other research participants. I often gained no response from letters, was passed on to various departments and, on occasions, the telephone call was ended. When I visited some businesses, no one was available to speak to me or believed that they did not have anything valuable to contribute.

As with other research groups, sampling involved both a purposive and snowball sampling framework, however, the successes experienced with the police and local authority officials were considerably lower with local businesses. It was felt that the role of local police and local authority officials to 'serve' the public enabled the comparative ease with which I had researched these groups.

Recording interviews with local businesses proved to be the greatest difficulty in researching this group. Of the nine interviews undertaken, only three interviews were recorded by Dictaphone, in comparison to all six focus groups, all ten interviews with local authority officials and nine of ten interviews with local police. The reasons stemmed from the interviewees' lack of consent and upon my discretion. Some interviewees did not wish to have the interview recorded, and, in other instances, I felt that it was inappropriate to record the interview, due to the location in which the interview took place.

Of the six interviews that were unrecorded by Dictaphone, two interviewees asked for the interview not to be recorded. Desmond (45, white, director), from a development company, stated that he wanted to remain anonymous throughout the research and did not want to have the meeting recorded. He felt that his involvement in the research may have some impact upon the company and his reputation. John (55, manager) similarly wished to remain anonymous, but also commented that the recording of meetings was not a normal occurrence within the business community. Rather, minutes of meetings are generally made, and he preferred to employ this method in the interview.

A further four interviews were not recorded, due to the inappropriateness of the interview location. All four interviews were undertaken at the interviewees' place of employment. Three interviews were undertaken in a cafeteria-type venue, where similar meetings were taking place on tables next to each other. Due to the closeness of adjacent tables and the belief that it would have been inappropriate to record the interview and other people's meetings, I decided not to record the interview. Though I could have asked those parties on opposite tables if they consented to the recording, I felt that this would have become a difficult task, due to the transient nature of the cafeteria.

The fourth interview that I chose not to record was based upon the nature of the job held by the interviewee. He was employed as a caretaker at a large commercial property, which was occupied by numerous businesses. He explained at the beginning of the interview that he would have to leave at certain times, answer telephone calls, reply to occupants' requests and deal with the running of the front desk of the property. In light of these issues, I made the decision not to record the interview, instead making notes, as I had done with the five similar unrecorded interviews.

Being a sex work researcher

Hammond and Kingston (forthcoming) have explored some of the experiences of being a sex work researcher in the UK. This work has highlighted some of the stigma that sex work researchers can face in both their professional and personal lives when researching a stigmatized topic. As they argue, the stigma associated with prostitution can, as Goffman (1963: 43) suggests, 'spread out in waves'. It was through research reflectivity that our experiences demonstrated some of the problems that sex work researchers can encounter when researching a sensitive and stigmatized topic. I often found myself avoiding discussions about my research in my personal life, because I had experienced occasions when people I had only just met wanted to engage in a heated debate about prostitution and because my research was considered to be somewhat of a joke, being laughed at when people discovered the nature of its focus. The stigma associated with prostitution became associated with my research and was often met with criticism and ridicule.

The nature of sex work research and my experience of researching this topic also meant that I expected that, often, people would decline to be involved at the last minute; not only for general reasons, such as changes in circumstances or an inability to take part, but also because this is a sensitive research area. I found that a number of councillors pulled out at the last minute, when incidents involving prostitution taking place in the area that they represented were publicized in the local newspapers. This meant that I needed to be adaptable to different context and groups. I often found myself employing different strategies to gain access to different groups and taking on different 'personas', depending on the type of participants that I was working with. For example, when meeting business employees, I often ensured that I dressed appropriately and spoke in a more formal and professional manner. I would of course, wear less formal clothing and speak in a less formal way when conducting research at youth and community centres, as my clothing and manner in which I spoke could have deterred participants from engaging in the research.

Being a sex work researcher can often be fraught with many challenges, both personally, as Hammond (2010b) has explored, and professionally, within academic contexts and beyond (Sanders 2006b). As Sanders (2008b) and Hammond (2010a) describe, they both felt that they needed to employ 'emotional labour' in conducting their research on men who buy sex. Similarly, Shaver (2005) has documented some of the methodological and ethical challenges of researching this hidden and controversial subject. Researchers in this sensitive field of study need to understand the wider implications of their research, not only for research participants, but also for themselves, both as researchers and human beings.

Conclusion

The following chapters will explore the data gained through the methods employed and described in this chapter. Each chapter will consider some of the key themes that emerged from my research, as well as reflections on previous academic research in this area and additional research undertaken through an examination of international news' reports.

Note

1 For a critique of a geographically based notion of community, see Cohen (1985).

4 Community attitudes

It has been commonly assumed that the media, politicians and the general public know what people think about prostitution. Although it has been argued that public attitudes are evident in the laws and policies that a country implements or in the media reporting of prostitution-related activities, others have challenged this assumption (see, for example, Kingston 2010). It is often the most vocal members of society who have their voices heard and those who feel wronged who make their feelings known (O'Dell 2003). Those who tolerate and accept the existence of prostitution are frequently overlooked, because they express their tactic acceptance in silence. Research that has been conducted on public attitudes towards prostitution has demonstrated how views range on a spectrum from tolerance to intolerance. Rather than either supporting or disapproving of prostitution, attitudes are much more divided. Previous research has included Bellis *et al.*'s (2007) analysis of a consultation in Liverpool for a managed zone; Pitcher *et al.*'s (2006) research that explored how communities and those involved in prostitution co-exist; Jakobsson and Kotsadam's (2011) survey of attitudes in Norway and Sweden; and Brehman's (2010) Master's dissertation, which explored residents' attitudes towards prostitution in the United States. My research sought to feed into this existing research to determine what people who live and work in areas known for prostitution think about the existence of sex work in their neighbourhoods.

This chapter will explore attitudes towards prostitution generally, moving on to consider views about prostitutes and, finally, community perceptions of clients. What is demonstrated is that many people often hold contradictory and conflicting views and express tolerance in some instances, while in others, they express intolerance. Furthermore, as the chapter will show, many of the perceptions held reflect academic research in this area, demonstrating that those who do not engage in prostitution (or who did not identify as doing so) have an awareness of the complexity of the sex industry.

Prostitution: the oldest profession

Monto (2010) suggested that there is a widespread assumption with some scholars and the public that prostitution is the world's oldest profession. Prostitution has been culturally referred to as 'the oldest profession' for decades (Bassermann 1967; Milman 1980; Parsons 2005; Snell 1994), suggesting that women have always engaged in prostitution and will continue to do so (Overall 1992). Many participants in my research referred to prostitution as the 'oldest profession', arguing that this specific industry has existed for hundreds of years:

> It's one of the oldest industries.
> (Gemma, 46, Afro-Caribbean, Area 1 resident)

> Well as they say it's the oldest occupation.
> (Anne, 64, white, Area 2 resident)

Because many believed that prostitution has existed for years, they also argued that it can never be eradicated:

> I mean it's gone on for hundreds of years aint it ... It's something I don't think you'll ever get rid of it.
> (Carol, 68, white, Area 2 resident)

> Prostitution will be there forever, because there are people who are prepared to go and do it and there are men who are prepared to go and buy it.
> (James, 60, Afro-Caribbean, Area 1 resident)

> Oh I think it's engrained in people's psyche is that. You know even when the news comes on they always hark back to roman times and I think it is just part and parcel of the British psyche, that it is the oldest profession. I don't think it's frowned upon.
> (Clive, 42, white, Area 1 chief inspector)

Matthews (2008: 22) contends that the claim that prostitution is the oldest profession is often utilized to suggest that intervention in changing or improving prostitution is limited, which he claims is a 'defeatist statement'. Similarly, Jeffreys (2009) believes that such views are fatalistic, whereas she asserts that prostitution can be brought to an end and that such an aim is not unrealistic, when we consider examples of good practice, in terms of legislation, education and services to victims. What these defeatist views demonstrate, Matthews (2008) proposes, is that such commentators have a limited understanding of the history of prostitution and, thus, employ this statement because they do not wish to engage in serious discussion about social reform.

Yet, when we examine the history of prostitution, it is clear that prostitution has existed for many centuries. Historical studies have documented prostitution throughout the Victorian era (Bartley 2000), and its existence is also referred to in the Bible. Clarkson (1939) claims that the earliest human records, which charts the existence of prostitution, dates back to the fourth century before Christ (BC), whilst Sanger (1858) argues that it can been seen even earlier in eighteenth century BC, through references made in the book of Moses. Although hunting and gathering or agriculture are more likely to be the oldest profession, historical records suggest that the exchange of sex for monetary or material gain does, indeed, have a very long history.[1] Arguably, then, this old cliché is an accurate reflection of prostitution's existence. As Matthews (2008: 19) states: 'most myths have a rational core', which may explain their 'widespread adoption'.

The commonly held view that prostitution is the oldest *profession* may also be related to beliefs that sex work is an industry and that those involved are engaging in a business transaction. Again, it is clear that the association between prostitution and work has a long history. Brothels, commonly defined as business establishments where clients pay for sexual services, were first documented in London in 1058 and arguably existed much earlier than this (Linnane 2003). Many of my research participants made reference to prostitution being a job for sex workers, and the work that they do is providing a service to their clients, arguably demonstrating tolerance towards prostitution. They often viewed prostitution from an economic perspective, highlighting demand and supply and the basic economic principles of prostitution:

> It's the oldest bloody profession in the world. I mean [men] are always going to pay for sex. They're going to find women that will provide it.... I'm not being prude, its business. You've got a service and there's a demand for it.
>
> (Angela, 27, Afro-Caribbean, Area 1 resident)

> Everybody says they do a service.
>
> (Patrick, 53, white, Area 2 resident)

In recent years, sex worker rights' activists have called for greater rights and powers to be awarded to sex workers who freely choose to sell sexual services and for the recognition that prostitution can be a form of work for some (Hardy 2010; Weitzer 2007a). Debates from pro-sex work feminists and sex worker activist groups, such as the UK Network of Sex Work Project, the English Collective of Prostitutes; AMMAR, Argentina; Scarlet Alliance – an Australian sex workers association; and Desiree Alliance, US, have argued for greater protection for sex workers in terms of labour rights and have sought to increase awareness that some, but not all, sex workers actively choose to work as prostitutes. In Europe, the Declaration of Human Rights for Sex Workers initiative seeks to challenge 'current violations of the rights of sex workers in Europe which occur across health and social care, housing, employment, education, administrative law and criminal justice system' (The International Committee on the Rights of Sex Workers in Europe 2005: 13).

If prostitution is regarded as a legitimate form of work by the state, this, Weitzer (2009) asserted, may enable sex workers to gain equal employment rights and improve their working conditions. In South Africa, Victoria

(Australia), Germany and the Netherlands, for example, sex workers' rights as workers are recognized and have been upheld in courts of law, where wrongful dismissal cases have been won and sex workers' working conditions have been considered (Harrison 2010; Kelly *et al.* 2009). Although prostitution is responded to in different ways, the fundamental recognition of sex workers as workers is central for some commentators and campaigners. Yet, it must be recognized that not all women choose to sell sex as freely as others, and some prostitutes are forced and coerced into prostitution.

Perceptions of prostitutes

Prostitutes have remained in the public imagination for centuries. Historical records and literature demonstrate how the presence of prostitutes has been controversial in many cities and towns in the UK (Bartley 2000; Linnane 2003). The prostitute's presence on the street has been the issue of much contestation, as it still is today. Given this context, it is unsurprising that participants expressed views about prostitutes.

Women

Prostitutes were commonly assumed to be women. All of the participants in my study made this assumption; not one person discussed male, transsexual or transgender sex workers. This may have been a direct reflection of their experiences of female sex workers in their neighbourhoods and the wider national context of the UK sex industry, which has predominantly catered towards male clients. For instance, research has estimated that over 4 per cent of men in the UK have paid for sex over their lifetime (Johnson *et al.* 2001; Ward *et al.* 2005).

Historical records somewhat mirror these assumptions about prostitution and who is involved. Proverbs 23:27–28 of the Bible, for instance, state that: 'For a prostitute is a deep pit and a wayward wife is a narrow well. Like a bandit she lies in wait, and multiplies the unfaithful among men.' Yet, female prostitution is not the only form of prostitution referred to in biblical texts. In the Old Testament, the selling of sexual favours by men in sacred shrines was claimed to be a 'pagan practice'. Earlier still, Ancient Greece and Ancient Rome saw the existence of male brothels (Dynes 1990). In more recent years, there has been growing evidence from academic research in the UK that male, transgender and transsexual prostitutes operate in cities such as Brighton, Manchester and London (Browne *et al.* 2010; Whowell 2010). Similarly, in Argentina, Indonesia and India, for example, research has documented the existence of prostitutes who are not women (Ford *et al.* 1993; Lorway *et al.* 2009; Scott *et al.* 2005).

Despite the existence of both male and female prostitution, it was women who were most commonly assumed to be prostitutes. Traditionally, research, discussions and debates have focused on the 'female sex-worker, male client'. Researchers and academics have thus fed into the social construction and conceptualization of prostitutes as women. Without realizing, I myself have often unknowingly spoken of sex workers as women and men as clients, arguably because the cultural context in which I am situated perpetuates these gendered assumptions. This is particularly the case in many Westernized countries, such as the UK, US, Australia and New Zealand, where media portrayals depict female sex workers and male clients, and political discussions predominantly focus on women (Weitzer 2009). Feminist debates have also similarly focused on the female sex worker, with radical feminists arguing that prostitution is symbolic of patriarchal power (Kesler 2002). Perceiving prostitutes as women is crucially informed by the cultural stereotypes that permeate the societies in which we live. In the UK and the US, concerns over female victims of sex trafficking certainly fuel these gendered ideas.

Choice and agency

Although there is increasing recognition that some sex workers make an active choice to enter sex work and work as a prostitute, there are others whose choices are constrained or who are abused or coerced into prostitution (Kingston and Sanders 2010). Participants recognized that there is a distinction between forced prostitution and that which is more freely chosen. Four residents, for example, identified trafficking and the abuse of young women by men as a concern:

> How many young girls have been taken from places like Romania and the go to countries, brought here with the pre-text of a good job and then they've been put up in houses and people using them like.
> (Gemma, 46, Afro-Caribbean, Area 1 resident)

> Trafficking rife though isn't it.
> (Karen, 36, Afro-Caribbean, Area 1 resident)

Trafficking has become an increasingly important area that is in need of further investigation. Many have argued that trafficking is a new form of modern day slavery and that many women and children are being forced to sell sexual services against their will (Baldock 2009; Wilson 2011). Accounts made by trafficked women have described how they were offered the opportunity of employment in a foreign country, but, once they arrived, they were housed in brothels and forced to sell sex under conditions of violence, threats and abuse (Stanton 2011). These disturbing accounts highlight the more negative aspects of the sex industry and how criminal gangs and networks have exploited vulnerable men, women and children.

A distinction must also be made in this context between trafficking and migration, as not all foreign prostitutes are trafficked victims. Some women actively migrate to sell sex in foreign lands. For example, Gulcar and Ilkkaracan (2010) document how women from Eastern Europe travel periodically to Turkey to sell sex. Augustin (2007) has highlighted some of the problems with defining and responding to trafficking and migration, as recognition of women's agency

Community attitudes 59

is ignored. As she suggests, often 'women's presumed greater disposition (along with children) to be deceived, above all into "prostitution", and their lesser disposition to migrate, the consent of the woman victim is sidelined' (Augustin 2007: 40).

Despite the concern of some, other participants expressed their view that not all prostitutes are forced to sell sex:

> Nobody's forcing her to do it. She just went out and do it for the money.
> (Frank, 55, Afro-Caribbean, Area 1 resident)

Others appreciated that generalizations were not appropriate and considered that some prostitutes made a choice to sell sex, whereas others did not fully choose to engage in prostitution. This, for Paula, could be related to the different types of prostitution, in that those on the street may be more likely to have made constrained choices and those who sell sex indoors are more likely to have freely chosen prostitution as a form of work:

> Some are forced into it, but others actually make that choice, because of the benefits that they get from doing that and they don't see any other way of living their lifestyle.... Sometimes I think when we talk about prostitution we tend to look at the lower end of prostitution, those that are on the backstreets.... Whereas there are high class prostitutes are very different.
> (Paula, 42, Afro-Caribbean, Area 1 resident)

For some, the distinction between choice and force was considered a murky area. Some participants felt that a prostitute's motivation to enter prostitution may blur the boundaries between choice and force. As Gemma explains:

> That's alright for the persons who've got what they've got going on for themselves, but if people are at a low esteem or they've no money or no drive, no life and the only way that they can see forward.
> (Gemma, 46, Afro-Caribbean, Area 1 resident)

Discussions about choice and agency were also related to women's motivation to sell sex. The two main views were that prostitutes were either motivated by drug dependency or a desire to earn money to buy material goods. Many participants believed that prostitutes sold access to their bodies 'to fund their habit' (Angela, 27, Afro-Caribbean, Area 1 resident) and that, in the majority of cases, '[n]ine times out of ten there's drugs related to it, though isn't there. It's to feed their habit' (Emma, 27, Afro-Caribbean, Area 1 resident). There was also a strong view that drug dependency often led to desperation and that this was one of the reasons why women entered into prostitution.

The link between drug use and prostitution has long been established and highlighted in academic research. In particular, street prostitutes are commonly associated with the use of heroin, crack cocaine and other drugs that are deemed

60 Community attitudes

most dangerous. Research has highlighted that the use of drugs and dependency on drugs is high amongst street prostitutes (Spice 2007). Similarly, the use of more recreational drugs in indoor sex markets has also been documented (Colosi 2010). These views are, thus, somewhat in line with much academic literature in this area, especially in relation to street sex work (Potterat et al. 1998; Surratt et al. 2004). Yet, as Sanders (2005b: 10) has argued, the academic and public focus on drug use and disease 'blurs the whole picture of prostitution but also distorts the realities of prostitution for many workers'. For some, drug dependency has led men and women into prostitution, while, for others, drugs offer a means of coping with the realities of sex work (Sanders 2005a). Furthermore, not all sex workers are drug users or take recreational drugs. This view was echoed by one resident, who described how: 'they're definitely not all drugs users. They're not all on drugs. I mean that one on the bike.... That's her career' (Patrick, 53, white, Area 2 resident).

For those participants who believed that prostitutes were not on drugs or solely motivated by drug dependency, many stated that they felt that some prostitutes sold sexual services for monetary gain or simply in order to live a normal life. Some participants felt that 'there's always people who want the quick money' (Tina, 31, Afro-Caribbean, Area 1 resident) or who have 'got to get rich quick' (Linda, 62, Afro-Caribbean, Area 1 resident). Whereas others believed that they engaged in prostitution to bring up a family:

> Sometimes it's just as simple as giving their children the best things.
> (Gemma, 46, Afro-Caribbean, Area 1 resident)

> There are a small percentage that do it to get money to feed the family, to lead a decent life, even as well. But then there are the others who do it as a job, a lucrative job as well.
> (Tina, 31, Afro-Caribbean, Area 1 resident)

Some participants, particularly in Area 1, identified women who they had known to have sold sex, in order to support their family.

Putting themselves in danger

Many residents voiced their views that 'women of the night' were either wholly or partly to blame for any sexual and/or physical violence perpetrated against them. Kate (26, white, Area 2 resident) made a comment that epitomized the general perspective of residents, deeming any violence or abuse perpetrated against sex workers as their responsibility. As Kate claimed: 'In a way they're to blame for it. They know they're putting themselves out on the street or whatever, and they know what could happen, so in a way they're to blame for it I'd say.' Similarly, Naomi stated: 'they're putting their lives at risk' (Naomi, 32, Afro-Caribbean, Area 1 resident). Responsibility for avoiding violence was apportioned to women:

Women that take that road put themselves at risk, massively of getting raped..., it's hard to decide what it is that might be a punter that didn't have no money today.... That might be a punter that was drunk.... Some prostitutes say that's the risk. The one who had her arm severed ... she could have had her neck severed. It could have been her life that she lost. I mean look at what happened in, in Ipswich the other week there ... when this guy went on a killing spree. So I think.... It's part of the risk you take.

(Brian, 47, Afro-Caribbean, Area 1 resident)

They're putting their lives at risk. So why are they putting their lives at risk when they know.

(Naomi, 32, Afro-Caribbean, Area 1 resident)

Violence, sexual assault and abuse were considered to be 'part and parcel' of the job of a sex worker. In their discussions about the risks taken by sex workers, Emma (27, white, Area 2 resident) and Angela (27, white, Area 2 resident) identified clients as 'occupational hazards', using comparisons with other types of jobs to express their views:

It's like a builder getting hit by a pole or something.

(Emma, 27, white, Area 2 resident)

It's like certain professions carry certain risks.... You're a formula one driver; you might just crash your car and lose your life. If you are a prostitute selling sex ... then violence, because of the kinds of clients you might attract ... some of these clients ... are nasty and I'm sorry but if you get into that industry then you've got to appreciate the risks.

(Angela, 27, white, Area 2 resident)

This comparison suggests that such occupational risks are to be expected in this context and that, through choosing such risky behaviour, sex workers are well aware that such dangers may arise. According to Debbie (27, Afro-Caribbean, Area 1 resident), it is 'not a career where you can have, well if you can call it a career ... you don't have that kind of trust [with clients], you don't have that security so you're obviously bound to get like dodgy people'. Thus, it was assumed that female sex workers make individual decisions at the level of everyday life and must take the risks involved in sex work into account when choosing to sell sex. The individual must judge the likelihood of violence and/or abuse, making risk calculations as part of their decision making, ideas which feed into Beck's (1992) suggestion that we live in a 'Risk Society'.

The murder of five sex workers in Ipswich, UK, in December 2006 may have informed these views, due to the intense media publicity surrounding the murders (Lewis 2006; McGurran 2006; Troup 2006; Wright et al. 2006). As Craig (46, Afro-Caribbean, Area 2 community worker) explained: 'They [the media] don't really report if a prostitute dies unless there is about three and four and four and six in line, like what happened in Ipswich.' A similar 'moral panic' around the dangerous client in the form of the 'Yorkshire Ripper' (Hay 1995) was also identified by numerous participants, when discussing the dangers that sex workers experience while working in the sex industry. According to Kylie (54, white, Area 2 resident): 'some rapists start with prostitutes, that's what the Ripper did hadn't he'. The notorious case of the 'Yorkshire Ripper', which involved the murder of thirteen women and the attempted murder of a further seven women by Peter Sutcliffe during the 1980s, fuelled women's fear and anger of victimization. The media frenzy throughout the 1980s of a single male client who posed a serious threat to the safety of all women exaggerated the threat posed by men who buy sex on the street (Segal 1994; Smith 1989). Public perceptions of violence in the sex industry have been profoundly influenced by the serial murders of sex workers by Peter Sutcliffe – an acclaimed 'typical' punter in the 1980s (Kinnell 2008).

Research suggests that violence from clients is a daily hazard, both nationally and internationally (Nixon *et al.* 2002; Penfold *et al.* 2004; Sanders 2004a), with more than half of sex workers experiencing violence from clients in the previous year in Miami (Kurtz *et al.* 2004). Research into the extent of violence experienced by sex workers at the hands of their client shows that standardized mortality rates for sex workers are six times higher than any group of women from the general population in the UK (Goodyear and Cusick 2007: 52). Furthermore, research suggested that UK sex workers are sixty to 100 times more likely to be murdered than non-prostitute females (Salfati *et al.* 2008: 505).

Violence perpetrated against sex workers is not only perpetrated by clients. Pimps, drug dealers, other sex workers, community activists or family members have also been identified in UK research as perpetrators of violence towards sex workers (Kinnell 2008). The Sweet Project's *Violent Incident Report* (2007, cited in Kinnell 2008: 50) identified that while 34 per cent of violence reported was perpetrated by clients, 31 per cent was perpetrated by a partner/ex-partner/pimp, 3 per cent by family members and 31 per cent by others, such as vigilantes, muggers, drug dealers, other sex workers, acquaintances and men committing sexual violence who did not approach as clients.

Research within Liverpool, UK, has demonstrated how the police and local authorities in the city are now viewing violence and sexual abuse against sex workers as 'hate crime', because of the levels of violence that sex workers have experienced (Campbell 2011). As Campbell has demonstrated, comparisons made between female sex workers and non-sex working women's injuries sustained from sexual assaults show that sex workers' injuries are far more severe. This, it is believed, is related to negative societal views against sex workers. These women are considered to be unwanted and unmissed within society; evidence of a 'discourse of disposability' towards sex workers (Lowman 2000). Sex workers are generally despised within society and thus violence is justified, as they are deemed unworthy and lesser women.

Rape myths

Angela (27, Afro-Caribbean, Area 1 resident) expressed how she found it peculiar that sex workers can be raped. The peculiarity, she noted, was based upon the sale of sex: 'It's strange you know that you could actually get raped by a punter, coz you're selling sex, yourself aren't you. It's weird isn't it. I think that's the main thing.' Similarly, Joanne (25, white, Area 2 resident) also questioned rape claims made by prostitutes: 'What they classing as rape, not being paid for it?' Because prostitutes sell access to their bodies, it is assumed that they will consent to any sexual act and, thus, that rape claims are likely to be unfounded or will not be awarded sympathy.

Sexual promiscuity has long been associated with perceptions that women who are raped have in some way 'asked for it' (Suarez and Gadalla 2010). Debates surrounding rape trials have demonstrated how women who have had more than a handful of sexual partners are deemed to have 'invited' the sexual advances of men, because they are known to be sexually open (Smith and Skinner 2012). Women who do not adhere to dominant ideologies around femininity, which emphasize modesty and chastity, have been held partly responsible for any sexual aggression perpetrated against them (Chan 2001). Cotton *et al.* (2000) argue that such rape and prostitution myths are part of a cultural milieu that normalizes violence against women. Prostitution myths such as these, they assert, justify the existence of prostitution, promote distorted information about prostitution and sex workers and contribute to a social climate that justifies the exploitation and harm caused, not only to women who sell sex, but all women (Lonsway and Fitzgerald 1994). The belief that sex workers cannot be raped has been 'associated with culturally supported attitudes that encourage men to feel entitled to sexual access to women, to feel superior to women, or to feel they have the license as sexual aggressors' (Cotton *et al.* 2000: 1790). As sex workers do not conform to social norms that proscribe women's sexuality as more passive and reserved than men, their transgression of moral boundaries leads them to be considered as deviant, as they help to undermine deeply rooted cultural beliefs (Duncan 1996).

Despite the widespread belief that sex workers place themselves in situations where they are open to sexual attack, three female participants expressed their views that anyone, regardless of whether they are a prostitute or not, is open to being attacked. As Fiona and Ruby state:

> It could happen to you on your way with your friends at night you could get attacked or anything.
> (Fiona, 27, white, Area 2 resident)

> But everybody is though whether they're prostitutes or not.
> (Ruby, 23, white, Area 2 resident)

Interestingly, research into violence against women supports this view, but it, furthermore, challenges the belief that the street is a space where violence takes place. Research clearly shows that women are more likely to be attacked or murdered by someone they know, such as a partner or family member, and this more likely to take place behind closed doors (Berrington and Jones 2002). It would seem absurd that these women would be accused of placing themselves in a dangerous situation and were encouraging any violence perpetrated against them. Sex workers, because of the stigma associated with prostitution, are often seen as unworthy victims.

Dirty and diseased

A small number of participants (seven) made reference to how they felt that prostitutes were dirty or diseased. For instance, Angela (27, Afro-Caribbean, Area 1 resident) described how: 'the perception I had of them was that they were pretty dirty'. Similarly, Karen (32, Afro-Caribbean, Area 1 resident) stated how she would often see sex workers on the streets, and 'I just want to take them in and scrub them.' For others, they felt that selling sex 'increases the risk of picking up these infections' (Mary, 44, Afro-Caribbean, Area 1 resident).

Links between dirt, contagion and disease can be seen to stem as far back as the Contagious Diseases Acts 1864, 1866 and 1869 in the UK. These Acts firmly established the belief that women working as prostitutes, not their clients, were the source of contagious diseases (Walkowitz 1980). These acts sought to monitor and manage the spread of sexually transmitted diseases in the armed forces and allowed police officers to arrest prostitutes and subject them to compulsory checks for venereal disease, while their male clients went unchecked. Similarly, in more recent years, sex workers were seen as likely vehicles or spreaders of HIV/AIDS in the 1980s and thus a source of sexually transmitted diseases (Matthews 2008).

Although some may argue that such links are justified because sexual liaisons can often lead to an increased risk of contracting sexually transmitted infections, research indicates that sex workers and their clients consistently engage in safe sex practices. In the UK, research has found condom use to be high. In Glasgow, 68 per cent of men who contacted prostitutes on the street used a condom on their last visit (Barnard and McKeganey 1992). More recent research in the UK shows similar results. Sanders (2008: 56) found, in a sample of fifty men, 60 per cent identified that they had used condoms throughout the history of their engagement in the sex industry. Internationally, there are similarly high levels of condom use amongst clients (Fox *et al.* 2006; Marino *et al.* 2004; Wong *et al.* 2005).

Yet, despite this research, links between prostitution and sexual infections remain in the public imagination. Some of my participants referred to the risks of clients catching infections and diseases from sex workers and then transmitting them to their wives or partners. Although a minority suggested that some prostitutes were clean and disease-free, such as Liam, who said that: 'There's some very clean and healthy prostitutes, course there is' (54, Afro-Caribbean, Area 1 resident), many identified prostitutes as 'dirty', 'mucky' and 'riddled' and that men who buy sex are 'going to pick up these germs' (Joanne, 25, white, Area 2 resident). According to one lady, they 'don't think about catching a disease or something.... And then you take it home to your lovely wife' (Mary, 44, Afro-Caribbean, Area 1 resident). Similarly, in New Zealand, members of the Papatoetoe Community Patrol group believed that some sex workers carried diseases and posed a risk to their clients and client's partners (New Zealand Herald 2009). Many of the female participants in my study explained how they felt sorry for the wives of men who buy sex, because they have no knowledge of their partner's sexual deviancies. This sympathy, for some, related their personal reflections upon their own relationships with men. Placing themselves in the position of women whose partners paid for sex, they empathized with them. Values around monogamy and social disapproval of adultery seemed key to some of these women, and these are ideas that relate to a specific cultural context, in which family values, relationship commitment and marriage are often emphasized (Weeks 2007).

Sympathy for plight

Despite numerous negative views and attitudes expressed towards prostitutes, residents demonstrated a degree of sympathy for sex workers in some instances, often despite simultaneously holding negative views. Many participants expressed how they felt sorry for female sex workers, as they perceived the work that they do as something they would not undertake themselves:

> I think it's a shame for the women ... it must be horrible.
> (Joanne, 25, white, Area 2 resident)

> It's awful. They've just destroyed themselves.
> (Emma, 27, Afro-Caribbean, Area 1 resident)

For others, their sympathy related to seeing women on the streets late at night and during the winter months, when temperatures can often drop to below freezing:

> I mean it's really sad ... I've noticed that some of the workers now don't even wait until it gets dark ... and I'm driving from work and ... there's girls there in rush hour traffic ... you just think it's really desperate.
> (Vicky, 31, white, Area 2 researcher)

> I do feel sad for the prostitutes and I'm really concerned coz when I drive past it's so cold sometimes and raining.
> (Mary, 44, Afro-Caribbean, Area 1 resident)

Interestingly, even those who, at the time of the research, were actively campaigning for the removal of prostitution from their streets and who often held the most negative views, because of the nuisance caused by street prostitution, expressed their concern and sympathy for sex workers. Some residents also gave local prostitutes assistance and help when they were in need. For example, Patrick described many instances where he called the police, because of his concerns for the safety and well-being of local prostitutes:

> There's one, she was so hammered, whether she was drunk or I think probably more drugged up. She's nearly getting knocked down and its right rat run is this road, you know at rush hour. So cars come up here, they come shooting a long here and she's that hammered as the cars are sort of like pulling up because the traffic. She thought they were pulling up for her. And she's staggering.... And I phoned police. I said look you'd better take this one away coz basically she' going to get killed coz she keeps stepping out into the road. Anyway they came and took her away.
> (Patrick, 53, white, Area 2 resident)

Therefore, despite some negative attitudes that some residents 'hate prostitutes' (Brian, 47, Afro-Caribbean, Area 1 resident), participants also expressed empathy and sympathy. Although sex workers often face widespread stigma and sometimes participants did not want sex workers in their area, they still demonstrated compassion and expressed concern for their well-being.

Attitudes towards clients

Men

As with the gendered perceptions of sex workers, clients were often assumed to be male. This perception is similarly reflected in the media, political debates, policy documents and research literature. This may, overall, be an accurate reflection of the nature of prostitution, as studies show that men are more likely to pay for sexual services. For instance, US research has suggested that the purchasers of commercial sex are predominantly male (Jordan 1997; Shrage 1999). In the UK, it has been estimated that £534 million is spent each year in escort and parlour sex markets (Moffat and Peters 2004: 684), with estimates that between 4 per cent (Johnson *et al.* 2001; Ward *et al.* 2005) and 10 per cent of men in the UK have paid for sex in their lifetime (Groom and Nandwani 2006: 364). In London (UK), research conducted by Johnson *et al.* (1994, 2001) indicates that the number of men reporting having paid for sex has doubled over ten years, with up to 8.9 per cent of men reporting that they have paid for sex over the previous five years (2001: 1837). Similar increases were evident in Glasgow (UK), as research has highlighted that some men contacted at least five sex workers in the last twelve months (Barnard and McKeganey 1992). Two years later, in a separate study in Glasgow, this figure was 10.7 times (McKeganey 1994: 291). Internationally, research has shown that over one-quarter of men in one survey had paid for sex in their lifetime in Spain (Belza *et al.* 2008) and 15 per cent of men in the United States (Langer *et al.* 2004). Red-light districts, such as Amsterdam (Netherlands), Prague (Czech Republic), Phuket (Thailand) and Nevada (US), predominantly cater to men who buy sex.

Male clients were also perceived as *always* willing to buy sex, which fed into discussions around prostitution being the oldest profession. According to one resident: 'prostitution will be there forever, because there are people who are prepared to go and do it and there are men who are prepared to go and buy it' (James, 60, Afro-Caribbean, Area 1 resident). Participants proposed that, for some men, 'it's their way of life to use' sex workers (Angela, 27, Afro-Caribbean, Area 1 resident) and that 'there'll always be men wanting sex' (Linda, 62, Afro-Caribbean, Area 1 resident). Research on male clients both supports and challenges these views. Sanders' (2008b) research catalogued different typologies of clients, with some that bought sex throughout their lifetime, others who were sporadic users and some men who bought sex once or twice over the course of their life. Similarly, Hammond (2010) found that some men had been involved for decades, others less consistently and some who found it difficult to stop buying sex.

This is not to say that women do not buy sex, as research has documented female clients. Research into female sex buyers has predominantly focused upon relationships between North American and European female tourists, who go to underdeveloped countries for a holiday and have sexual relations with local males (Herold *et al.* 2001). Studies of relationships between female tourists and local males have been conducted in the Dominican Republic (Herold *et al.* 2001; Sánchez-Taylor 2001), Cuba (Cabezas 2004), Jamaica (O'Connell Davidson and Sánchez-Taylor 1999; Pruitt and LaFont 1995), Barbados (de Albuquerque 1998), Costa Rica (Romero-Daza and Freidus 2008), Indonesia (Dahles and Bras 1999) and Greece (Lazaridis and Wickens 1999). The extensive documentation of female sex tourism thereby evidences the degree to which women also buy sex and questions the assertions made that conveys the 'prostitute user' as 'a man'. Similarly, statistics that identify the extent to which men buy sex must take into account the number of men buying sex from other men or transgendered individuals (Bloor *et al.* 1992; Elifson *et al.* 1993a; Elifson *et al.* 1993b). Furthermore, given that the sex industry is an under-researched and hidden area, statistics must be considered with caution and are merely a representation of a much broader picture.

Although female sex tourism is well recorded, it would appear that the UK's sex industry is still predominantly catering for male consumers, and, on the whole, female sex tourists are in the minority in the UK. For example, internet searches, reviews of newspapers, website searches advertising sexual services, lap dancing clubs, strip shows and research in the UK establishes that the gendered nature of the sex industry is catered more towards heterosexual male desires. This lack of research into women who buy sex and the gendered nature of the UK's sex industry require further consideration and investigation.

Motivations

Participants described many reasons why they believed male clients purchased sex, which, in each case, somewhat reflected the literature and academic research in this area.

Lonely

Five participants identified that male clients buy sex because they are lonely and engage in prostitution because they want emotional or social intimacy. Kate (26, white, Area 2 resident) and Stacey (20, white, Area 2 resident) classified men who buy sex as, typically: 'A lonely, old man.' Others expressed their view that men often did not want to have sex; instead, they often wanted someone they could talk to and would pay sex workers for their time:

> Prostitution doesn't necessarily mean that somebody's going to have intercourse with another person. Some of those guys go and meet women and they do other things. Some guys just go for somebody to talk to.
> (Brian, 47, Afro-Caribbean, Area 1 resident)

> It's not always about sex, coz this one was saying to me that she had a lot of clients and she was well paid and at the end of the day the person just wanted to come and talk, talk for an hour.
> (Linda, 62, Afro-Caribbean, Area 1 resident)

Research similarly suggests that sex workers provide more than sexual services. In some cases, the service involves more than just 'sex', but also emotional intimacy (Jordan 1997; Pickering et al. 1992; Sanders 2005a; Vanwesenbeeck et al. 1993). Evidence of emotional intimacy may be drawn from research that indicates that some clients disclose personal information (Marina 1993). McLeod's (1982) interviews with clients in Birmingham also revealed that men sought out the services of sex workers because their marriage was emotionally and sexually unfulfilling. Rather than being an uncontrollable urge whereby men have sex with the nearest women, McLeod argues that male sex buyers seek sexual and emotional connection. Similarly, Jordan's (1997) in-depth interviews with thirteen indoor clients found that men visited sex workers to relieve their sense of intense loneliness.

The 'girlfriend experience' has been identified by some male clients as something that they are looking for when purchasing sex. They are also looking for friendship, conversation, intimacy, affection and providing, what some call, the 'GFE' or 'girlfriend experience' (Sharp and Earle 2002: 36). Some men show a preference for the use of only one or two sex workers, maintaining regular contact – in one case, for up to thirteen years (McKeganey 1994: 293). In some instances, clients will remain with a prostitute for a whole night having sex once, in fewer cases, twice and, in even fewer instances, three or more times (Pickering et al. 1992). This experience is sought by some men who want to feel 'special', not just another client. The desire for the girlfriend experience may be linked to a client's loneliness and/or inability to form non-commercial sexual relationships (Campbell 1998). Some men visit prostitutes due to their difficulty in establishing non-commercial relationships, because they lack self-confidence or because they are unattractive (Jordan 1997; Xantidis and McCabe 2000). For men living with an impairment who are prevented from engaging in everyday social and leisure activities where relationships can begin, such experiences may provide company and sexual relations (Sanders 2007). Similarly, some single men in Sanders' (2008b) study highlighted that they have problems meeting single women. For men in relationships, this loneliness may stem from feelings of emotional and physical dissatisfaction in their current relationship. A lack of intimacy in a long-term relationship or marriage was the reason given for why some men buy sex (Sanders 2008a).

Excitement and fun

Excitement and fun were identified as reasons why participants believed some men buy sex, as Kylie explained:

> I think from a man's perspective it might be that there's a sense of adventure ... it's a bit risky, you know it's out of your normal comfort zone and the sense of a sexual adventure.
>
> (Kylie, 54, white, Area 2 resident)

Engaging in an activity deemed dangerous, risky and different to a man's 'normal' everyday life was also described:

> For some men, it's just another way of getting kicks and there's the excitement and there's the kind of like this danger, oh you know it's very kind of like it's almost like another life.
>
> (Paula, 42, Afro-Caribbean, Area 1 resident)

The suggestion that men who buy sex do so to engage in an activity that is different and out of the ordinary was also expressed by some participants, when they shared their beliefs that men buy sex to be 'dirty'. A small number of participants believed that men bought sex to bring excitement into their lives, through engaging in an activity considered to be 'dirty' and 'seedy'. As two participants explained:

> Some of the prostitutes are so dirty and so dirty looking ... but they live in such a clean world ... with probably a clean wife, a clean house and they want to live dirty for a split second.
>
> (Brian, 47, Afro-Caribbean, Area 1 resident)

> He needs that one bit of dirt in his life.
>
> (Emma, 27, Afro-Caribbean, Area 1 resident)

Research has demonstrated that the illicit nature of prostitution, for many men, offers excitement and an added thrill to their lives (Campbell 1997, 1998; McKeganey 1994; McKeganey and Barnard 1996; Monto 2000). The thrill or excitement of engaging in the sex industry was the most frequently cited motivation in Campbell's study (1997). Some men found the illicit and taboo nature of the sex industry enduring and exciting. Similarly, the possibility of being caught by the police makes the sexual transaction a risky but thrilling pursuit. Others stated that such engagement fulfilled a sexual fantasy. Sexual experimentation was a motivation identified by ten men in Sanders' (2008b: 35) sample, all of which were aged over 55 years. This, for some men, may be seen as their final chance to experiment in different and diverse sexual relationships.

Dependency and sexual needs

Emma and Angela both described a sexual need and dependency as one reason why some men buy sex. Explaining their attitudes, they stated that:

> It's like fix.... Some people smoke cigarettes, some people drink alcohol.
> (Emma, 27, Afro-Caribbean, Area 1 resident)

> Some people are just nymphomaniacs, just obsessed with sex.
> (Angela, 27, Afro-Caribbean, Area 1 resident)

The fulfilment of a 'sexual urge' is a reason explicitly given by some male clients. The majority (43.8 per cent of 612 clients surveyed) of Pitts *et al.*'s (2004: 356) study identified that the reason why they purchased commercial sex was to satisfy their sexual needs. In some studies, they described their sexual urge as an overwhelming desire that needed to be satisfied. Likewise, in other studies, male sex buyers have catalogued feelings of sexual frustration and often shared a belief that their behaviour was a normal, reasonable expression of male sexuality (Campbell 1997, 1998; Monto 2004). For some, this expression of heterosexual male sexuality was fuelled by a desire to reassure themselves that they were normal and subvert any homosexual tendencies (Gibbens and Silverman 1960). Such sexual subversions support the idea that male sexual desire is socially constructed as an expression of a powerful urge to seek sexual gratification from women. Within this discourse, men are constructed as 'active predatory sexual initiators' (Campbell 1998: 167).

Research by Jordan (1997) supports this male sexual desire discourse, as male clients discuss men's higher sex drive compared to women. According to some men in the study, women generally tended to lose interest in sex, while the male sex drive remained strong. This discrepancy between men's and women's sex drives is the rationale for why some men purchase sex acts, as these clients did not believe leaving their current partners was an option. Women's lack of sex drive was thus used by some men as a means of justifying their involvement in the sex industry (Prasad 1999). The ability to have the type of sex they want, when they want it, may be seen, by men, as an essential part of masculinity and male sexuality. This assumption has underpinned popular culture and science for centuries, which Carpenter (1998) argues is evidenced by the suggestion that prostitution is an inevitability and is motivated by natural male tendencies. For some men, sexual stimulation is the only motivating factor in their involvement in the sex industry. This sexual stimulation is predominantly vaginal, with oral sex being the second most popular sexual service desired (Pickering *et al.* 1992). For many men who buy sex, prostitution has an enduring appeal, due to the ability that these men have to purchase specific sexual acts. Men who are not in a personal relationship often seek specific sexual services as a means to release sexual 'frustrations', while avoiding any emotional involvement (Kinnell 1989).

Specific sexual acts

The belief that men engaged in prostitution to purchase specific sexual acts was a key motivation indicated by participants. Many participants believed that men bought sex from a prostitute because 'they do things that their wives or their regular girlfriend won't do' (Linda, 62, Afro-Caribbean, Area 1 resident). As Craig (45, Afro-Caribbean, Area 2 community worker) further explained: 'Some people just want a quickie, some people want a hand job, everybody wants different things.' Others felt that the sexual services bought were either those 'that they can't get from their wives or they can't get from their girlfriends' (Gemma, 46, Afro-Caribbean, Area 1 resident) or those 'that they can't do with their wife' (Liam, 54, Afro-Caribbean, Area 1 resident). Men who buy sex have identified a lack of specific sexual acts, such as oral or anal sex, within their non-commercial relationships as the motivating factor in academic research. Some men have indicated that their partners were unable or unwilling to satisfy their sexual needs (Campbell 1997, 1998; Jordan 1997; Kinnell 1989; Monto 2000). The sexual transaction is cited as compensation for the shortcomings in such relationships (McKeganey and Barnard 1996) and is often justified on the grounds that it keeps a marriage together (Campbell 1998).

The relationship shortcomings that some male clients suggest are not always a shortcoming on the part of the clients' partners. Sex workers are often, to some men, deemed as professionals, who are able to fulfil their sexual fantasies. Some men believe that it is often unreasonable to expect a partner to satisfy some of their sexual preferences, while others deem their partners unable to provide specific techniques. Such specialist services include bondage, sadomasochism and other forms of physical acts, such as being urinated or defecated on (Campbell 1998; Gemme 1993; Monto 2001; Plumbrige 2001; Vanwesenbeeck *et al.* 1993). The pursuit of sexual services for some male clients allows their sexual desires to be central and relieves the concern of how their sexual preferences might be judged by a non-commercial partner. Such sexual gratification has led some to argue that men view sex workers as nothing more than sexual objects (McKeganey 1994).

Relationship status

The majority of participants identified men who buy sex as married or in a relationship. Only one participant classified a man who buys sex as someone who 'doesn't have a girlfriend or a partner or anything' (Ruby, 23, white, Area 2 resident). Throughout many conversations and discussions, participants made reference to 'girlfriends' (Tara, 20, white resident) and 'wives' (Mary, 44, Afro-Caribbean, Area 1 resident) and research somewhat reflects these attitudes. For instance, in the UK, New Zealand and Ecuador, the average client was found to be married (Barnard *et al.* 1993; Gutierrez *et al.* 2006; Jordan 1997; McKeganey 1994; Sanders 2008b) or in a long-term relationship (Campbell 1998; Coy *et al.* 2007). Whereas, in the US, men who buy sex were less likely to be married (Monto and McRee 2005), and, in Gambia, two-thirds were single (Pickering *et al.* 1992). The differences in the marital status of men who buy sex from women may be attributable to different methodological techniques (Kinnell 1989) or differences in international cultures. The purchase of sex by single men may be relatively more acceptable or non-commercial sexual interactions less common in the US and Gambia, which would account for the higher incidence of single male use. Alternatively, these differences may stem from increased cultural stigma afforded to the purchase of commercial sex by married men in these two countries. Men who buy sex in Gambia or the US may be less likely to reveal their marital status, because of fear of reprisal.

Although the majority of men who buy sex are categorized as married by the research cited, the differences between single, divorced or widowed men may not be overwhelming. For instance, in Sanders' (2008b: 34) research, eighteen out of a sample of fifty male sex buyers identified themselves as married, in contrast to twelve single men, nine divorced or separated and four widowed.

For those clients who are married, the perceived nature of the commercial sexual transaction as emotionally uninvolved and relatively anonymous is the attraction for some men who buy sex (Campbell 1997, 1998; Gibbens and Silverman 1960; Kinnell 1989; McKeganey 1994; Vanwesenbeeck *et al.* 1993). Many men feel that paying for sex is not dissimilar to taking a woman out for a drink or a meal, with the implicit understanding that sex would ensue (Campbell 1998; McKeganey 1994). In essence, by contacting a sex worker, the same interaction can be stripped down to its component parts, thus allowing for greater convenience and minimum prior effort. Such an uninvolved interaction appears to appeal more to men who are involved in long-term relationships. Prostitution, for these men, offers a means of having sexual variety, without posing a threat to their primary relationship (McKeganey 1994). Some men have claimed that such sexual relations posed less risk than having an extra-marital affair (Jordan 1997).

Buying sex as a leisure activity

The belief that buying sex is 'harmless fun' or is simply part of male leisure activities emerged when participants discussed male stag parties. According to

Rachel, having sex with prostitutes on a stag night out: 'it's like a day out at Blackpool, you go on the rides' (Rachel, 43, Afro-Caribbean, Area 1 resident). In recent years, the proportion of men visiting places such as Estonia from England has increased, as a result of travel companies that arrange 'stag parties' (Lawrence and Aral 2005: 23). This increase may have led to cultural assumptions that deem stag parties a marital rite of passage. As a rite of passage, marriage is seen as including specific rituals and practices (Bernardo and Vera 1981). For men on bachelor or stag parties, engaging in the purchase of sex may be socially considered as a ritual, which, O'Connell Davidson (1998) suggests, has been historically situated. Thus, as Joan Smith (2006: 1) concurs: 'In the world of stag-night excess, lad mags and lap dancing, paying for sex is losing its stigma and more and more men do it.'

As a ritualized male practice in some Western nations, stag parties may be considered as a context in which dominant masculine practices, such as male virility and risky sexual behaviour, are exercised. Research illustrates that young men in male peer groups have been shown to compete with each other, measuring their own and others' sexual success in terms of sexual conquest and experience (Kimmel 1994). Such sexual conquests are deemed an enviable achievement (Curry 2002). Research has highlighted that, while men generally do not discuss commercial sexual contacts with each other, there are situations where this does occur, which include 'stag party' trips and holidays, where commercial sex may be a 'collective experience' (Ward *et al.* 2005: 470). In Pakistani culture, men display and demonstrate their economic power to their peers through engagement with female dancers. As Brown (2007: 417) explains, elite men would often give female dancers thousands of pounds in a 'very visible prelude to pursuing a more intimate relationship with the tawa'if'. The purchase of sex during stag parties may, therefore, be considered a desirable accomplishment, as it reaffirms a sense of masculinity or power. However, the context in which this takes place is significant, as distance and place are important issues that inform these beliefs, which are explored further in Chapter 8.

Big men in high places

A theme that emerged from my research was the belief that men who buy sex are likely to be wealthy and hold a position of power or be employed in a high-status job. Rachel (42, Afro-Caribbean, Area 1 resident) emphasized social class status when she stated:

> They're all big men in high places aren't they a lot of them and they'll just go from work, do a quick thing and go home.... Coz then you get the big hierarchy in prostitution don't you where you have the judges and everybody.

Similarly, Claire (57, Afro-Caribbean, Area 1 resident) and Brian (47, Afro-Caribbean, Area 1 resident) identified seeing 'prestigious councillors' and 'known consultants' visit areas known for street sex work.

Alongside social status, residents distinguished male sex buyers as wealthy. This wealth was represented by the types of cars that the men drive. The types of cars were described by three male and one female resident: 'it was proper money men that was coming in the area in flashy cars and stuff like that, yeah, so it was obvious' (Terry, 27, Afro-Caribbean, Area 1 community worker). Similarly, Patrick (53, white, Area 2 resident) established that, where he lives, 'you get a lot of them like, older blokes, but you get a lot of businessmen. I've had a lot of them. The best one was there was a brand new BMW, and Mercedes.' Arguably, expensive cars are more distinguishable and obvious to residents in the areas that they live; therefore, residents' perceptions are informed by the vehicles that they have seen kerb-crawling in their area.

The perception of male clients as men with money was the basis of two male resident's lack of understanding for the motivation behind purchasing sex on the street. Brian found it difficult to conceive why 'rich' men decided to kerb-crawl, when, as Brian suggested, they could arguably go to a club in the city centre and meet women:

> if I go down to city centre I can walk into lots of clubs, this evening and if I'm spending money I will pick up a woman.... That's, coz, that's the beauty of the beast.... But he doesn't he chooses to pay ten pounds to take somebody to [Area 2] park or to take somebody down the woods.... Why, why's this rich guy. You can see he's rich. Why does he need to come down [Area 2 street] and pick up a woman? Why?
>
> (Brian, 47, Afro-Caribbean, Area 1 resident)

Yet, what residents did not identify was that such cars may potentially belong to 'pimps' or 'drug dealers', who may similarly be economically wealthy. Residents assumed that flashy cars are driven by male clients.

Interestingly, the perception that men who buy sex from women drive 'flashy cars' is coupled with the perception that men who drive nice cars are less likely to be violent or abusive. Angela suggested that: 'not every client is going to be driving a nice shaped Audi or a nice Merc, some of these clients are coming there are nasty. They're nasty men' (Angela, 27, Afro-Caribbean, Area 1 resident). Research has identified that sex workers use signs of wealth to assess whether their client is a 'good type'. According to Sanders (2005b: 55): 'a man who is well dressed in a suit or designer clothing, wearing gold jewellery and driving an expensive car, displays enough signs to convince a sex worker he is a good type'. Residents therefore examine what Posner (2002: 21) calls 'conspicuous consumption' and 'cultural competence', in order to assess whether a client is a good or bad type. Previous research in other areas has documented the impact of cultural socialization on perceptions of the drivers of particular vehicles and social class, with the predominant identification of the driver of vehicles being middle class (Luken *et al.* 2006). Flashy cars may be deemed a signal of 'middle class respectability' (Bao 2004: 125).

'Hypocritical Muslim men'

The perception that men who buy sex from women are predominantly Muslim or Pakistani was held by a local authority official, a resident and was also expressed as a community view by a second official. This community view was expressed by Eli (55, Afro-Caribbean, Area 1 community worker), who believed that: 'Muslims, particularly Pakistanis' are the sex workers' 'best customers, most fanciful customers'. But despite being sex workers' best customers, Eli explains that: 'come Friday they would spit at them and all this "go away, go away" because they were going to Mosque. But it was the best place to attract customers.' In 'using' and then 'disowning' sex workers, Muslim and Pakistani men were accused of being hypocritical.

The hypocrisy alluded to was attributed to religion by Craig (45, Afro-Caribbean, Area 2 community worker). He claimed that religion played a pivotal role in the reasons why some communities complain about prostitution and, in the same sense, engage in the sex industry. Stereotyping the Asian community, Craig explained that:

> Certain communities, like the Asian community they are complaining about it ... some of the religious leaders are complaining says 'oh we do not like the prostitution in our area' ... but it's them who's buying it.... It's all about religion, it's nothing about what men want ... in them countries they arranges marriage so everybody have a woman so you don't need to look at another woman. But it's not so when they come here, they says oh, everything's out in the open, showing, so they can look so when there's places for them to buy they will purchase that bit there, but in their own environment it doesn't happen.
>
> (Craig, 45, Afro-Caribbean, Area 2 community worker)

The 'hypocrisy' identified may be the result of cultural beliefs that expressions of sexuality outside of marriage are considered inappropriate and immoral (Okazaki 2002). Asian and Muslim men, they argue, thus protest about the existence of street prostitution, because it challenges their sexually conservative beliefs, but they do so in order to 'mask' their 'deviant' sexual behaviour.

In some Muslim communities in the Midlands, local residents attempted to deter street sex workers by standing outside their houses (Hubbard 1998a). Similarly, in Jakarta, Muslim groups ordered that local government close a known brothel, and, following dissatisfaction with the Jakarta Government's response to prostitution, the Islamic Defenders Front broke into the City Hall (Yamin 1999). Similarly, an initiative led by Oldham Muslim Centre launched patrols in the local area, confronting kerb-crawlers, drug dealers and prostitutes in an attempt to reclaim the streets (Begum 2008a). More than 100 men formed a vigilante group to drive the problem out of the area through naming and shaming offenders who live in the local area by informing their families of their actions (Begum 2008b).

The perception of Asian, Muslim men, noted by Craig, may be considered illustrative of a significant shift in the perception of Asian, Muslim masculinities, from being hyper-feminized and passive towards a hyper-masculinity (Alexander 2000b). These shifts and re-imagination of Muslim masculinities 'has drawn on a legacy of radicalized pathologies ... which ... transfixes Muslim men as the new dangerous "Other"' (Alexander 2000a: 123). This 'other-ing' is evident in Craig's suggestion that the Asian, Muslim community is not in their own environment. What Craig may have been suggesting was that the Asian community and religious leaders, to which he referred to, were immigrants and not British citizens and that their engagement in prostitution was related to their culture, rather than religion. Arguably, Craig was indicating that such communities were 'out of place', despite literature from second generation Pakistani immigrants, which has documented that they identify themselves as British citizens (Hussain and Bagguley 2005). What may be suggested is that, through proposing that men who buy sex from women are from immigrant communities, Craig is distancing the Asian, Muslim community from himself, in order to create a sense of the 'other'. Highlighting the hypocrisy of this ethnic and/or religious group fuels this 'other-ing'.

Interestingly, the identification that Asian, Muslim men are purchasing sex is only made by participants who lived or worked in Area 1. This stereotyping may therefore reflect the ethnic and religious make-up of the area. Two of those who stereotyped Muslim men as purchasers of sex came from the Afro-Caribbean community, and the third person who identified this community perception represented the community in Area 1. Tension between African-Caribbean residents born in Leeds (or those living there for a considerable period of time) and 'outsiders' has been deemed inevitable (Hylton 1999). 'Outsiders' to the African-Caribbean community may be considered to be any other communities, according to a survey that mapped the religious groups in Area 1 (Fotiou *et al.* 2007). A distinct lack of integration between all religious groups in Area 1 was identified as contributing towards a sense of segregation between religious communities (Fotiou *et al.* 2007). This context may have contributed to the identification of 'outsiders' as Asian/Muslim men who buy sex from women.

Chapter summary

This chapter has examined perceptions of female sex workers, their clients and prostitution, in order to demonstrate the diverse views held about the nature of prostitution and those involved. Attitudes explored often mirrored academic literature in these areas and recognized the complexities of the sex industry. Yet, in some instances, views captured often related to cultural assumptions and stereotypes about who was involved in sex work and why. In particular, it is concerning that people held the view that sex workers were in some manner responsible for any acts of violence and abuse perpetrated against them when they choose to sell sex. This tells us more about the cultural context in which these people are situated, rather than intrinsic beliefs that the participants held themselves. As discussed, sex work goes against moral and family values, which see the sale of sex as an immoral act. Furthermore, this chapter has highlighted interesting comparisons between men who buy sex during stag parties and those who buy sex on the street, which will be explored further in the following chapters. Yet, here, it can be seen that, while buying sex during stag parties is sometimes seen as a leisure activity, kerb-crawling was linked to dirt and disease.

Note

1 For more detailed examination of the history of prostitution, see Sanger (1858) and Bassermann (1967).

5 The impact of prostitution on communities

Previous research has highlighted the nuisance that prostitution has caused to communities, such as noise, litter, anti-social behaviour, public sex, reduction of business investments, lowering of property prices and reputational damage (Hubbard 1998a; Matthews 2008; Pitcher *et al.* 2006). These concerns have mainly centred on the impact that street prostitution has on residential and business neighbourhoods, despite indoor sex markets existing in many cities and towns. Similarly, in my research, street prostitution was considered to have the greatest negative impact on local communities, because of the related nuisance caused, the presence and visibility of prostitutes and also the associated stigma. Although indoor sex work is considered in this book, the discussion here focuses on mainly on-street prostitution, because of the nature of my research. This chapter aims to show some of the detrimental consequences that street prostitution can have for residential and business districts. Yet, it is often assumed that prostitution has an adverse influence on communities. By challenging this assumption, the chapter will also examine the positive and beneficial role that sex work can have for communities – in particular, the impact on local economies through increased visitors and local trade, as well as crime prevention.

The negative impact of street prostitution

The negative impact that street prostitution has on businesses and residential neighbourhoods was a significant concern raised by residents, businesses employees, councillors and the police. Many identified the negative impact that street prostitution has upon local businesses' and residential districts' image and reputation, as well as concerns about the presence and visibility of environmental debris, such as litter and used condoms in these areas. These anxieties correspond to existing literature, which has documented concerns over the negative impact that street prostitution has had on business trade, the stigma of being associated with living in an area known for street prostitution, concerns for safety and the displeasure of having to dispose of debris, such as condoms, needles and other environmental waste (Edwards 1991; Hubbard 1998a; O'Neill and Campbell 2006). According to Matthews (2008), the nuisance caused to local neighbourhoods led to a significant change in public attitudes and was the

The impact of prostitution on communities 79

reason why many communities decided to take action to rid their streets of prostitution. Matthews' (2008) research highlighted how some residents complained about finding used condoms and other paraphernalia on their premises, whereas others objected to the increasing number of cars visiting the area and the public arguments between prostitutes, clients and pimps.

Reputation and image

Many residents and business employees indicated how street prostitution in the areas where they lived and worked had a negative impact on their business, their neighbourhood and themselves. Residents felt that street prostitution 'created a negative impact on this community' (Brian, 47, Afro-Caribbean, Area 1 resident) and, as a result of this association, 'It's like giving us a bad name' (Angela, 27, Afro-Caribbean, Area 1 resident). As James (60, West Indian, Area 2 resident) explained: 'Everybody tried to get [street prostitution] away from [Area 2 street] because it brought a bad impression on the people who live in this area.' These concerns mirror those of many other UK and international residential and business communities' concerns about the negative impact that street prostitution has upon the reputation and image of an area, the people who live there and their businesses. In Michigan (US), residents argued that the presence of street prostitution 'brings the whole reputation of our neighborhood down.... It makes us look like trash' (Field 2009: 1). For residents and businesses in Preston, Dundee and Southall, London (UK), street prostitution was deemed to give these areas a negative reputation, which often impacted negatively on business trade (Lancashire Evening Post 2008; Wilson 2011).

Maintaining a good reputation and projecting the 'right' image was identified by seven business representatives as a key interest. Street prostitution was considered a source of embarrassment and believed to project the wrong image of a company. Roger (57, white, director) illustrated the effects that an association between prostitution and particular buildings and streets can have upon local businesses. As Roger (57, white, director) described, the building that his company owned had been used by the media as a poignant image of prostitution and murder in Leeds:

> I own a building down the road ... whenever there was any programme on prostitution on television, if there were murders this building was always, always on television (laugh) you know it was always featured for the wrong reasons. So it was very embarrassing.

This embarrassment stemmed from the associations that residents and businesses had with prostitution, because it took place in the areas in which they lived and worked; as Goffman's work (1963: 43) suggests, they experienced stigma by association. Because prostitution is often stigmatized, 'the problems faced by stigmatized persons spread out in waves' (Goffman 1969: 43). The stigma associated with prostitution became fused with residential and business properties, because of the close geographical proximity. They, too, believed that they would be seen in negative ways.

The associations made between street prostitution and local business premises were highlighted as a potential hindrance and business problem by five of the nine business representatives that were interviewed. Street prostitution was considered to be 'bad for business', because 'customers get put off from coming into the area' (Anthony, 34, white, manager). In particular, three police officers identified how street prostitution was tolerated in the industrial site of Area 2, but that it was not until business and residential groups moved into the district that street prostitution became a problem:

> They've got a load of brand new flats like for half a million pounds.... So obviously they're complaining about it.... They're spending millions and millions and millions of pounds and there's going to be people living there ... that's why they're trying to tidy it up.
> (Dean, 30, white, Area 2 police constable)

> [Area 2] had an unmentioned tolerance zone. It was somewhere where they could forget about it, and it kept the problem away ... from the city centre. Very affluent city centre, didn't want prostitutes. But the police knew they were going down there.... It was only when we started to get the multi-million pound apartment developments down there where a lot of people were paying big money to buy apartments and don't want to be looking down to watch, you know, men and women having sex in alleyways. Girls walking around the area, that [Area 1] started doing something about it.
> (Terry, 53, white, Area 1 police constable)

The existence of street prostitution in an area over a period of time was categorized as creating a particular reputation, both in the business and non-business world. This reputation was perceived as tainting the image of a business and was identified as a 'deal-breaker':

> You know word gets around ... in the market place. And in terms of being able to let your premises it causes a problem. So from a developer's perspective there is that issue of you can build a lovely scheme that at the end of the day once it gets a reputation for being a bit risky and a bit dangerous, then it can put tenants off.
> (Roger, 57, white, director)

Concerns regarding the reputation of an area, because of the presence of street prostitution, were equivalently expressed by residents in Northampton (UK) and Lisbon (Portugal). According to one resident in Northampton (UK): 'whenever a person hears the place name Semilong [people say] "ah that's where the street prostitute problem is"' (Semilong Northampton Residents Group 2009). This negative image was also seen as impinging upon residents' ability to sell their homes, and many residential developers' capacity to sell the properties that they built. Patrick (53, white, Area 2 resident) described how a neighbour had hoped to sell his home when police intervention in the area had led to a reduction in the presence of street prostitution, as he detailed:

> That's why that house has been done up next door. I think he's seen a window of opportunity, coz these two houses have been empty here for a couple of years. Seen people coming to look at them; they've seen a prostitute at end of street and they've gone, oh. And they've just drove off.
> (Patrick, 53, white, Area 2 resident)

Similarly, in Area 2, residential housing developers saw the presence and visibility of street prostitution as 'a threat to their ability to let or sell these flats' (Paul, 56, Area 2 Chief Superintendent). As Sian explained:

> They're wanting to bring a new image to the area and they're getting all the new flats there and they're trying to attract young professionals, the little cafes and bars there I think if the prostitutes started coming back, that would just ruin in their eyes.... I think that would put people off coming. They people they are trying to attract to the area will just get put off by it won't they.
> (Sian, 29, Area 2 police community support officer (PCSO))

Home ownership and a concern for property prices was a key issue for residents in Preston (UK), Helsinki and City Island (US), as residents were anxious that street prostitution would have a negative impact on the value of their homes and may cause problems if they decided to sell in the future (Helsingin Sanomat 2000; Lancashire Evening Post 2008). In City Island (US), Stanton residents were reluctant to speak out about the presence of prostitution in their area, 'because people are worried about their property values' (Jaccarino 2009: 1).

Cycle of decline

Street prostitution is often seen as encouraging a cycle of decline. Residents in Berlin (Germany) feared that the area where they lived would descend into seedy chaos, because of the presence of street prostitution (Reimann and Preuss 2007). In Portugal and London (UK), residents believed that street prostitution would lead to other social problems, such as other forms of criminality, as well as health and safety issues, robbery, substance misuse and theft (Gates 2008; The Portugal News Online 2008). Concern over the use of drugs and other associated crime was a worry for residents in both Beurton (US) and Coventry (UK) (Field 2009; The Swish Project 2008). As one resident explained: 'Prostitution has a way of filtering back into larger criminal problems' (Field 2009: 1). Similarly, Alan (58, white, security guard) and John (55, white, manager) felt that the existence of street prostitution in a particular area can be an indicator that other crimes will arise. Alan (58, white, security guard) noted seeing the use of drugs, and he believed that street prostitution and its visible aftermath encouraged such illegality. The view that street prostitution encourages additional crime and criminality is further illustrated by John (55, white, manager), who attributed local robberies to those involved in street prostitution, despite citing no evidence to support this claim:

> John explains that local businesses are concerned that prostitution brings other crimes with it. He says that colleagues and other businesses are concerned about the safety of their property and personal belongings, in light of a number of local break-ins in the area. These break-ins he believes are related to prostitution.
> (Interview notes with John, 55, white manager)

Similar concerns led residents of Basall Heath, Birmingham (UK), to put pressure on local police to respond to residential concerns, as they feared that the area would decline without intervention (Hubbard 1998a). Such nuisances are seen as contributing to a general feeling of criminality, signalling to people that the area is vulnerable to crime (O'Neill et al. 2008). It has been suggested that the visibility of low-level crime can lead to an increase in lawlessness and a breakdown in community controls, which corresponds with the ideas maintained within the 'broken windows theory' (Wilson and Kelling 1982). This theory maintains that a focus on minor offences of disorder deserve greater police attention than robbery or murder, due to the spiralling effect produced by such minor offences (Herbert 2001; Xu et al. 2005). In this scenario, those involved in street prostitution and the environmental aftermath represent a 'broken window' (Brock 1998). If this window is left unrepaired – in other words, if prostitutes, their clients, drug dealers and pimps are tolerated on the streets – then more serious crimes will follow (Wilson and Kelling 1982).

In making sense of these attitudes, it appears that they do somewhat seem to be context-specific and dependent upon spatial boundaries. These spatial boundaries dictate what is acceptable and unacceptable in public spaces, thus reaffirming the public/private divide. This construction gives way to the notion that 'everything "has its place", and that things (e.g. people, actions) can be "in-place" or "out-of-place" is deeply engrained in the way we think and act [...] when individuals or groups ignore this socially produced common sense, they are said to be out of place and defined as deviant. Frequently, this labelling of out of place is metaphorical, based on analogies which themselves refer to common sense expectations' (Cresswell 1997: 334). Thus, as one resident from City Island (US) explained: 'It doesn't belong here. It's not the type of business we want here.' (Jaccarino 2009) As such, public spaces 'are constructed around particular notions of appropriate sexual comportment which exclude those whose lives do not centre on monogamous, heterosexual, procreative sex' (Hubbard 2001: 51), which, as Hubbard (2012) demonstrates, has a history that goes back many centuries. Thus, street prostitution is considered inappropriate, because the engagement in sexual relations in public goes against these cultural norms, and local residents and businesses are embarrassed by being associated with those who do not adhere to cultural standards of acceptable moral behaviour. It is interesting to note, as Hubbard (2004) does, that the spatial displacement of street sex work into high-class 'lap-dancing' bars seems to be accepted by corporate 'gentrifiers'.

Noise and nuisance

Noise and other associated nuisance, such as environmental debris and drugs paraphernalia, have been commonly associated with the street sex scene. Litter, used condoms, tampons, syringes and human excrement have all been identified as items that many residents and businesses have complained about finding in their neighbourhoods, both nationally and internationally (Lancashire Evening Post 2008; Tapaleao 2009a, 2009b; The Swish Project 2008; This is Walsall Online 2009). As Terry (53, white, Area 1 police constable) explained, residents and businesses were concerned about:

> Used condoms in gardens, girls loitering at half past, seven, eight o'clock in the morning when women are taking their kids to school, shouting and arguments outside houses on a night between punters and the girls or drug dealers and the girls, erm, needles being found, er in the garden ... where you know you've got girls stood outside your house erm, day in day out, shouting, balling, having sex in your front garden is quite common.
> (Terry, 53, white, Area 1 police constable)

Alan (58, white, security guard) similarly stated that street prostitution impinged upon the image of the area and local businesses in the vicinity. Alan referred to a particular area in which he worked as 'condom alley', due to the amount of discarded condoms left in the area. The following extract from my fieldwork notes illustrates Alan's concerns:

> Alan raised his concerns about the environmental problems prostitution caused in the area. His main concern was the litter i.e. used condoms which were discarded by sex workers in the local vicinity. He referred to the rear of the Embankment as 'Condom City', due to the sheer amount of condoms which were left. He was concerned that this would impact upon local businesses in the area.
> (Alan, 58, white, security guard)

Residents in Birmingham (UK) have also raised their concern about finding condoms in nearby streets and alleyways (This is Walsall Online 2009). In Preston, residents and business owners complained about finding discarded condoms and tampons, which they were left to dispose of (Lancashire Evening Post 2008). Drug use and the remains of drug paraphernalia have also caused anxiety in Edinburgh and Coventry (UK), with drugs being used in full view of the public and sexual acts being performed in residents' backyards (The Christian Institute 2001; The Swish Project 2008). However, for one business owner, who swept up condom wrappers from outside her premises each morning, the reason that she does not complain is because she can go home at the end of her working day (*Lancashire Evening Post* 2008).

Yet, concerns over environmental debris and the nuisance caused by those involved in the sex industry are not limited to the UK. For instance, in South Auckland (New Zealand), residents have voiced their frustration at the sight of used condoms and bodily waste in their neighbourhood, as well as the noise and verbal abuse caused by street sex workers (Buckley 2009). In Toronto (US), residents have also expressed their distaste over finding used condoms in their area and encountering visible acts of a sexual nature. For one resident, this disquiet was linked to his two-year-old daughter's curiosity and subsequent potential for catching diseases, as 'she sees something on the ground, she wants to pick it up' (City News 2006: 1).

Disrupted sleep was a further cause of distress for some residents. In Manhattan, residents complained that their sleep was being interrupted by the street sex scene (Mittelmann 2008). Similarly, Patrick maintained that his sleep was often disrupted by sex workers and their clients:

> I have seen stag nights come this way and used the prostitutes. I got woke up with a gang of them 'arhh'.... That is the problem. And, they do come down but I don't know if you've ever had sleep deprivation, but if you're trying to do a fulltime job and you're only having three, four hours sleep a night, you just don't need it.
>
> (Patrick, 53, white, Area 2 resident)

As a result of the disruption that Patrick continued to experience from the existence of street prostitution outside his home, he expressed some understanding as to why the Ipswich Ripper may have murdered local prostitutes. As Patrick indicated:

> That's why this guy in Ipswich, and they were joking at work 'oh, you been driving down to Ipswich have you and got rid of them' ... you don't want anybody killed. But I say, 'it will be somebody local who doesn't want them on his doorstep' and the bloke they got was actually a local bloke.... He's probably got to the end of his tether. I can understand that, when you've had three or four hours sleep. You know, you just lose it, you do. I mean, I think other people are phoning, but nobody seems to get together, to do anything.
>
> (Patrick, 53, white, Area 2 resident)

Clearly, for some, taking action to contact the police with little or no response may lead them to take further, more serious action. Although Patrick did not appear to be the type of person who would undertake such horrific acts, it does raise questions about the police's response to community concerns and was one of the reasons why vigilantism was experienced in another part of the city, which is more fully explored in the following chapter.

A visible problem

The visible presence of street prostitutes was a key problem for some residents and businesses, as many did not want to see sex workers and their clients outside their homes or places of work. Neither did they wish to see sexual activities taking place or semi-naked women walking the streets. As Terry explained:

> It was the visible side. The attitude of the community was hardened due to the visible presence, the visible evidence of prostitution ... it wasn't a moral objection of the girls ... it is all about the visible aspects and audio aspects of having to live in a community.
> (Terry, 53, white, Area 1 police constable)

Similarly, in Manchester (US), residents expressed their dissatisfaction with street prostitutes: 'they're in broad daylight.... They stand in front of our building. They stand on the sidewalks. They laugh if you ask them to leave.... We see the girls in the middle of the street flagging cars down.' (WMUR 2007: 1). For others, the visibility of the sexual liaisons caused annoyance: 'People have told me they have seen them lingering in taxis around The Broadway, either signaling to other girls or waiting for customers. They take their customers and go down nearby alleyways.' (Gates 2008: 1).

However, a significant concern was related to the presence of children in residential areas and the possibility that these children might see street prostitutes, their clients or sexual transactions taking place. Patrick described many incidents in which he saw people having sex outside his home in bushes or car parks and expressed his anger that: 'There are mothers and kids walking up and down and there's one outside pulling her knickers.' Similarly, residents in Manchester and Montreal (US), Delhi (India), Coventry (UK), Auckland (New Zealand) and Berlin (Germany) revealed their frustration that children may see prostitutes on street corners on their way to school and may observe people having sex in the street (CBC News 2009; India eNews 2009; Tapaleao 2009b; The Swish Project 2008; WMUR 2007).

Mistaken identity

Living and working in an area known for street prostitution sometimes meant that residents and business employees were mistaken for those involved in prostitution. For many men and women involved in my research, being mistaken for a client or prostitute was considered a negative experience, impacting upon their daily lives and how they behaved.

Mistaken for a prostitute

Many residents identified how they or their friends and family members had been approached and propositioned by kerb-crawlers. Female residents identified: 'The amount of times I've been asked how much' (Gemma, 46, Afro-Caribbean, Area 1 resident); 'Yeah, yeah tell me about it' (Karen, 32, Afro-Caribbean, Area 1 resident). Many residents held the view that kerb-crawlers assume that anyone is potentially a sex worker:

> They tend not to differentiate between who is a prostitute or not ... and so it's any woman who's walking by herself.
> (Paula, 42, Afro-Caribbean, Area 1 resident)

> I think if you're just walking along in that area and you're on your own and maybe you, you have a skirt on or some high boots or something they just automatically assume ... for instance when I, if I need something from the Indian shop and I go up and park on [Area 2 street] that's the first thing that enters my mind coz I'm walking on my own ... I think gosh I hope nobody that I know sees me walking here.
> (Mary, 44, Afro-Caribbean, Area 1 resident)

For some, they felt that certain features should have diffused a kerb-crawler's curiosity and differentiated them from sex workers. Such circumstances included the presence of children in the near vicinity or when they were out walking with their own children. Vicky (31, white, Area 2 researcher) detailed a situation in which an Area 2 resident was propositioned by a kerb-crawler, while pushing a pram:

> [O]ne of the ladies was saying that she's lived in [Area 1] for years and because [Area 1] is kind of like a through road from the motorways and you do get people that are getting lost in Area 1, so she's quite used to or she was quite used to people stopping and asking for directions. But in the last years she's stop doing that because even though she was pushing a pram along with ... people were stopping and asking her for business.
> (Vicky, 31, white, Area 2 researcher)

Similarly, in Area 1, Emma (27, Afro-Caribbean, Area 1 resident) stated that:

> I've got a four year old daughter and, do you think that makes any difference? And that's the one thing that really rattles me when I'm with my kid. I can't even have a man give me a compliment in front of my child, coz I think it's disgusting.
> (Emma, 27, Afro-Caribbean, Area 1 resident)

Participants also reported that residents with physical impairments had been approached:

One of the female members was in a motorized wheelchair. The lady talked about an experience in which she was propositioned by a punter in the locality. She said that she couldn't believe that she was propositioned and that they must have nothing else better to do if they are approaching her on her scooter.

(Field notes, over 55s group, Area 2)

Features that participants perceived as indicating a woman was a sex worker included 'a skirt on or some high boots or something' (Mary, 44, Afro-Caribbean, Area 1 resident) or '[a] woman walking by herself' (Paula, 42, Afro-Caribbean, Area 1 resident).

Being propositioned was presented as an unpleasant experience, as some women declared that they felt insulted, shocked and fearful of what could happen. Terry and Patrick highlighted the negative impact of being propositioned for women:

> That was the horrible thing about it ... a woman walking past or standing outside the door just talking and be seen as one. And it would be bad as well because a lot of black women some of them like stand outside the garden and have a chat and so you get that kind of thing as well. It's insulting.
>
> (Terry, 27, Afro-Caribbean, Area 1 resident)

> Susan who I used to go out with she's thin and I told her not to come down on bus and she got pulled three times from the bus stop to the pub down here and she never came. She says if you want to live down there, I'm not talking to you. She wouldn't come down here again, definitely not.
>
> (Patrick, 53, white, Area 2 resident)

Some female residents expressed how they felt intimated by kerb-crawlers' advances. For one woman, as Vicky explained, this affected her confidence in walking the streets in Area 2:

> But as she was saying now when she's walking along through [Area2] she walks with her head down and doesn't communicate with anyone because she just doesn't want to see what's going on around her ... she doesn't want to help people, she doesn't want to be stopped by people that are kerb-crawling. So for her, that individual it's obviously had an impact on her confidence and you know the ways she feels about living in the area so, Prostitution's bad ... prostitute are bad for the area. Kerb-crawlers made residents feel intimidated. Just generally that feeling of is that person genuinely lost, should I stop or is there something more sinister to it are they out; you know are they looking for business.
>
> (Vicky, 32, white, Area 2 researcher)

These findings reflected those of Pitcher *et al.*'s (2006) study, whereby female residents would avoid particular areas late at night or would avoid travel altogether, in order to avoid kerb-crawlers' advances and increase their sense of safety. As with Hubbard *et al.*'s (2007) study, female residents disclosed how kerb-crawlers had impinged negatively on their use of public space. Similarly, in Helsinki, 40 per cent of Harju residents revealed that the presence of street prostitution in the area in which they lived influenced their choice of walking routes, and 29 per cent said it had affected their life to the extent that they were wary of moving about in the area in the evening or at night (Helsingin Sanomat 2000).

Matthews (2008) remarked how many women who lived in inner-city areas operated under an unofficial curfew and did not feel safe going out alone at night. These fears were then compounded by reports from women living in these areas of being propositioned, harassed and, on some occasions, he suggests, assaulted. Although documentation of women's experiences of living in red-light districts rarely mention women being assaulted (Koskela and Tani 2005), there have been reports of women being propositioned by kerb-crawlers. For instance, in Birmingham (UK), an advisor on crime in local communities for the Local Government Association declared that he was informed 'about situations where respectable women walking in the street were mistaken as prostitutes by men kerb-crawling in their cars' (This is Walsall Online 2009). Similarly, in Berkshire, Thames Valley, police explained how women who lived in the area were sometimes being stopped by kerb-crawlers (Wheeler 2009). Abbey Ward, West Midlands (UK), also witnessed increasing numbers of complaints from women who have been harassed by drivers pulling up and propositioning them (Bearwood Blog 2010). Furthermore, local business owners in Preston (UK) conveyed concerns for their clients, who had been propositioned by kerb-crawlers – an experience that was described as 'very intimidating' (*Lancashire Evening Post* 2008: 2).

Women's experiences of being mistaken for sex workers and approached by kerb-crawlers are also evident internationally. For instance, in Manhattan (US), a resident indicated how local women 'were being harassed, sometimes followed, groped and threatened' as they went to work (Mittelmann 2008: 1). Residents in New Zealand also identified being propositioned by aggressive and noisy clients (New Zealand Ministry of Justice 2008). A survey conducted with 1714 women who lived in Harju (Helsinki) revealed that female residents were being called 'whore' by the drivers of passing cars, stared at while waiting at bus stops, propositioned for sexual services and asked how much their sexual services would cost (Helsingin Sanomat 2000). At the time of the study, during May to June 2000, as many as 67 per cent of the female residents claimed to have experienced these incidents over the previous twelve months. For 13 per cent of the Harju residents, these incidents occurred on a weekly basis over that period of time. According to a news report: 'The harassment prompted feelings of indignation, anger, a certain amount of fear, some shame, and even in some cases a measure of mirth and amusement – perhaps at the unselective behaviour of those doing the name-calling and requesting.' (Helsingin Sanomat 2000: 1)

Although some women felt uneasy walking around certain areas, others demonstrated that being propositioned did not affect their daily lives and instead challenged kerb-crawler advances with verbal retaliation. As one resident of Vallejo, California (US), stated: 'I've been approached on the street right by my house by johns who thought I was a prostitute ... I'll get in their face and yell at them, "No, I'm not a prostitute. Go home to your wife!"' (McNichol 2011: 1). Like respondents in Koskela and Tani's study (2005), many female residents and employees employed strategies of resistance in response to unwanted propositioning by kerb-crawlers. In particular, female residents and employees employed verbal strategies, asked family members to pick them up after work or would walk with them to the train station and often avoided particular streets. Female community members have also been shown to carry tools for active resistance and dress more conservatively in response to kerb-crawler advances (Koskela and Tani 2005). Interestingly, the employment of such 'strategies of resistance' is strongly correlated with increased fear levels (Scott 2003), despite being at less risk of attack than men (Holloway and Jefferson 1997).

Mistaken for a kerb-crawler

Men, too, were mistakenly identified as clients in my research, some by the police and others by prostitutes. For instance, local business representatives expressed their concern that male employees were being mistaken for kerb-crawlers by local police. Following a police crackdown on street prostitution in Area 2, Anthony (34, white, manager) described an incident, in which an employee was stopped by police on suspicion of kerb-crawling, while on his way home from work:

> A guy that does our painting and decorating and stuff ... he's got this big white van. He was here early evening doing some work and he was stopped. His van was searched on his way home. Which is, he phoned me up and it was tongue and cheek about it and I thought well in a way I'm pleased that they're doing their job and they are stopping people and saying what are you doing down here.
>
> (Anthony, 34, white, manager)

The experiences of male employees being mistaken for kerb-crawlers were echoed by three residents and two local authority officials. For one local authority official, anxiety concerning mistaken identity stemmed from an experience in which his vehicle was checked by local police, while he was attending a local community partnership meeting in Area 2. Local police ran a vehicle check, in order to determine the vehicle's ownership, and subsequently informed the councillor of their inquiries. Furthermore, Vernon (57, Afro-Caribbean, Area 1 resident) complained about being apprehended by the police while walking around late at night, specifying one particular occasion when he was meeting his daughter:

> You get the odd, you get the innocent person going down to the dentist ... so if [you] stop somebody to ask them a question, some of them will think

well hey hey he goes again, he's chasing a women.... The guy might be totally innocent. He might be lost ... I'll give you a personal experience my daughter, took her one night to somewhere, it was just after midnight ... and there was this cop car, he was more concerned about me then, then the prostitutes ... these overzealous people create more problems than they solve.

(Vernon, 57, Afro-Caribbean, Area 1 resident)

These sorts of incidents led to concerns such as those raised by Alarna, who became worried that her boyfriend might be apprehended for kerb-crawling, while waiting outside the centre to collect her after a meeting:

If I've got a meeting in [Area 1 Community Centre] and my boyfriend comes to pick me up and he waits in the car, I'm always like don't wait in the car for too long ... because you'll either get picked up by the police or someone else will come up and ask and then if the police think he's a kerb-crawler then you know so you have to be careful of that as well.

(Alarna, 32, white, Area 2 community safety officer)

Similarly, a female resident from Area 2 recounted an incident when her son had visited her and the unease that she felt. My field notes depict this incident:

A lady stated that she was concerned about her son as women would tap on the window of his car when he came to visit her. She was worried that the police may see this occur and assume that he was looking for business.

(Over 55s group, Area 2)

Increased policing in Area 2 resulted in concern from local authority officials, business representatives and residents that they may be misconstrued as a kerb-crawler – an experience that Chief Superintendent Paul (51, white, Area 2) could relate to. Following his attendance at a community centre in Area 2, Paul was propositioned by a street sex worker when he left the premises. He recognized that this incident could have been interpreted as something more than him merely walking in the area. For some residents, the possibility of being apprehended for kerb-crawling led them to feel intimidated and apprehensive when strolling around the district:

There's a lot of police presence sometimes around there to catch kerb-crawlers and ... a lot of residents feel quite..., not intimidated but generally a bit pissed off that when they're walking home from the pub, they're being asked why they're walking and where they're going to and being hassled as they see it by the police all the time coz they're assuming that they're kerb-crawling.

(Alarna, 32, white, Area 2 community safety officer)

Similarly, research conducted by O'Neill and Campbell (2006) illustrated that some men feared being approached by a sex worker for business and felt nervous when they drove over speed bumps, in case they were mistaken for kerb-crawlers. For male participants, their family and friends in my study, these worries were justified by direct experience of being misunderstood as men who buy sex, but, more acutely, a fear of being mistaken for a client by the police. From my own experience of a sex worker assuming that I was a kerb-crawler in Area 2, I, too, felt concerned when I was approached. An absence in the literature around the 'mistaken client' suggests that further research is required to fully understand the nature of these concerns and the extent to which 'innocent' men are being accosted by the police.

Fearing those involved in street prostitution

A further negative impact that the presence of street prostitution posed was the fear of those involved in the street sex scene. This fear appeared to be gender-specific, as female participants feared being approached by kerb-crawlers, while male participants identified pimps as a potential danger. Rather than evidence based anxiety, it appears that these fears were informed by a cultural context that has perpetuated and socialized women into fearing 'stranger danger' and the sexualized male, while, for male participants, 'pimps' were deemed as a threat.

Women's fear of being propositioned on the street

The fear of being propositioned on the street was voiced by female residents and male employees, speaking on behalf of women that they worked with. It was claimed that female employees feared being approached by kerb-crawlers when leaving work premises. Moreover, some female residents expressed a deep sense of fear concerning what could happen to them when strolling around the area in which they lived.

Four of the nine local business representatives recognized that female employees feared being propositioned. As Roger (57, white, company director) asserted, this fear has impacted upon female employees' daily lives, as 'it affected the girls going home'. This effect upon female employees was believed to stem from the view that 'it was the fear that you might (be accosted), which was almost as bad [as being propositioned]' (Roger, 57, white, company director). The experience of being approached by male clients was similarly disclosed by female residents. Female residents also expressed a sense of fear and stated they had felt intimidated by kerb-crawlers' advances:

> I got propositioned from people ... coz I used to walk home from town and spend my last pound on ten cigs and walk home and I always used to try and avoid [Area 2 road], but sometimes it kind of like gets, it gets to the stage where it's difficult to kind of avoid it.... It's intimidating when you're that young ... I used to have this, this man ... he always used to 'how much?'
>
> (Karen, 32, Afro-Caribbean, Area 1 resident)

> My grandma actually lives on Spencer Place and when I was younger as well ... sometimes like there were men coming up along the street and they do like slow down and ask you loads of questions about yourself, which is, it is quite scary when you're such a young age coz you don't know what to say to them.
>
> (Hannah, 23, Afro-Caribbean, Area 1 resident)

Some residents revealed their concern for their partners or daughters being approached by kerb-crawlers:

> It's not necessarily you think of yourself, but for you know if you've got teenage children, I mean I have a teenage daughter who's you know, you know walks home from her friends or her cousins or whatever. Times she's come back and she's said his guys followed me.
>
> (Paula, 42, Afro-Caribbean, Area 1 resident)

These gendered fears were linked specifically to the street and advances made by male clients. A relationship between women's fear and public spaces has long been established, as it is women who are considered to be most at risk on the street (McGuire 2011; McNichol 2011). In reality, it is widely shown that women are more likely to be attacked or murdered by someone they know, rather than the dangerous stranger (Edelstein 2007). For example, Her Majesty's Crown Prosecution Service Inspectorate report, *Without Consent* (2007: 159), found that out of 573 recorded sexual crimes, the suspect was known to the victim in 491 of the cases. Given that rape by strangers is the fear most commonly reported by women, despite being very rare, it may be unsurprising that women have identified being fearful of kerb-crawlers, who are on the street looking to buy sex. This context arguably exacerbates women's fear, as they perceive this encounter increasing the likelihood of rape by a stranger. Therefore, these fears can be understood as socially constructed, rather than as a rational fear of kerb-crawlers. This social context has demonized the image of a lone sex-crazed male, for which, the kerb-crawler can be seen to epitomize this dangerous figure.

For male employees, as Roger (57, white, company director) suggests: 'From a man's point of view I think it was probably an image of their customers coming down and their feeling, you know wasn't the right image for the company. So I don't think men are particularly worried.' Instead, 'pimps' were the source of male employees' fear. Yet, as Koskela and Tani note (2005: 428): 'gender relations are reciprocal and comprised of complex power relations which include the possibility of resistance'. Assuming that female employees are victims only denies their agency and does not acknowledge the potential for resistance.

Male employees' fear of pimps

Male employees' fear was predominantly associated with a fear of 'pimps'. Culturally, pimps are characterized as being aggressive, violent and hypersexual

The impact of prostitution on communities 93

(Giobbe 1993). Interestingly, Roger (57, white, company director) identifies 'pimps' as 'rather threatening looking blokes driving around in big black cars and blacked out windows', which arguably fits the stereotypical image of a pimp. Roger explained the perceived danger that 'pimps' pose to local businesses and their employees:

> It's not only the girls but you got the pimps as well ... very threatening ... talking about the pimps, they were there in droves, er and that was quite dangerous. A lot of people felt they felt very, very threatened, er, down there. Now we were worried about that.
>
> (Roger, 57, white, company director)

It is questionable whether there was the presence of a high volume of 'pimps', implicit in his suggestion that 'they were in droves'. Increased levels of policing in Area 1 had been attributed to a reduction in the number of street sex workers in the city. This may suggest that Roger's fear of a high volume of 'pimps' may be disproportionate to the actual number of pimps in Leeds' red-light districts. Fears of crime levels in respect to prostitution locally in Leeds have been shown to be disproportionate to the relative level of crime perpetrated. Nationally, these perceptions have been shown to be linked to a person's socio-demographic characteristics (Jansson 2006; Jansson *et al.* 2007). The results of a Leeds Community Safety audit in 2003 revealed that, while many people identified prostitution and related crime as one of the main problems facing the area, these accounted for a small percentage of the total crime (Leeds City Council 2005). The disproportionate belief that crime rates are higher than those recorded by official statistics is documented as having a psychological effect, as people attempt to avoid victimization and protect themselves (Liska *et al.* 1982). The outcome of which may explain vigilantism, community protest and campaigns to rid the many streets of towns and cities throughout the UK of street prostitution (Hubbard 1998a; Hubbard and Sanders 2003; Sagar 2005; Sanders 2005c; Shead and Hamilton 2002).

However, the perceived threat posed by the presence of pimps in Area 2 was similarly represented by Alan (58, white, security guard). Alan experienced increased levels of fear in recent years, which he attributed to an assumed change in the ethnic background of pimps. This change in the ethnicity of men defined as pimps may explain Roger's suggestion that they were 'in droves', as this shift may have led to the appearance that there was an influx of pimps. Over the previous seven years, Alan (58, white, security guard) recalls how Afro-Caribbean pimps were replaced by Asian pimps, and, in recent years, Asian pimps were replaced by Eastern European pimps. Interview notes taken at the time of interview recount these points:

> Alan firstly referred to changes in the ethnicity of pimps. He had seen a change over the last seven years. First, Alan recalls that West Indian men were the pimps over six years ago, over a period of a number of years.

94 *The impact of prostitution on communities*

Following this period he saw a change from the West Indian pimps to Asian men. Asian pimps were seen in the area for a short period of time. The Asian pimps have been replaced in the last year, by Eastern European men, Albanian or Lithuanian. Alan believed that potentially the Eastern European pimps had scared the other pimps off because they were more violent and had guns; although this he admitted was pure speculation. Alan said that he had seen a lot of rivalry and fighting between pimps, especially the West Indians who covered the area for some years. The disputes between pimps were over their working girl's patches. He said that he would see a pimp drop off a woman and then another car would pull up and have an argument with the other pimp about where his women were standing.

(Alan, 58, white, security guard)

The notion that criminal movements of racial others are destroying 'our' moral and lawful way of life has been described by Berman (2003), when identifying the portrayal of trafficking in Western Europe and of 'Eastern' criminals who deal in 'white flesh'. Hubbard (2006a), for example, highlights the extent to which press coverage of sex work in London (UK) and Paris (France) dwells on the role of Albanians, Russians, Serbs and Ukrainians in instigating a flood of criminality and immorality. This dwelling on the role of 'Eastern Europeans' in the media is somewhat mirrored by the suggestion made by Alan – that Eastern European men have taken over the role of pimp in Leeds, through their brutality and violence.

Positive impacts

Although prostitution is most often seen in a negative way, my research demonstrated that prostitution also led to a number of positive impacts on the community. In particular, the monetary gain that may arise from the presence of prostitution and sex work in an area, as clients and sex workers may spend money in local shops. Also, sex workers can have an impact in terms of preventing or detecting crime.

Local economies and entertainment

The relationship between local and national economies and prostitution is well established. As Jeffreys (2009) indicates, prostitution is now a significant part of the market sector within national economies. In Thailand, Amsterdam (Netherlands), Prague (Czech Republic) and Nevada (US), prostitution is a key part of the tourist industry, attracting millions of travellers each year to these destinations, specifically to engage in the sex industry. Although it is difficult to estimate the profits of the sex industry, because of its hidden nature and illegality in many nation states, the literature suggests its vast economic worth. According to Nuttavuthisit (2007), sex tourism in Thailand was established as a mechanism of economic development in the 1970s following the Vietnam War, in order to benefit from the influx of male tourists from Europe, America and Japan. Lim (1998) argues that 1.5 per cent of the female population in the Philippines, Malaysia, Thailand and Indonesia work as prostitutes, which highlights the size of the sex industry and influence of foreign tourists. In China, it has been estimated that income generated from prostitution constituted 8 per cent of the Chinese economy (Zhou 2006). As Peterson and Runyan (1999, cited in Croucher 2003: 164) explain, the sex industry has become 'a major pillar of the global economy, erected literally on the bodies of women'.

Although my participants did not state that prostitution impacted on the local economy, they did discuss how some stag parties would visit local brothels and massage parlours in the area, and one resident claimed seeing a stag party engaging with street sex workers near his home. Though this may not be on the same scale as some of the well-known locations listed above, there may be some less obvious impacts on the local economy, in terms of the money spent in local businesses. The sex industry could, in this way, be seen as part of the much wider entertainment industry.

Prostitution was also viewed as a form of entertainment for some local businesses. For instance, Ian (30, white, shop proprietor) and Judith (37, white, shop proprietor) outlined that those involved in prostitution became a source of daily entertainment. Ian and Judith recited how they would play a 'is she or isn't she game' or 'is he or isn't he game' during their working day, in order to entertain themselves when their shop was not busy, suggesting some level of tolerance. Anthony (34, white, manager) explains, even though prostitution may be in a public place, he never found prostitutes and their clients 'offensive really ... I think when you live in a city; sometimes they're just part of the wallpaper in a way, to a certain extent ... you know you kind of becomes acclimatized to it I think.' The perception that those involved in prostitution become part of the wallpaper of a city supports Simmel's suggestion that the city impacts upon social psychology (Simmel 2000). According to this argument, city dwellers learn to ignore aspects of the city that are of little importance to their daily lives. This 'attitude of indifference' allows city dwellers to live and work in areas of sex work and ignore the presence of prostitution, due to its insignificance in relation to their residency and employment (Hubbard 2006b).

Crime prevention and information gathering

Prostitutes, their managers and clients are often considered to be useful sources of information about other crimes. Sanders' (2005a) ten-month ethnographic study of indoor prostitution markets during 2000 and 2001 suggested that brothel owners and independent workers often strike up informal relationships with local police officers. In such instances, brothels are able to ply their trade undisrupted, on the basis that owners and workers provide information on other crimes.

Similarly, in my research, the police specified that prostitutes are often a wealth of information, because they stand on the street for many hours and sometimes observe crime or criminal activities in the area. They often know local criminals or know about the activities of people committing crime nearby. Moreover, street sex workers are often involved in the reporting and capture of 'dodgy punters', as they will often note down the number plate of a vehicle that a friend or co-worker gets into. They also sometimes report acts of violence or sexual abuse perpetrated against them by punters or those impersonating clients (Kinnell 2008). In this way, street prostitutes have a positive impact, in terms of the policing of crime in a local area.

Indoor prostitution can often also bring benefits to the local community. An interesting benefit that Paul (56, white, Area 2 Chief Superintendent) identified, from the existence of indoor prostitution in his policing division, stemmed from the reduction in crime-related incidents, when a local bingo hall was converted into a brothel. Paul compared the complaints received about the establishment on the main road in Area 2 to when it was operated as a bingo hall. As Paul detailed:

> What was interesting about that was before they took over that was a bingo hall. And in terms of crime and disorder we had more recorded crime and disorder when it was a bingo hall than when it got taken over by this company and turned it into allegedly a brothel. Much more, I think we've had about two incidents in the three of four years it's been there. And we were going to two or three a week when it was a bingo hall.
> (Paul, 56, white, Area 2 Chief Superintendent)

This, as the police explained, was the reason why residents and businesses did not protest against local brothels, because they did not cause any nuisance. Because of this, there was support, both from the police, as well as business employees, residents and officials, for prostitution to move indoors, as it was considered to be a means through which the problems associated with street prostitution could be better managed.

Chapter summary

The presence of prostitution in residential and business neighbourhoods has been shown to have a number of impacts on residents, business employees and proprietors. The majority of these impacts have been negative, ranging from affecting the reputation and image of an area, encouraging further crime, leaving environmental waste, noise and nuisance, visible sex acts, people being mistaken for kerb-crawlers by local police, women being propositioned by kerb-crawlers to increased feelings of insecurity and danger. In addition, this chapter has noted that there are a number of positive consequences, in terms of economic wealth and industry, as well crime prevention and detection through collaboration with sex workers. The next chapter will examine – what could be described as a further positive impact – solidarity and community cohesion, as it explores how, when and why some communities take to the streets in an attempt to make their neighbourhoods better places for them to live and work.

6 Community action and resistance

Many communities, both in the UK and internationally, have protested against the presence of prostitution in their neighbourhoods. These protests have predominantly focused on the removal of street prostitution from streets, cities and towns, largely because of the negative impact that street prostitution is perceived to have upon residential and business districts and in response to the unwanted propositioning of female residents. This chapter will explore how some communities have responded to prostitution in the areas that they live and work. In particular, the chapter will examine community activism in the form of protests against street prostitution, complaints, petitioning, vigilantism and violent marches to eradicate the industry. The chapter will also consider the means through which communities come together to take action as 'active citizens' and their common or divergent goals. Finally, the chapter will also explore the action taken by communities to embrace and support the presence of sex workers in the areas that they live and work, in order to demonstrate that not all communities want to rid their local neighbourhood of prostitution.

Community action

Communities have sought to take action against the presence of prostitution in residential and business districts for many years. Kantola and Squires (2004) suggest that UK parliamentary debates surrounding prostitution in the mid-1980s and 1990s, which were characterized by persistent attempts to criminalize kerb-crawlers, were introduced in response to local community activism. This community activism focused on the public nuisance that prostitution caused to local communities, as prostitution was seen as encouraging a cycle of crime. Local authorities, the media and protesters employed what Kantola and Squires (2004: 77) identified as 'a public nuisance discourse', which focuses upon the social stigma that prostitution brought to the local community.

Significant changes in community responses to prostitution during 1980s in the UK, particularly those who live in red-light districts, are similarly acknowledged by Matthews (2008). He argues that neighbourhood protests emerged during the 1980s and 1990s in the UK cites of Bradford, Cardiff, Glasgow, Leeds, Liverpool, London, Sheffield, Southampton, Stoke and Walsall, despite prostitution existing in these urban areas for many years. This, he suggests, demonstrates a significant change in the nature of public attitudes. No longer were many residents all over the UK tolerant of street prostitution. Rather, they began to campaign for the removal of prostitution from 'their' neighbourhoods. More widely during this period, the UK Government embraced situational crime control policies and sought to encourage greater involvement of communities to prevent crime, which arguably gave greater recognition to this type of community action. As Crawford (1997: 34) describes: 'by the 1990s the message had become a familiar one: crime prevention is an important responsibility of all institutions (be they public or private), associations, communities and individuals'.

Growing concerns over the impact of street prostitution on the community, Matthews (2008) indicates, has served to galvanize a number of different residents' groups. These concerns provided the rationale for vigilante movements throughout the 1990s in many towns and cities across the UK and encouraged police to undertake periodic crackdowns. In particular, Hubbard (1997, 1998a, 1998b) identified how community activism in Birmingham and Bradford was driven by local residents' desire to rid the streets of prostitution. Local residents organized regular street patrols and pickets, which targeted kerb-crawlers. Residents armed themselves with placards wielding messages such as 'Kerb-crawlers – We Have Your Number' (Hubbard 1998a: 277). Given the perceived effectiveness of the campaigns, 'it is perhaps not surprising that it spawned a number of imitation campaigns' (Hubbard 1998a: 278). Sagar (2005) and Williams (2005b) similarly identified how Street Watch schemes were initiated in response to street prostitution in Cardiff and a particular West Midlands city. These schemes usually involved members of the public patrolling the streets voluntarily and in partnership with the police. In both instances, local communities attempted to remove street prostitution from residential streets as a means of dealing with community concerns.

In the two areas in which I undertook research, two distinct approaches to tackling street prostitution were evident. In Area 2, residents and businesses took 'formal' action to deal with street prostitution in their neighbourhood, through contacting councillors and the police and attending community meetings. In Area 1, residents and businesses actively protested against prostitution on their streets with placards, surveillance and a visible presence. As a result of this community action, street prostitution was displaced from Area 1 into Area 2, from the north to the south of the city.

Types of action

Residents in both UK and international cities and towns have campaigned against the presence of street prostitutes and their clients utilizing various techniques to deter and displace them from residential neighbourhoods. These have included forming action groups, designing the local landscape to deter prostitutes and their clients, as well as, in some instances, committing acts of violence and vigilantism.

Action groups

Some communities have taken to the streets to protest against prostitution and formed community action groups. For example, in Scotland (UK), a residents association launched nightly patrols to drive prostitutes out of the area, after residents suffered threats from female sex workers, kerb-crawlers and their 'pimps' (Swanson 2010). In Berkshire (UK), residents patrolled their streets following complaints that local people felt uncomfortable by the visible presence of sex workers on residential streets, as well as young girls and women being stopped by men in cars (Wheeler 2009). The establishment of community action groups to deal with prostitution has also been observed internationally. In the US, residents in Manchester decided to take matters into their own hands and documented the problem of street prostitution, reporting what they had seen to local police (WMUR 2007). Whereas in South Auckland (New Zealand), the Papatoetoe Reclaiming our Streets group, which was made up of local residents, patrolled the area, recording kerb-crawler registration numbers and sending warning notices to their homes, as well as breaking up negotiations between sex workers and their clients and warning them of the health risks involved in prostitution (Tapaleao 2009a). Furthermore, local residents in Vallejo, California (US), formed an action group called the Kentucky Street Watch Owls, who patrolled the local district, walking the streets to discourage prostitutes and their customers from plying their trade in the community (Nicholson 2007). Moreover, in Vancouver (Canada), CROWE (Concerned Residents of the West End) took to the streets to reclaim their neighbourhood and deter clients from entering the locality (Ross 2010). Such action has been undertaken, both with and without police and/or local authority supervision or guidance, which raises questions about the legitimacy and accountability of those who take action to deal with prostitution.

Other, more 'innovative' approaches to tackle prostitution can also be seen through communities' use of less traditional methods of action. In addition to conducting patrols several times a month, the Kentucky Street Watch Owls met regularly to discuss neighbourhood problems and maintain a Facebook page, which posts photos of suspicious activities (McNichol 2011). Similarly, in Montreal (Canada), residents also set up an online Facebook group, where people could discuss the nuisances associated with prostitution and post photographs of sex workers who work in the local vicinity (CBC News 2009). Furthermore, an online forum was established by a group of residents in Semilong, Northampton (UK), who set up an online site that discusses issues of concern regarding prostitution (Semilong Northampton Residents Group 2009).

Residents of Area 1 and 2 formed 'community action groups' to deal with the issues of prostitution, crime and blight in 'their' neighbourhoods. These groups brought together local organizations, residents and local government officials to assist in the removal of street prostitution. The groups met on a regular basis to update on any progress, discuss initiatives and in order to prompt the police and/or local authorities to take action. Although these meetings and groups were less organized in Area 2, Area 1 formed a much more mobile and organized action group to eradicate street prostitution from the suburb. Efforts to 'reclaim' Area 1 focused around community protests and patrols of the area, mirroring those in Hubbard et al. (2007), Hubbard (1998a), Hubbard and Sanders (2003), Sagar (2005) and Williams (2005b) research, whereby residents protested against street prostitution, noted down registration numbers of kerb-crawlers and marched against street prostitution.

Similarly, in my research, residents from Area 1 identified how they would 'march along [Area 1 street] with placards saying "Get Rid of the Prostitutes, get them out" and stuff like that. But it's all gone now, there's nothing there whatsoever … that's how they got rid of it' (Terry, 27, Afro-Caribbean, Area 1 resident). In addition, the Area 1 action group took part in a number of initiatives aimed at deterring sex workers and their clients from working and entering the area. These included engaging with prostitutes and asking them to move on from their street or area, as Tony explained:

> About fifteen to seventeen years ago I used to be the one that used to tell them to get off the street and don't stand outside of my door. I managed to engage with a couple of them as well. It can be very irritable you know, but there was one experience one time I remember I was telling the prostitutes, I was telling a prostitute to move because she was stood opposite where I lived so any of the prostitutes that do that and I ask them politely to move.
> (Tony, 27, Afro-Caribbean, Area 1 resident)

Others voiced their concerns and made complaints to the police and local council, while also informing the local press, in order to raise awareness of their concerns:

> They complained continually on [Area 1 street]. There was a group on there who, for the right reasons, and I don't think it was on moral grounds. It was mainly about the nuisance of having girls working on the corner of their street with the punters coming round and the other reason of course was the drugs and needles. Used Durex and things like that. Their kids are in the area. Of course it's bringing process of houses down. So they used to have [Area 1] Action Group who used to be continuously complaining. Actions groups for the [local newspaper], coz of course the papers would like something like this.
> (Clive, 42, Area 1 chief inspector)

When some residents felt that their actions were deterring street prostitution from Area 1, some local people took to the streets to march against prostitution with placards, in order to maintain a visible presence:

> There was a committee called the [Area 1] committee that was different agencies that worked together to get [Area 1[rid of all them [prostitutes and clients] and the stereotypical images and that. They used to campaign

fiercely. I remember them going on their little march along [Area 1 street] with placards saying 'get rid of the prostitutes, get them out, prostitutes out' and stuff like that. But it's all gone now, there's nothing there whatsoever.

(Tony, 27, Afro-Caribbean, Area 1 resident)

In contrast, the majority of residents and business employees from Area 2 took a more formal approach, through attending community meetings, contacting local politicians and phoning the police. Rather than actively taking to the streets and marching against the street sex scene, the majority of Area 2 residents took a less direct approach. One police officer claimed that: 'The action group, they were very reactionary as an action group. And they just vilified prostitutes full stop ... it was just like a lynching mob type thing. Am exaggerating, but it wasn't far off' (Peter, 35, Area 2 police constable). However, discussions with many residents, councillors and businesses employees demonstrated a greater tolerance of street prostitution. I attended numerous community meetings, which were established to discuss local concerns; one of those raised was prostitution. Unlike Area 1, Area 2 residents voiced their concerns at community meetings and contacted local police when they saw a prostitute or client nearby. They did not form an action group or mobilize in any coherent way during the study. The reasons behind this will be discussed below.

Violence and vigilantism

Although the majority of campaigns and marches against prostitution identified in the literature are non-violent, some evidence demonstrates that physical force and violence has been used by local people to remove prostitution from the areas where they live and/or work. In some instances, community action could, therefore, be labelled as vigilantism. Johnston argues that vigilantism

> has six necessary features: (i) it involves planning and premeditation by those engaging in it; (ii) its participants are private citizens whose engagement is voluntary; (iii) it is a form of 'autonomous citizenship' and, as such, constitutes a social movement; (iv) it uses or threatens the use of force; (v) it arises when an established order is under threat from the transgression, the potential transgression, or the imputed transgression of institutionalized norms; (vi) it aims to control crime or other social infractions by offering assurances (or 'guarantees') of security both to participants and to others.
>
> (Johnston 1996: 220)

Adopting this model to analyse the actions of Street Watch schemes, Williams (2005: 528) argues that it is when force is used or threatened 'that is the crux, and thus would be the tipping at which actions would be deemed vigilantism'.

Physical force was used in Delhi (India), where over 100 residents of the Mahipalpur area tried to physically barge into a guest house, after the police failed to act on their complaints that the property was a brothel (Carey and

102 *Community action and resistance*

Smith-Miles 2008). Similarly, in Jakarta (Indonesia), it has been claimed that 4000 activists from a group called the Islamic Defenders Front (FPI) broke into city's local government offices and occupied it for the day, apparently paralyzing the city administration's activities, because they were not satisfied with the government intervention provided to deal with prostitution. In Tangerang, 30 km west of Jakarta (Indonesia), seventeen brothels were set on fire, while in Bekasi, east of the capital, two brothels were also burned down, while angry mobs destroyed hotels, restaurants and cafes that were known locally as sex hot-spots (Baeva 2005). Violent behaviour was similarly observed in Christchurch (New Zealand), where residents claimed that disruptive behaviour was being caused by members of the public, who regularly drove to the area specifically to shout and harass sex workers, as well as throwing eggs at them. Yet, violence was also identified as being perpetrated by sex workers in Manukau (New Zealand), as residents claimed that sex workers had thrown rocks at them, as well as attacking them with crowbars on their cars and kicking their vehicles. This violence, it was claimed, was in response to resident campaigns to remove street prostitution from the area (*New Zealand Herald* 2009).

In the UK, sex workers have claimed that male patrollers of a Street Watch scheme in Cardiff would physically move them on, putting their arms around them and forcing them to walk (Sagar 2005). Sagar (2005) found that there was an absence of checks made by the police to determine whether a violent member of the public had been recruited to the Street Watch programme. This clearly raises significant issues in terms of accountability, guidance, supervision, training and partnership working with the police. Those who join such action groups need to be monitored and their backgrounds checked, in order to ensure that acts of violence or vigilantism are prevented. These issues were more pronounced in the context of reports from prostitutes in Basal Heath, Birmingham (UK), where it emerged that they had been subjected to death threats, bricks being thrown at them and one girl being shot at with a crossbow. According to the English Collective of Prostitutes, Street Watch patrollers were responsible for the attacks, and they, therefore, claimed that such schemes were 'a guise for vigilantism' (cited in Sagar 2005: 107). Clearly, police supervision is needed to ensure that such instances are dealt with appropriately, in order to protect the safety of prostitutes and their clients. Yet, as Sagar (2005: 108) claims:

> When the mission is a popular one, then, regardless of the tactics employed, the criminal actions of the community are often exonerated. Arguably, Street Watch members are not; nor are they likely to be held to account for vigilante actions against street prostitutes.

Evidence emerged from my research suggesting that some of the protests and marches were not always peaceful. Although some residents in Area 1 did not identify that the action taken to remove street prostitution from their neighbourhoods was violent, Terry explained how some of the campaigns involved violent behaviour and that certain members of the community were targeting prostitutes:

Community action and resistance 103

> I remember a few years ago we was all campaigning together ... when prostitution first came into [Area 1] ... the kerb-crawlers they came and they were kind of like getting robbed and stoned.... So eventually the kerb-crawlers they weren't coming no more and the prostitutes weren't making no money ... and eventually they've just fizzled out.... Young kids as well used to like throw stones at them [prostitutes] and all sorts like that. That on our streets was the most detesting thing there was. But yeah I'd say that's how they got rid of it.... The women and the cars ... robbing them when they came kind of worked to help get rid of it.
>
> (Terry, 63, white, Area 1 police constable)

Similarly, in Area 2, a police officer claimed that a group that was established by residents to remove street prostitution from the area was somewhat like a 'lynching mob'. Not the police, councillors, residents nor business employees identified anyone who was prosecuted or arrested for violent conduct in either Area 1 or 2, which raises concerns about how the violence documented was dealt with, particularly when perpetrated against sex workers and their clients.

In recent years, however, there has been an important reconceptualization of how violence perpetrated towards sex workers is viewed by the authorities in the UK and how these matters are dealt with. In Liverpool, during the summer of 2005, images of Peter Sutcliffe were spray-painted on the walls of the beat, which has been interpreted as a means of intimidating prostitutes from the area. Since 2006, Merseyside police believe that acts of violence against sex workers is a form of 'hate crime'. This demonstrates an ideological shift in how violence against sex workers is seen, as it is often believed that they are in some way responsible for the violence perpetrated against them (Campbell 2011). However, sadly, this initiative has yet to be taken forward by other forces in the UK.

'Designing out' street prostitution

A further strategy sometimes employed by members of a community to deal with prostitution has been to design the area that they live and work in a way that attempts to exclude sex workers and their clients. As residents and business employees sought to reclaim their streets, they redesigned the local area to exclude those who were not considered to be welcome. Some members expressed a sense of 'ownership' over the areas where they lived, despite the local streets being public property; they sought to remove prostitutes and their clients from 'their' area, as they were clearly deemed to be 'out of place'. They were seen as 'outsiders', who brought disruption and problems to the local area, despite some sex workers living in the areas that they work. Matthews (2008: 7) explains: 'the changing sense of space involved new notions of "ownership", which in many areas became linked with new forms of privatisation, as neighbourhoods became more fragmented. This change was, in turn, linked to the changing nature of communities.' In this sense, the concept of 'community' is problematic, as such activism cannot be said to fully represent the goals and objectives of the whole community. As with Sagar's (2005: 1001) research, this 'supports the argument that *who* represents the community determines *whom* the community is made safe *for*'. Clearly, notions of 'citizenship' and 'belonging' became visible in terms of how areas are designed and structured, as those who are deemed to belong to the community influence how the area is made and remade. As Hubbard (1998a: 271) states: 'space is where discourses about power and knowledge are transformed into actual relations of power'. In this context, the boundaries around what is considered respectable sexuality are marked, as the removal of prostitutes marks them as sexual Others. In this sense, it could be argued that 'the location of street prostitution reflects the differential ability of social groups to purify space' (Hubbard 2011: 61).

The ways in which public and semi-public spaces have been designed and developed have sought to aim towards the 'designing out' of prostitution. For instance, residents in Bristol (UK) introduced a series of measures to make it difficult for sex workers and their punters to meet and engage in sexual activities. These measures included the installation of improved street lighting in dark corners, as well as hedges being planted to prevent people leaning against the walls of local property and regular cleaning and clearing of undergrowth and landscaping in an effort to make criminal activity more difficult (This is Bristol. co.uk 2011). Also in the UK, residents of Bolton developed an action plan in conjunction with the local council, which sought to improve the local environment and image of the area through refurbishing open spaces, footpaths and a local park, addressing issues of the poor management of privately rented properties, improving the security of business premises through CCTV, installing shuttering and better lighting and developing community facilities (Hughes 2008). In France, parking restrictions have been used to deter sex workers and their clients from Lyon. Gräbener *et al.* explained:

> [T]he City Hall has enforced a series of municipal bylaws aimed at prostitutes, under the guise of parking regulations.... Following the criminalization of solicitation in 2003, many prostitutes who worked on the streets in Lyon adapted to the law by purchasing vans and working inside them; some claim, under the advice of law enforcement authorities. In response, City Hall has passed six bylaws over the last seven years to restrict parking in designated areas of the city during certain hours. The most recent bylaw affected the prostitutes parked in Gerland, a gentrified neighborhood in Lyon, where they had congregated because of parking prohibitions in other parts of the city. The bylaw led to the arrest of a number of prostitutes, as well as the impoundment of twelve vans.
>
> (Gräbener *et al.* 2010: 1)

These bylaws can impinge on prostitutes' private property rights and make working conditions more dangerous, as they move to other areas of the city to escape prosecution. Furthermore, as Gräbener *et al.* (2010: 1) suggest, this method of attacking prostitution 'has diverted attention from its underlying factors, such as poverty, gender segregation and discrimination in the labor market, systematic male domination of women, and cultural beliefs that condone such practices'.

In both Area 1 and Area 2, public and semi-public spaces were designed to deter prostitutes and their clients. In Area 1, speed bumps were installed on a street known locally for street prostitution. The aim of these traffic calming measures was to deter kerb-crawlers, because they would no longer be able to accelerate quickly to exit the area, in order to escape being apprehended by the police. However, as Clive describes, these speed bumps had the opposite effect. Rather than deterring kerb-crawlers, it offered them an excuse for the slow speed at which they drove down local roads:

> The council put speed bumps on Spencer Place, which was perfect for them, because of course they've got to slow down. You know. Whereas before you'd see them up and down, up and down. All of a sudden they've got these speed bumps as an excuse as well 'well I was just slowing done to have a look at them' 'no I was slowing down for the speed bumps' and they needed the speed bumps because obviously you've got a lot of kids on there and the dangers with the speed was too much so it was catch twenty two.
>
> (Clive, 42, white, Area 1 chief inspector)

Similarly, Area 2 saw the introduction of traffic calming measures as a means of deterring kerb-crawlers. Yet, rather than using speed bumps, the local council installed a number of road narrowing methods and give way signs. In addition, they also made changes to local carparks where sexual activities often took place, as well as funding the installation of gates and fencing for residents whose yards had been used for sex. For some residents, the impact of such interventions had a positive impact on their quality of life, as Patrick explains:

> Since the roads been closed down here, it's been quite quiet ... they've been doing some road works [to narrow the road].... So this last five weeks have been brilliant. I've been having great night's sleep, sleeping through; you know a good nights kip and everything. But, I expect, when I saw road opening again I thought oh they'll be back.
>
> (Patrick, 53, white, Area 2 resident)

The industrial part of Area 2 also underwent significant aesthetic changes with the introduction of residential buildings and the redevelopment of run-down business premises. As new developers and residents moved into the previously industrialized area, they began to view the presence of prostitution as a problem and sought to exclude prostitutes and their clients. This process of redevelopment and exclusion can be linked to the process of gentrification. Gentrification is defined as:

106 Community action and resistance

> A physical, economic, social and cultural phenomenon. Gentrification commonly involves the invasion by middle-class of higher-income groups of previously working-class neighbourhoods or multi-occupied 'twilight areas' and the replacement or displacement of many original occupants. It involves the physical renovation or rehabilitation of what was frequently a highly deteriorated housing stock and it's upgrading to meet the requirements of its new owners.
>
> (Hamnett 1984: 284)

Gentrification has been hypothesized as a major impetuous to anti-prostitution protests (Winchester and White 1988), which may be understood as arising from concerns over property prices and a desire to purify 'redeveloped' spaces. With the 'redevelopment' of Area 1, the city would be 'cleansed' and the 'immoral' designed out. In this context, street sex workers and their clients, pimps and drug dealers all become a target population (Flint and Nixon 2006).

Matthews (2008) argues that shifting views towards prostitution during the 1990s led to the growth of gated communities and introduction of security systems on council estates. These changing attitudes towards street prostitution, he argued, were bound up with the process of gentrification. With poor and deprived areas being regenerated through development grants, a change in class composition of an area led to a change in local politics. While poorer disempowered residents often lacked the organization and political clout and, thus, 'put up with' street prostitution, new residents moving into these regenerated areas were not prepared to tolerate its presence. The impact of regeneration and the shift in class composition of an area can be seen in Edinburgh (UK), where residents displaced a tolerance zone from their area (The Christian Institute 2001). The tolerance zone in Leith, Edinburgh, was moved, following the regeneration of the area, which then led to an increase in residential properties and an influx of new families.

Marginal populations then begin to feel 'out of place in spaces devoted to affluent consumption' (Hubbard 2004: 669), due to their inability to afford to engage in such practices. Thus, as street prostitution does not fit with the 'newly remade' city centre, those involved are displaced into the ungentrified area. This suggestion is supported by Roger (57, white, director), who explains how the regeneration of a neighbourhood may, in fact, result in the displacement of street prostitution, because those involved feel spatially excluded from the area:

> As more and more businesses come down and there's more pressures I suppose the prostitutes themselves feel a bit uncomfortable, in a way, I don't know. Maybe they felt a bit uncomfortable ... they must have known there was pressure so I think at that particular time it moved.
>
> (Roger, 57, white, company director)

This displacement led one resident to claim that the ungentrified site of Area 2 was Leeds city centre's 'dumping ground' (Patrick, 53, white, Area 2 resident).

Residents claimed that prostitution had been displaced out of the city centre, where local business representatives worked, and pushed into the surrounding area in line with recent 'redevelopments' of the city. This form of displacement has been explained by Winchester and White (1988), who claim that it is only when more affluent gentrifiers return to the city that anti-prostitution campaigns are acted upon by the police and local councillors. This was observed in San Francisco (US) at the beginning of the 1900s, where the influx of business and economic investment led to increased levels of policing, which, in turn, pushed prostitution away from the more desirable and cosmopolitan areas of the city (Shumsky and Springer 1981). As Hubbard (2011) has argued, the visibility of street prostitution is often located in already marginalized and socially disadvantaged areas, which lack the necessary political power to deal with social problems.

The importance of informal mechanisms of social control in crime prevention has continued to have a lasting impact for policymaking and academic debates. Crawford argues that three influential American criminologists made significant contributions to academic developments in this area. Drawing on the work of Jacobs (1961), the first influential contributor, Oscar Newman (1972),

> [a]rgued that the nature of certain built environments (notably large public sector housing estates constructed in the 1950s and 1960s) can have a suffocating impact upon important 'natural' social processes which prevent or lessen the likelihood of crime. He argued that through design modification 'defensible spaces' can be reconstructed and, consequently, processes of informal control revived.
>
> (Crawford 1997: 29)

This work was then developed by Alice Coleman (1985), whose work was influential on British Government thinking. She argued that poor physical environments can lead to social breakdown, as the notion of 'community' is eroded, and outsiders are able to enter the area. Furthermore, the work of Clarke (2002) has argued that most crime is opportunistic, suggesting that the majority of crime can be deterred by designing and managing the immediate environment in a way that deters criminals from committing an offence. This can be achieved through altering or redesigning the physical environment to make it more difficult to commit a crime, such as installing surveillance cameras, or taking steps to reduce the attractiveness of a particular crime or object, by, for example, reducing an item's value on the illicit market.

Naming and shaming

A small number of residents in Area 2 took action by supporting the naming and shaming of kerb-crawlers, through noting down registration numbers of persistent kerb-crawlers and shaming them by informing their family, employers or the local press. Residents identified a number of occasions where they contacted the police to inform them when a persistent kerb-crawler was seen in the vicinity. As Patrick explained: 'I often rang the police and told them when a guy was in the area looking for sex.' There was widespread support for such schemes, as it was believed that clients '[s]houldn't be doing it. Should be named' (Tina, 31, Afro-Caribbean, Area 1 resident); 'put their names in the paper and everybody knows who they are' (Carol, 68, white, Area 2 resident). Resident involvement in the naming and shaming of prostitutes and their clients was supported and encouraged by the police:

> It's worthwhile, even though it captures a small part of the overall strategy; you know part of the overall publicity. You throw that in with newspapers and adverts and even posters on lampposts in the area are letting them know we area around erm, you know it all adds to people being worried about being down there and deterring them from using the area so good work.
> (Malcolm, 36, Area 1 detective inspector)

The naming and shaming of kerb-crawlers has also been observed in other parts of the UK. For example, in 2000, Sanders (2008b) observed how in Balsall Heath, Birmingham, the Street Watch campaign targeted men who drove their vehicles through the neighbourhood. Uniformed residents took photographs of suspected kerb-crawlers and noted registration numbers, which they then passed on to the police. According to Sanders (2008b), there appeared to be no criteria for judging who was a kerb-crawler. Similarly, in Oldham (UK), over 100 men formed a vigilante group to drive prostitution out of the area, through naming and shaming men who used the services of prostitutes and through patrolling the local streets (Begum 2008b). One of the Muslim campaigners, Said Salik, explained how: 'We warned people on the streets that we will tell the mosques and even their families if they are seen approaching prostitutes or using drugs' (cited in Begum 2008a: 1). Williams' (2005b) and Sagar's (2005) research also identified how residents would send warning letters to the registered keeper of a vehicle seen frequenting the district and would also pass the information on to the police. Finally, in Kensington, London, MP Louise Baldock claimed that 'the community are all very keen that prostitution in our area should be stopped' and supported initiatives to name and shame kerb-crawlers entering the area for sex (Baldock 2009: 1).

Internationally, this practice has also been utilized to tackle street prostitution. In Manhattan (US), residents began monitoring those suspected of engaging in prostitution and sometimes detaining them for a police arrest (Mittelmann 2008). Similarly, in the US, residents in Manchester documented the names of prostitutes and recorded the license plate numbers of their clients (WMUR 2007). In Spain, residents of a central Madrid street threatened to film negotiations between prostitutes and potential clients in an attempt to scare the men away (Tarvainen 2007). Furthermore, in New Zealand, residents sent letters to suspected kerb-crawlers and tracked them down through their car registration plates. The letters, posted in pink envelopes, alerted kerb-crawlers to the fact that they had been spotted in the local area and warned them of the dangers of their actions (Buckley 2009).

The naming and shaming of sex workers and their clients raises important issues around human rights, freedom of movement and the right to be deemed innocent until proven guilty. Sending letters to the registered keeper of a vehicle seen in a known red-light area may act as a deterrent; however, it may also lead to family or employment problems for those who were in the area for innocent purposes. Furthermore, some local men in my research identified occasions when they had been apprehended by the police for kerb-crawling, while walking home at night. Other participants also identified occasions when their vehicles were checked against police databases when they were visiting the area on official business.

Rationale for action

In many areas where community activism takes place, there are some members of the community who take action and protest on the street or contact the police, while others do very little. For example, Patrick explained how he and his neighbour seemed to be the only people in his area who took action to remove prostitution. He also stated how his actions led some members of the community, as well as sex workers themselves, to criticize him for passing on information to the police. This left him questioning whether it was only him and his neighbour who considered street prostitution to be a problem in the area:

> There only seems to be me and Kate bothered, you know what I mean, you know. So I think there's just two of us phoning up, probably just think its just them two, they're trouble makers maybe. I mean one of the prostitutes told me and I was just letting him in. I didn't even know they were there and she's across the road and there's a car there. 'I'm just talking to friends, so they're no need to come out', I says 'look I'm just getting the cat, right' and I says 'and it makes a change for you to be talking to friends who you haven't just met on the street', 'you get in, the police hate you with always phoning up' ... I was fuming, so I phoned them up and came down 'oh no no no. Just keep phoning. We don't mind you, you ringing up. Just keep letting us know what's going on'.... Well I just thought it was just me and Kate, you know that were complaining. But when we've been at these meetings you've heard. Like there was one poor old lady who said they drove up her drive and were doing it right outside her house.
> (Patrick, white, Area 2 resident)

Sagar's (2005) research demonstrated that some residents claimed not to have seen prostitutes in the area in which they lived, while others had seen prostitutes, but said 'it really doesn't bother me'. Yet, for some residents and business employees, taking action was considered the best approach for them.

Characteristics of activists

In understanding why some members of the community take action and others do not, Sagar (2005) claims that concerns expressed by Street Watch patrollers in Cardiff may be more of a consequence of the composition of its members. By considering Shapland and Vagg's (1988) suggestion that it is generally older people who report suspicious activity, Sagar (2005) argues that because neighbourhood watchers and Street Watch patrollers were mainly retired, this may explain the anxiety of some members of the community. Shapland and Vagg (1988: 70) state that increased reporting of suspicious behaviour stems from 'moral connotations of people who did not fit into watchers' views of how life should be lived within the area'.

Yet, Street Watch members in Sagar's (2005) research claimed that the reasons why young people were not involved or were less concerned about the presence of street prostitution stemmed from their busy lifestyles, because they were either at work or too busy with their families and, thus, did not always see street prostitution occurring. This was supported by Craig, who believed that the reason why some people did not complain was because they have more important issues to think about in their daily lives:

> I don't think a lot of people complain about it really because it's been going on for so long ... I don't think people put too much thought in to that really. I think they put more thought in the poll tax, the er the rent increase, the electric bills, food I don't think a lot think it concerns them really. I don't think they put too much thought into that at all. It's not a big issue.
> (Craig, 46, Afro-Caribbean, Area 2 community worker)

For others, they felt that the reason why some citizens complained more often related to their social position within society – in particular, their social class. Social class and its relationship to the sex industry has been considered by academics (Bernstein 2007; O'Connell Davidson 1995; Sanders 2008b), local government (Adams 2008) and central government (Home Office 2007c) and is, furthermore, evidenced here. The belief that a person's class influences a person's perception of prostitution was mentioned by a local councillor and police officer. Daniel suggested that there were differences between those who complained and those who did not take action, attributing this difference to a person's social class. As Daniel explains:

> People ... in the leafy lane areas ... first they hear of it ... they're on the ball and if there's protest, masses of people, they're protesting. Whereas in the ... inner city areas ... tend to be on low income; not as well educated; have day to day problems because of their low income, they're struggling to live; and their priorities are sort of the immediate environment; bringing up their family ... they don't really bother going to meetings and getting involved in the wider community.... So they ignore things and then suddenly when

everything's agreed and starts to happen it hits them and then they're not happy with it and they want to do something about it.

(Daniel, 62, white, Area 1 Labour councillor)

Working-class people's lack of action towards prostitution was not deemed as evidence of empathy for those who sell sexual access to their bodies for economic gain, but was due to the fact that they themselves had more immediate priorities to consider. Yet, this is questioned by Thorpe and Wood's (2004) analysis of the *British Crime Survey*, which suggests that people living in social housing estates or poorer areas tend to report more anti-social behaviour problems. According to Hancock (2001), perceptions of disorder are accentuated for people experiencing deteriorating standards of living or those who live within deprived or declining neighbourhoods. Therefore, the assumption that people of lower social classes are less likely to complain about the existence of prostitution in the areas in which they live appears to be misplaced.

In contrast, Clive believed that class impacts on whether a person views something to be wrongful or not. People of lower social classes, Clive believes, are more tolerant of behaviours committed for 'survival'. Whereas those from a higher class background are less tolerant and more critical:

> I think that class comes into it a little bit more.... I think your sort of working class stroke lower class person will have the view of you know there is a need, I keep going back to the woman who is doing it to feed her kids and there used to be the same idea of you're a burglar because you need to feed the kids it was socially acceptable.... Whereas your middle classes, because they have never understood the sort of feeling of hunger.... It's very easy to have morals to say that its wrong ... it's very easy when you've had everything all your life to have a social view that something's wrong as to when you've had nothing. I think you're more understanding and accepting of something that maybe is wrong.
>
> (Clive, 42, white, Area 2 chief inspector)

This class-related intolerance may explain why street prostitution was displaced into the less affluent location of Area 1, following the regeneration of the newly remade city centre. The lack of understanding as to why women engage in prostitution and the desire to cleanse and claim the newly remade city centre resulted in the displacement of street prostitution, as 'wealthy developers, businesses and individuals moving into the area ... spending lots and lots of money on the area, being confronted by street prostitutes.... So they, they were up in arms about it' (Paul, 56, white, Area 1 Chief Superintendent). The impact of this lack of understanding and 'compassion' may be observed in the difficulties that Kevin identified when attempting

> [t]o get an agreement for a kind of drop-in centre for women, not big sign saying prostitute drop-in centre health thing from there, a drop-in centre with health. NHS would of actually paid for. The [Area 1 development

group] was totally against that. They didn't want that in the area so to speak, you know even if it was covert in its identity, just didn't want that facility there and you know in truth business investment in the city has a considerable clout in decision making in the city.

(Kevin, age unknown, white, drug intervention)

The idea that people of a lower social class status tolerate crimes of 'survival' because they themselves struggle to survive suggests that the commonality between those of a low social class status impacts upon the perceptions held. People from higher social class backgrounds are intolerant, because they lack the commonality held by the lower classes. The importance of being able to relate to another person due to their social class was also identified in Bernstein's research, which described the experiences of a female sex worker, who suggested that her success was related to her social class background. As Amanda explained: 'I have the same kind of background as they do and I seem easy to talk to. White educated women like me have a lot of appeal to professional white men.' (cited in Bernstein 2007: 479) Similarly, Clive (42, white, Area 2 chief inspector) states that he can make such a claim, 'because I'm from ... that sort of community myself'. Through identifying himself as coming from a working class background and suggesting that people of lower social classes are more tolerant of prostitution, Clive's suggestion may be deemed as an 'embrace of these ideals', which 'serves as a means for members' of the working class 'to distinguish themselves from the' upper classes (Bernstein 2007: 477). The aim of distinguishing himself from the upper classes can be understood as a means of creating and confirming social distance between himself – as a working class man –from those he perceives as less tolerant – the upper classes. The desire to create social distance will be explored further in Chapter 8.

Concern for female residents

Evidence from my research demonstrated that people of all ages were protesting against street prostitution, particularly in Area 1, because of concerns that female residents were being approached by kerb-crawlers. Residents in Area 1 explained that they were annoyed to hear of female residents being approached by kerb-crawlers and propositioned for sex. Some residents expressed fear for female family members and friends. Rachel (43, Afro-Caribbean, Area 1 resident) explained how:

> There used to be some big set to's in [Area 1 road] I think the women and the fathers used to come out and try to run the prostitutes off the streets. They were probably thinking that she was being followed and might be attacked or something.

As a result, Brian (47, West Indian, Area 1 resident) identified that local residents protested against street prostitution, because:

[i]t was an everyday occurrence, anytime of the night. Again as guys, we're like if your girlfriend comes in and she says I was walking you're out there and you're looking for this guy. So it's a really crazy thing but to me it's always happened, you know and that's why we didn't want to live, that's why we marched against prostitution in the seventies, we fought against them as a kid, we did everything to get them out of the area but it never happened.

(Brian, 47, Afro-Caribbean, Area 2 resident)

Concerns over being propositioned were echoed by female residents; this was explored in depth in Chapter 5, so is only briefly mentioned here.

Removing the problem

In both Area 1 and Area 2, resident community meetings were set up in response to resident complaints and concerns about the existence of street prostitution locally. In the first community meetings that were held to deal with prostitution in both areas, sex workers were considered the main 'problem'. Nine of the ten local authority officials interviewed stated that residents deemed street sex workers as the problem and suggested their removal as a means of dealing with their concerns. According to residents, this focus would result in a reduction in the number of kerb-crawlers in Area 1 and Area 2. As Daniel (62, white, Area 1 Labour councillor) stated: 'The concentration was on the women ... rather than the kerb-crawlers.... Get rid of the women and ... the men will go.' This focus was also apparent from some discussions that I had with residents, as they often saw sex workers as the cause of nuisance. For instance, Peter explained that street prostitutes were more visible and became easily recognizable to residents. As a result of this continued visibility:

> The residents seem to ... have their anger more at the women than at the punters ... they're ... in their eye all the time coz obviously the men come and go, but ... the same women will be walking the same patch ... and I suppose they're more instantly recognizable. I suppose residents will look at it and say well if the women aren't there the men won't come.
>
> (Peter, 35, white, Area 2 Labour councillor)

Similarly, Clive (42, white, Area 1 chief inspector) identified residents' beliefs that sex workers were the main source of anxiety because of their visibility: 'It was sex workers who were the focus of public concerns, seeing them on the streets, outside their homes ... taking drugs.... They just wanted them off their streets.'

Matthews (2008) described concerns that arose in the 1980s and 1990s, which led to 'the growing objection to vagrancy, street begging and young people "hanging around" reflect a change of public sensibilities' (Matthews 2008: 7). McKewon (2003) also illustrates that the tensions caused by the public visibility of prostitution can similarly be observed in Perth (Australia) during the early 1990s, as local people protested against its presence, due to concerns that it might affect the image of the city. More recently, the increased visibility of street prostitution and those involved has been cited as a problem for some residents in Coventry (UK). Local people complained about seeing sex workers outside their business premises and homes (The Swish Project 2008). Concerns over increased visibility may be resolved for some, as residents in Manhattan (US) suggested, through moving street prostitution into an industrial area, where it is deemed as less of a problem (Mittelmann 2008).

Despite such opposition to visible forms of prostitution, Matthews (2008) asserts that the majority of residents were opposed to prostitution, not prostitutes. Residents, for the most part, saw women working on the streets as victims of their problematic drug use, poor health and physical condition. Their hostility, he suggests, has increasingly turned towards their clients, 'either because it became evident that many of those cruising around the streets were voyeurs and were attracted to red light districts as sites of entertainment' or because their clients 'were the persistent and sometimes aggressive punters who intimidates local women and created a sense of disorder and lack of control' (Matthews 2008: 9–10). The shift to focus more on clients was similarly observed in my research. According to local authority officials, clients began to be perceived as the main source of the 'problem'. This was documented by Ivor (40, white, Area 1 development officer), who suggested that residents began to realize that prostitution involved more than one party and focusing on kerb-crawlers may be the solution to dealing with community concerns:

> I think the focus has definitely changed from the women ... to actually saying well in actual fact you can't have a prostitute without having a man ... so ... the focus seems to have shifted ... in general, not only with policy makers, but with the community, that ... maybe the way to deal with this is to target the people who use prostitutes ... I think that is the right approach.
>
> (Ivor, 40, white, Area 2 development officer)

Through the direction of local authority officials, some Area 2 residents began to perceive kerb-crawlers as equally responsible for the presence of prostitution in their neighbourhoods. Many residents believed that 'if the men weren't coming down the prostitutes wouldn't be there' (Ivor, 40, white, Area 2 development officer). O'Neill *et al.* (2008: 84) suggest that a shift from 'don't blame the women, look at men' illustrates some tolerance of women working the streets.

The move to focus on sex buyers was identified as stemming from the input of local police and officials, rather than originating from within the community. As Daniel (62, white, Area 1 Labour councillor) explained, residents began to recognize that men who buy sex are equally to blame for the 'nuisance' caused to residents. Daniel identifies the shift of focus to kerb-crawlers as something that he influenced:

> The early meetings it was get rid of them [street sex workers], they should be locked up ... put in prison ... get em in court and fine them and we argued and the police argued, yeah but what about the men, if the men weren't there the girls wouldn't be there ... and we were insisting on targeting kerb-crawlers ... as the meetings went on ... they got to understand ... men were to blame as well ... and the attitude changed a little bit towards kerb-crawlers, especially ... coz we'd told them to note registration numbers to get them reported.
>
> (Daniel, 62, white, Area 1 Labour councillor)

Similarly, Edward (33, white, Area 2 police sergeant) documents how:

> They just vilified prostitutes full stop ... and it wasn't until we said you know you can't really do that, it's not just the women who are the problem.... Well actually these people when we actually sat down and introduced, well actually they've got needs. These are their problems. This is what we're trying to do to try and solve them.
>
> (Edward, 33, white, Area 2 police sergeant)

As with Williams' (2005b) research, one group of residents from Area 2 appeared to accept suggestions made by the police and local authority officials, whereas others acted more independently and demonstrated acts of vigilantism.

Yet, much wider policy shifts in the UK, which began to identify sex workers less as offenders and more as victims, alongside a changing regulatory and ideological landscape, which began to see clients as perpetrators, may also explain the shift in attitude and action taken towards dealing with prostitution. Police interviewees suggested that the local authority officials' attitudes were similarly altered. This change in perception of the problem was attributed by Paul to officials being informed about prostitution law. As Paul explained:

> Councillors themselves have changed their minds, as times gone on. Coz certainly at that first meeting, I mean [councillor] ... his view was just get them locked up'.... So there was a tremendous lack of understanding of legislation and how effective it could be ... which we highlighted ... they started to realise it had to be tackled in a slightly more sensitive way ... the focus was very much on the kerb-crawlers ... from the policing activity.
>
> (Paul, 56, white, Area 1 Chief Superintendent)

This change to focus enforcement on kerb-crawlers may be deemed a result of the national drive to tackle demand (Association of Chief Police Officers 2004; Home Office 2006, 2008c). In this sense, changes to the prostitution law can be seen to have a 'trickle down' effect, as police officers raise awareness within local communities about changes to legislation.

Yet, despite this recognized shift in who the community perceived as the problem, it was still very evident from the people that I spoke with 'that they get

116 *Community action and resistance*

more annoyed with the women really' (Edward, 33, white, Area 1 police sergeant). Because women were more visible, due to their continued presence on the streets in both Area 1 and Area 2, they were often targeted more consistently than their male clients. This may be understood through exploring the work of Foucault and Bourdieu.

Foucault (1972, 1977, 1978) has described how social order is shaped and organized by authoritative knowledge, such as political institutions. With government direction to focus more on tackling the clients of sex workers, this political power can be seen to be reflected in policing practices and then observed in public responses to prostitution. Yet, resistance to that power was also observed and can be understood through exploring Bourdieu's (1989, 1992) work on symbolic power. While Foucault sees power as being everywhere and beyond agency or the capacity of social actors, Bourdieu sees power as culturally and symbolically created and re-legitimized through a continuous interplay between agency and structure. According to Bourdieu, social action is guided by socialized norms or through, what he calls, 'habitus'. Habitus is 'the way society becomes deposited in persons in the form of lasting dispositions, or trained capacities and structured propensities to think, feel and act in determinant ways, which then guide them' (Waquant 2005: 316, cited in Navarro 2006: 16). Important for Bourdieu's work is the idea that social actors are influenced by social norms, while at the same time developing strategies that are adapted to the needs of the social worlds that they inhabit. Thus, community members take actions that are influenced by social norms, yet reproduce those social norms in ways that are tailored to a given situation.

Responding to state and police inaction

State and police inaction was a motivating factor for some residents and business employees who sought to take action to remove prostitution from 'their' neighbourhoods. Matthews (2008) explained how residents in Birmingham and South London (UK) set up street patrols and, in some cases, vigilante groups, because the police and local authorities were seen to be unresponsive. Similarly, Liverpool (UK) group Residents Against Prostitution accused police of turning a blind eye to local brothels that were often common knowledge to the general public in the neighbourhood. Residents felt that if they did not take action, they would never be able to eradicate prostitution from their area (Traynor 2007). As Matthews (2008: 8) argues: 'Street prostitution became *the* major issue of public concern in certain locations.' Public meetings were often organized by local authorities in affected areas, with residents' groups demanding that something be done. This, he suggests, demonstrates communities' growing frustration with official bodies, which were seen to be avoiding taking the matter seriously.

Police and local authority inaction has been identified as the reason why over 100 residents in Delhi (India) decided to barge a guest house accused of being associated with prostitution (Sidhu 2009). Residents gathered outside the guest house to protest against their presence, with some engaging in altercations with staff. Similarly, in Jakarta (India), 4000 activists from a group called the Islamic

Defenders Front broke into local government offices and occupied them for the day, because they were not satisfied with the government's response to prostitution in the city (Yamin 1999). Activists claimed that the state was 'turning a blind eye' to prostitution, which thereby sent the message that they both accepted and tolerated its existence. And, finally, in Islington (New Zealand), residents and local businesses threatened to take legal action against the state and local government, because the council failed to enforce its own crime prevention plan. The group claimed that the government had breached its duty of care by not enforcing the law – specifically, sections of the Summary Offences Act 1981, which prohibits solicitation and acts of prostitution near dwellings, schools, churches or hospitals (Parliamentary Counsel Office 1981). As a result, the group issued a formal demand letter to both the state and local government to tackle street prostitution in their suburbs – specifically, to remove street prostitutes – because the state's negligence had caused significant emotional and economic damage, for which they sought redress. Acting on behalf of the residents and local businesses group, solicitor Leon Sokulsky explained that, although 'he ... was not aware of a precedent for the Islington Action Group's potential legal action', he was 'confident of establishing breaches of duty of care as well as a case for damages' (cited in *The Herald*, see Jones 2009: 1).

In addition, evidence from my study demonstrated that some community members sought to take action because the police, they felt, were not fulfilling their role of protecting community interests. As Patrick explained, his assumption that prostitutes would be removed from his area by the police was quickly undermined:

> I was like 'the police will move em off surely, they must know what's going on', so in the end we phoned the police, 'oh it's a prostitute.... Oh we'll come down and see', and they stand there arguing with the police and I got the impression that they thought they could stand here legally ... I mean I've no proof but I got the impression that they believed they were told they could actually come up here, so somebody.... Well there's one guy ... I phoned up [the police] and I said 'look I've phoned up about this guy at least for the last two years'. I say 'he's still here and he's still picking prostitutes up and I can't understand this, why he's still here and you're supposed to be doing something about it'. 'Oh we'll send somebody down, but it's not a priority'. I says 'yeah it is for me I've got to get up in two hours. You know I'd like some sleep tonight'.... That's why I've been so narked when I go to the meetings.
>
> (Patrick, 53, white, Area 2 resident)

This account was supported by Dean, who admitted that a policy of 'moving them on' was in place:

> At the time that I arrived there, there was a policy in place and that policy was effectively oh just go and move them on and record that you've moved

them on. That was for the purposes of public perception, which is a very, very, very short term strategy.

(Dean, 30, white, Area 2 police constable)

Similarly, a police officer in Area 1 admitted that the police regularly employed a short-term strategy to deal with prostitution, which often involved only responding to public complaints when they are made:

Typical, unfortunate knee jerk response from the police, which we're very good at doing, erm. We deploy resources to a place when people shout. Those who shout loudest get the resources and then when they quieten down we take those resources away, we don't, and we tend never to finish the job.

(Terry, 53, white, Area 2 police constable)

Police and state inaction were some of the reasons why residents in Area 1 also decided to take action by marching and protesting on the streets. They felt that it was their actions that moved street prostitution out of the district to other parts of the city.

Yet, as one resident explained, he believed that a policy existed that hindered some police officers' ability to deal with their complaints effectively:

Now who I really feel sorry for is the young coppers. They come down because we're phoning up all the time and they know they're here and they can see what agro it's really causing us and they can't do anything. Their hands are tied. They just don't seem to be able to do anything about it. You know they'll say move off don't come up here, but they know they'll come back.... I think they're hands are tied its coz its someone higher up obviously that's made this policy.

(Patrick, 53, white, Area 2 resident)

Community activism and vigilantism in response to police and state inaction has been well documented in Williams' (2005b) research. Sagar (2005) similarly describes how residents claimed that the police were not meeting agreed partnership responsibilities, because of their failure to act upon information that was passed on to them. Street Watch members felt that there had been a shift in the police's attitude towards the scheme, and, as a result, their engagement began to dwindle. In some instances, the police appeared unaware that the scheme existed or who were members.

In contrast, however, state and police *action*, which has been deemed inappropriate to the needs and desires of local communities, has also led some residents to take action. For example, residents in Soho, London (UK), began an anti-brothel campaign by organizing a petition, signed by 10,000 people, calling on the authorities to stop their activities, which had sought to remove prostitutes from the local area. Rather than seeking the removal of prostitutes from the neighbourhood, many residents supported sex workers and believed that they needed a safe place to work. Some residents claimed that the police were targeting sex workers, because they were 'easy targets', rather than pursuing drug dealers. One resident, Juliet Peston – a Soho Society member – said that she knew many of the women and some had even become friends (Dovkants 2009). In addition, Soho residents, including Father David Gilmore – rector of St Anne's Church – supported local sex workers during a court case that investigated the closure of a Soho brothel by the Metropolitan Police using antisocial behaviour legislation. Mr Justice Riddle refused the Metropolitan Police's application to have the closure order confirmed, stating: 'I am not satisfied that any person has engaged in antisocial behaviour on the premises.' (One News 2011: 1) Therefore, police action or inaction that contravenes community needs and interests raises questions about legitimacy and public confidence in policing.

The implications of activism

The final section of this chapter will explore the implications that community activism may have in terms of accountability and legitimacy, policing, citizenship and sex worker safety.

Accountability and legitimacy

Community action raises important questions about how these actions are made accountable and whether they are legitimate. Unorganized or uncoordinated action may contravene legal provisions for legitimate public demonstrations and may lead to violence and vigilantism. Given that sex workers and their clients, because of their social position within society, may be considered to be unworthy victims, any violence perpetrated against them may be deemed appropriate and blame apportioned to them.

Concerns that community activism may 'encourage vigilantes' or 'have a go heroes', because they are without police supervision and coordination, has been expressed by the UK Government in its guide for Neighbourhood Watch schemes.[1] Yet, as with Williams' and Sagar's research, the community action taken in Area 1 was extremely successful in removing street prostitution from the vicinity, while at the same time highlighting a number of concerns. As Williams describes, there are worrying possibilities

> that vigilantism as a method of policing may indeed be more effective at reducing levels of certain crimes than traditional methods of the police and secondly, that this type of resident involvement within policing could be encouraged or practised for precisely that reason.
>
> (Williams 2005b: 533)

Similarly, Sagar (2005: 100) claims that, following community action to remove street prostitution from Cardiff:

The police realized that not only had the campaigners successfully removed prostitutes and kerb-crawlers from the area, but that associated crime levels had dropped dramatically. Faced with such positive results, the police were, not surprisingly; keen to encourage community action of this type.

Sagar argues that it is vital that the police's responsibilities for reducing crime are not offloaded onto civilians. Indeed, the more effective that residents and business employees are in removing street prostitution from an area, the more frequently that this may result in the police being likely to pass this responsibility on to individuals or groups. Thereby, they become the victims of their own success.

In this context, ensuring that these groups and actions are made accountable can be problematic. Unlike the Street Watch schemes observed in the Basal Heath and Selly Oak areas of Birmingham and Grangetown Cardiff (UK), where volunteers were 'vetted and issues with an ID cars ... instructed to patrol the streets with yellow jackets and issued with walkie talkies, enabling them to act as the "eyes and ears" of the police and report suspected criminal activity' (Sagar 2005: 100–101), the communities in both Area 1 and Area 2 were less organized or formally recognized as action groups. Although they had the support of local councillors and the police, they were not in any way vetted or managed by the local police. It is in these unsupervised and unregulated instances that community action may slip into vigilantism and potentially violent or abusive instances. Thereby, sex workers and their clients may become victims of the violent protests and marches aimed at eradicating prostitution.

Active citizenship and belonging

Sagar's (2005) and Williams' (2005b) research have both highlighted how community activism feeds into debates about community policing and 'active citizenship'. In particular, the support or lack of intervention by the police can sometimes reinforce the activities of those individuals or groups who take action to rid an area of prostitution. In doing so, this leads to a district being made and remade in the interests of certain people. As Kearns (1995: 158) describes, active citizenship is often 'a selective, dual and elitist strategy. Only a small group of wealthy, professional citizens are expected, selected or provided with opportunities to exercise control functions, or power.'

Debates that surround this feed into earlier discussions, which considered the role of 'governance'. By encouraging citizens to become more responsible for local social problems, the 'longer-term project of reforming, curtailing and cheapening the welfare state' is facilitated (Kearns 1995: 158). Yet, as Kearns (1995: 159) identified, by being active citizens, there is a responsibility on citizens to make a 'personal effort and the exercise of moral judgement by citizens (*who have been educated in the right way*)'. Thus, as Heater (1991: 153) suggests, 'the activities in which citizens are to be engaged are to be far removed from any levels of real political power'. Being educated in the *right way* clearly removes any real power in decision-making. The exercise of 'moral judgement' is that which reflects and reinforces political power, which, in the context of prostitution in the UK, is the removal of street prostitution from residential streets.

Those who are educated correctly are often seen to belong and feel a distinct sense of belonging. Adrian Favell (1999) defined the politics of belonging as 'the dirty work of boundary maintenance'. As Yuval-Davis (2011: 20) describes: 'The boundaries the politics of belonging are concerned with are the boundaries of the political community of belonging, the boundaries which, sometimes physically, but always symbolically, separate the world population into "us" and "them".' Through taking action to remove prostitution from residential and business neighbourhoods, those who are seen as not belonging to the community or area are sought to be both symbolically and physically expelled. Those who take action may feel a sense of belonging, an 'emotional attachment, about feeling "at home"'. The 'other' is thereby rejected and may leave the area, as they feel that they do not belong. One impact of this action is often the displacement of street prostitution.

NIMBYISM and displacement

As with the targeting of an area by the police, localized community action can lead to the displacement of prostitution, because community members take a NIMBY (Not In My Back Yard) approach to dealing with their concerns. Displacement is a phenomenon whereby efforts to reduce the level of crime in one particular area can result in a change in criminal behaviour (Jones and Newburn 2002). Crime displacement, according to Gabor (1981), may occur along three dimensions: temporal, spatial or qualitative. These involve a significant change in criminal activity from one area to another or from one type of crime to another. Instead of removing street prostitution, the problem has often been displaced elsewhere (Lowman 2000) or for a small period of time (Hubbard 1998b). Sex workers, in their attempts to escape police crackdowns or community protests, have been known to temporally displace their activity by working later at night or at different times during the day, as well as spatially displacing to other less policed areas, commonly industrial sites away from residential neighbourhoods, and also functionally displacing by turning to other crimes.

The displacement of prostitution by police or community action has led to a number of criticisms and concerns raised about the impact that this may have for the safety and well-being of sex workers (Cusick and Berney 2005). In order to escape criminal sanctions, prostitutes simply move elsewhere, which may be to unknown or unsafe locations (Sanders 2005c). Displacing the problem of street prostitution to another location may place street sex workers in unfamiliar situations away from their familiar networks and support systems, which increases the risk of further victimization (Pitcher and Aris 2003). This was highlighted in 1999, when a sex worker travelled from Leeds to London as a direct result of a police anti-kerb-crawling crackdown and was subsequently murdered by a well-known convicted rapist. Sadly, because the woman was not from the local area, she was unaware of this man's previous convictions (Brooks-Gordon 2006b).

Furthermore, although employing such methods can be useful in reducing crime, they have been criticized for abandoning interest and concern for offender rehabilitation, as it 'represents a reorientation of the criminological gaze away from offenders and criminals towards offences and crimes' (Crawford 1998: 31). Although there has been a move towards seeing sex workers more as victims and less as offenders, it is still clear that those women who choose not to exit prostitution in the UK will still face the full force of the law. Yet, what this approach fails to consider is that exiting is a complex and difficult process.

Moreover, as this NIMBY concern tends to focus on particular locations and environments, it can lead to displacement into a neighbouring area. This was experienced following a crackdown in Area 1, which led to the emergence of prostitution in Area 2. As a result of this NIMBY approach to dealing with prostitution, some have questioned the overall effectiveness of these approaches. As Patrick explains:

> These people who do these things you know, it's just cosmetic, because they don't get rid of the problem, what's the point? That's my, at that meeting I says well, a nice little pond, for what? Nice new roads, so the kerb-crawlers can get in a bit faster and you know get away faster and to me it's just cosmetic and these people that work for the council and stuff like that and it goes on their CVs, yeah I've done this this and this and they don't get down to the basic problems.
>
> (Patrick, 53, white, Area 2 resident)

Critics of such local interventions in crime control have identified the short-sightedness of such an approach. Situational crime control methods have been criticized for many years, because of their limited geographical impact and short-term intervention. According to Clarke, there are seven main criticisms of situational crime prevention, which are identified as:

> it is overly simplistic and atheoretical; (2) it merely displaces crime or makes it worse; (3) it diverts attention from the underlying causes of crime; (4) it is a conservative and managerial approach to crime; (5) it promotes a selfish, exclusionary society; (6) it restricts personal freedom; and (7) it blames the victim.
>
> (Clarke 2005: 40)

Yet, despite these criticisms, situational crime prevention techniques are commonly used to respond to street prostitution in local communities.

Chapter summary

This chapter has explored some of the reasons why and how communities have taken action to deal with prostitution. As I have shown, not all communities take the same types of action, some are more formal and organized than others and some people do not take any action. Concerns have been raised regarding the accountability of action groups and the types of action that some have taken – in particular, questions need to be raised about how some groups are regulated, how inappropriate and violent actions are dealt with and how members are vetted, in order to prevent acts of vigilantism. These concerns appear justified in the context of evidence that demonstrates that acts of violence have been committed, both in my research and in that of others. Indeed, given that sex workers and their clients are often vilified within society, these issues should be given greater priority and recognition – as Liverpool (UK) police have highlighted – as such aggression can be conceived of as a form of hate crime.

Note

1 Vigilantism has been defined by Johnston (1996: 220) as involving

> six necessary features: (i) it involves planning and premeditation by those engaging in it; (it) its participants are private citizens whose engagement is voluntary; (iii) it is a form of 'autonomous citizenship' and, as such, constitutes a social movement; (iv) it uses or threatens the use of force; (v) it arises when an established order is under threat from the transgression, the potential transgression, or the imputed transgression of institutionalized norms; (vi) it aims to control crime or other social infractions by offering assurances (or 'guarantees') of security both to participants and to others.

7 Responding to community concerns

Local government and the police

This chapter will consider the police and local government responses to community needs and concerns and the way in which they have responded to sex work in their local constituencies. It will explore how local government and, in particular, the police have dealt with community concerns in my research, what strategies were put in place, considering what impact this could have on sex work and local communities. This chapter will highlight research that has focused on the impact of tolerance zones, police crackdowns and multi-agency strategies, as well as local, national and international crime prevention strategies (Matthews 2005, 2008; O'Neill 1997; O'Neill and Campbell 2006; Scoular and O'Neill 2007; Van Doorninck and Campbell 2006). In particular, the chapter will ascertain the implications that these strategies have in terms of displacement, sex worker safety, community quality of life and well-being and the wider organization of sex work.

This chapter aims to show how local authorities deal with, and respond to, prostitution in the areas in which they govern and represent, looking at the main mechanisms through which prostitution is managed in business and residential neighbourhoods. It will uncover the means through which local authority agencies govern, the policing strategies and policies utilized, planning and environmental law available and the political, legal and moral context that surrounds decision-making. In doing so, it will demonstrate how local authorities are often torn between local and national interests and how they balance community needs and demands with national and international law, policy and strategies (Kingston 2010; Weitzer 2009).

Policing street prostitution

The policing of street prostitution in the UK has predominantly focused on tackling street sex workers, rather than their clients. During the 1970s and 1980s, the police adopted an enforcement-led approach, which was mainly directed at street sex workers, in response to growing public concerns and within a legislative context that had focused primarily on street sex workers. This focus changed somewhat during the 1980s and 1990s, as the client began to be perceived as the main 'problem', with the sex worker increasingly being seen as a victim and less of an offender (Matthews 2005). Evidence of this shift can be seen in the number of sex workers arrested for soliciting. For example, the numbers of sex workers arrested for soliciting in the UK has dropped steadily since 1990. In contrast, there have been significant increases in the number of men convicted of kerb-crawling between 1999 and 2002 (Home Office 2004b: 92).

Changes in the law may account for these increases in arrests and convictions in the UK. For instance, the 1985 Sexual Offences Act created the offence of 'kerb-crawling', and, thus, police began to tackle this form of crime.[1] However, a number of limitations to kerb-crawling legislation emerged – in particular, limitations regarding the requirement of 'persistence' for the offence of kerb-crawling, which has subsequently led the police to adopt a range of different methods to deal with street sex buyers.[2] Such enforcement tools have included sending letters to the registered keeper of vehicles seen cruising areas known for sex work (Brooks-Gordon and Gelthorpe 2003b); charging the men with motoring offences (Matthews 2005), the use of Anti-Social Behaviour Orders by some local authorities against men persistently arrested for kerb-crawling (Coy *et al.* 2007) and the use of decoy officers to 'entrap' kerb-crawlers (Baker 2007; Dodge *et al.* 2005). These methods were employed by the police to tackle kerb-crawlers in Area 1. In contrast, Area 2 police focused enforcement upon street sex workers exclusively. These differing priorities had varying implications for sex worker safety and community well-being.

Differing priorities

The police and local authorities often exercise their legislative powers in a selective and inconsistent manner when dealing with prostitution, and these powers are generally exercised in response to public complaints (Benson and Matthews 1995; Penfold *et al.* 2004). Those with the most political and social power often have greater success in prompting intervention (Hubbard 1998a). As a result, there can be large differences between police forces, as to whether they target sex workers, kerb-crawlers or both (Benson and Matthews 1995). At the same time, the police and local authorities are directed from central government as to how they should tackle prostitution, with criminal law and prostitution policy guidelines stipulating how the sex industry should be dealt with. Therefore, the differing priorities between public needs and the wider political context can sometimes work against each other in responding to street sex work (Pitcher *et al.* 2006).

Differing priorities were evident in how the police and local authorities dealt with street prostitution in Area 1 and Area 2. In Area 2, the police focused enforcement on kerb-crawlers and street sex workers, combined with a diversion scheme for sex workers. The local authority supported the policing initiative, thus enabling the police to issue Anti-Social Behaviour Orders through local government. In contrast, Area 1 policing initiatives focused enforcement solely on street sex workers. Yet, this objective was often fraught with difficulties, as the general effect of police 'crackdowns' upon street prostitution has been the displacement of those involved. This outcome was observed in Area 1, as street prostitution displaced into Area 2. According to Paul, Area 2 policing strategy stemmed from a particular officer, who perceived street sex workers as the main source of the 'problem' and, as a result,

> [Named police office] is probably singly responsible for displacing that problem in the rest of Leeds ... spending huge sums of money and not actually dealing with the issues at all ... the policy at the time ... was very much around enforcement and I think there was a, a naïve belief that enforcement would prevent people from engaging in prostitution.... Nobody was interested in looking at the prostitution issue in a broader perspective [in Area 2].
> (Paul, 56, white, Area 2 Chief Superintendent)

The displacement of sex workers out of familiar locations and the detrimental impact that this can have has been well documented (Campbell and Storr 2001; Kinnell 2008; McKeganey and Barnard 1996). Sanders (2004b) argues that punitive policing operations have placed women in increasingly dangerous positions as they try to avoid being caught by moving to unknown and sometimes unsafe locations or take less time to assess their clients. Rather than deterring sex workers from selling sex on the street, they often move elsewhere. For instance, O'Kane (2002) found that out of 110 sex workers from eighteen towns and cities across the UK, only two women stopped selling sex as a result of police activities. Sixty-five per cent worked longer hours as result of police crackdowns to pay off fines, and 71 per cent worked later into the night to avoid the police.

In this context, it is clear that, without working together, the police, even in one city, merely move prostitution from one place to another, creating potentially dangerous situations for sex workers and their clients, as well as creating a new problem for residents and businesses in another area. Rather than 'designing out' prostitution, it simply moves to another location.

Area 1: Policing street sex workers

Street sex workers were the focus of policing activities in Area 1. This focus is evidenced by the first Anti-Social Behaviour Order to be issued to a sex worker in Leeds being made by the police in Area 1 during April 2005 (West Yorkshire Police 2005). The issuing of the order against a street sex worker, not her client, is indicative of the policing strategy of Area 1, despite resident campaigns launched against both parties and Area 1 police's perception that the use of ASBOs has been ineffective when applied to street sex work (Scurlock 2005). According to Terry (53, white, Area 1 police constable), focusing on kerb-crawlers was not a practical way to deal with street prostitution in his policing division, despite 'the government saying that we have to target kerb-crawlers.... I made a decision and said "no, we can't. It's not practical" there was two officers to run this whole [operation].... We had to target the prostitutes.'

The impracticality of focusing police enforcement upon clients was believed to stem from the fact that kerb-crawlers in Area 1 were primarily on foot and not in cars. In contrast, as Terry explains, clients in Area 2 were primarily in cars, and this difference between the two areas meant that the policing approach needed to be tailored to each district:

> [Area 2] has always targeted the kerb-crawlers ... because of the sheer geographical nature of the red-light district and the vast majority of their problems come from cars coming off the main arteries to the city. Our problem on our side was prostitute related because.... Immensely difficult to prove kerb-crawling on foot.... You ... see a guy go up to a girl or ... a guy walking down the street at two o'clock in the morning and the girl would go up to him.... And then they'd be a bit of a talk.... Well of course he hasn't done anything. She's approached him so ... she was getting arrested for soliciting.
>
> (Terry, 53, white, Area 1 police constable)

Terry argues that it was very difficult to prove that a man was soliciting a woman for the purpose of prostitution while on foot, despite being able to prosecute a man for kerb-crawling under the Sexual Offences Act 2003. This legislative difficulty was linked to the need to prove, under previous legislation in effect at the time of my research, that the man has kerb-crawled 'persistently'. Police in Dorset found this legislative requirement enabled a client to escape the conviction of kerb-crawling, because he approached the sex worker on a bicycle and not a motor vehicle (de Bruxelles 2007). This difficulty, as Terry identified, is indicative of an unequal legal system:

> I'm not saying ... that we shouldn't crack down on kerb-crawling. But again legislation has always been a man's world. And when you look at the legislation in respect of what you've got to prove in respect of a woman being a prostitute, compared to the lengths you've got to go to, to actually prove a man is kerb-crawling, miles apart. Certainly in terms of kerb-crawling it's very officer intensive and time intensive.
>
> (Terry, 53, white, Area 1 police constable)

Some have suggested that through the enactment of legislation that is sexually discriminatory, nation states have legally entrenched the explicit inequality between men and women, and, thus, sexual inequalities are manifested in law (Neuwirth 2005). As has been shown, historically legislative intervention into prostitution has predominantly focused upon sex workers and not their clients. Therefore, it could be argued that disparities in the legal requirements for prosecuting prostitutes and street sex buyers are deemed to be 'miles apart', because sexual inequalities have become legally institutionalized. Thus, according to Terry, Area 1 policing bias is not a result of negative perceptions of street sex workers, but is, instead, the result of legislative inequalities.

128 *Responding to community concerns*

Despite the legislative difficulties, however, the discretion exercised by the police in Area 1 and the varied methods employed by the police across the UK demonstrate some police officers' decisions to exercise their powers to deal with the perceived 'problem'. This police 'innovation' was recognized by Terry. Identifying the 'innovative' policing practice of officers in Area 2, Terry claimed that:

> With similar circumstances as a police officer I would have done the same. I would have gone to the Leeds City Council Anti-Social Behaviour Team and say 'I've got this sod continuously coming and kerb-crawling erm. I'm having difficulty getting enough evidence to prove beyond all reasonable doubt. I can't take him to court or I'm being told by CPS 'we're not going to blight this man's good name and put, we're not going to label him. So we'll let him off with a warning this time' ... I go to Leeds City Council, give them all the evidence that I've got and let's take it to the balance of probabilities, a lot lower level of proof and go for an injunction under section 222 of the Local Government's Act.[3]
>
> (Terry, 53, white, Area 1 police constable)

However, despite Terry's claims, the policing strategy identified by other officers in Area 1 did not mirror those that he recounted. Rather, Clive suggested that, instead:

> [w]e didn't have much to do with the prostitutes. And I've got to say that throughout my career I've never locked up one so I would never have been part of the team. I was always one that stopped to speak to them, because potentially they're always great sources of intelligence and information for us.
>
> (Clive, 42, white, Area 2 chief inspector)

Thus, it appeared that the policy strategy advocated by Terry and employed as the division's framework for dealing with prostitution was not shared by his colleagues. Justifying the enforcement focus upon street sex workers, Terry stated his belief that street sex workers are the main source of the 'problem' and that they

> [a]re not innocent victims, they are like any other person who has committed themselves to a lifestyle which is outside the boundaries of acceptable social behaviour. And by that I'm not talking about selling their bodies for sex. I'm talking about the drugs ... and I go on about street prostitutes because street prostitutes are primarily the main source of criminal activity ... I'm not anti-prostitute ... I am anti-street prostitution.
>
> (Terry, 53, white, Area 1 police constable)

This narrative locates street sex workers as individually responsible for their actions, rather than recognizing the reality of their lives, 'thereby justifying a punitive response' (Phoenix and Oerton 2005: 100). Street sex workers are perceived as the main source of the 'problem', because it is them, rather than their kerb-crawling and street walking clients, who behave in a manner outside the boundaries of acceptable social or moral behaviour. This, Terry attributes to the assumed criminal activity that street sex workers are engaged in. However, this fails to attribute criminal activity to pimps and drug dealers, thus further questioning the explanations that he gives for the police focus upon street sex workers in Area 1.

Instead, it is suggested that the perspective that street sex workers are the main source of the 'problem' mirrors the historical stigma afforded to street sex workers and the perception that it is them, rather than their clients, who are the source of social ills. Thus, although Matthews (2005) has documented changes in policing practice across the UK – particularly as regards conceptualizing sex workers more as 'victims' and less as 'offenders' – the policing practices of Area 2 police and less senior police activities in Area 1 appear to reflect pre-1980s and 1990s policing practices. Although Terry recognized the gendered inequality of the law surrounding prostitution, his comments and practices conformed to these sexual inequalities, by focusing police enforcement upon street sex workers, not their clients. As Terry explains, his perception is that men who buy sex are not the problem, as they are 'vilified within society. I'm not sure they should be' (Terry, 53, white, Area 2 police constable).

Area 2: Kerb-crawlers as a policing focus

The policing of street prostitution in Area 2 focused enforcement on kerb-crawlers, alongside a scheme that intended to help sex workers exit prostitution. The approach taken by the police in Area 1 closely correlated to the strategy proposed by the Home Office (2006) and the Association of Chief Police Officers (2004). In this context, the police in Area 1 focused enforcement upon street sex buyers, in line with senior officers' operational plans. As Edward (33, white, Area 2 police sergeant) explains: 'the focus upon kerb-crawlers within this division was a management steer, from the police side when they took the stance of "prostitutes are victims, kerb-crawlers are offenders, let's tackle the offender" '.

As a result of this management steer, the police launched two three-day operations to target street clients during 2006 and 2007. These kerb-crawler operations:

> [u]sed decoy officers, acting as lone females, stood on street corners, and we would have men in vehicles approaching these female officers asking for sexual services. To ask for a sexual service the offence is complete and they would be arrested.
>
> (Malcolm, 36, white, Area 2 detective inspector)

Twenty-eight men were charged with kerb-crawling, following the operation in June 2006 (BBC News 2006). Another operation during March 2007 resulted in the arrest of twenty-five men (West Yorkshire Police 2007b). Twenty-one men were charged with kerb-crawling, eighteen of which have been convicted of the offence (Rostron 2007; West Yorkshire Police 2007a). Similarly, during this period, a police operation in Doncaster (UK) resulted in the cautioning of fifty-four men, two of which were charged with kerb-crawling (BBC Inside Out 2007: 1), with ASBOs issued to kerb-crawlers in Edgbaston, Birmingham (UK), in 2007 (Birmingham Mail 2007).

Such police operations are, however, nothing new in the UK. For example, police in Southampton arrested 406 kerb-crawlers over four years between 2002 and 2006 (*Daily Echo* 2006); Liverpool police arrested more than 120 street clients in 2001 (Harvey 2001); in Middlesbrough, eleven men were charged with kerb-crawling in 1998 (*Northern Echo* 1998), and thirty men were charged in 2003 (Underwood 2003). Decoy officers were similarly used by police in Southend, London, in 2001 and also in London's King's Cross in 2004 (Echo 2001a, 2001b; Moore 2004), thus illustrating the extensive use of police powers to target kerb-crawlers years before the government's review of the prostitution legislation.

This will was further illustrated in Leeds in 1998, with the piloting of the UK's first kerb-crawler re-education programme. Furthermore, across the country, the number of men convicted of kerb-crawling hit its peak in 2001, with the lowest recorded level in 2005, which occurred after the consultation document, *Paying the Price*, was released (The Crown Prosecution Service 2008: 1). These figures illustrate 'the political will of a handful of local authorities and policing partnerships rather than a systematic attempt to implement the law or policy' (Sanders 2008b: 141). This political will was, however, extended much further than utilizing resources just to deal with street sex buyers in Area 2. Despite the lead from management to tackle kerb-crawlers and attempts to divert women involved in prostitution away from the criminal justice system, less senior-ranked Area 2 police officers continued to perceive the majority of sex workers as 'offenders' and not 'victims'. Sex workers were perceived as active agents, who were engaged in prostitution through choice. According to Malcolm (36, white, Area 2 detective inspector), the perception that sex workers are 'victims' is a 'myth', because

> [w]ithin the region of 90% of prostitutes were on drugs and were funding their habit through prostitution, and that a high percentage of them, something like 70, 80% of them, had also convictions for at least theft and shop lifting offences, and as high as 40–50% of them had convictions for more serious offences which we categorized as robbery, Class A drugs trafficking and burglary [no evidence was cited to support his claims]. So there was a myth at that time that said that these people were victims of crime, prostitutes were victims. To a certain extent one could sympathise with that, you know when you look at the lifestyle and upbringing what many of them had you could say yeah they are victims. But the fact remains that we've had to do something with these people because they were committing an awful lot of crime.
>
> (Malcolm, 36, white, Area 2 detective inspector)

Responding to community concerns 131

Matthews (2008) argues that this belief – that prostitution is a victimless crime and sex workers are not victims – is, in itself, a myth. According to Matthews (2008: 27): 'to adopt [the view] that prostitution is a non-victim crime is to adopt a very narrow and superficial definition of victimization'. This myth would suggest that sex workers freely choose to engage in criminal behaviour and disregard the difficulties that heavy drug users may face finding employment or, at least, finding employment that would be flexible or provide enough income to support their drug use.

Although Area 1 division had 'very much a hands off, don't hammer them, don't arrest them ... divisional steer' approach to responding to street prostitutes, the belief that was held was that 'the prostitution problem just carries on' (Edward, 33, white, Area 2 police sergeant). As a result of this perception, Edward suggested that:

> We went through a process of about a year, of struggling with the politics of it; both within the police service, within Leeds City Council and within the courts. To try and get to the point where, to cut a long story short, [Edward] you can hammer them.

What this comment appears to show is the antagonism between divisional lead and policing 'on the ground'. In this sense, changes in policy and law on prostitution may not lead to a change in policing practices, as often the views of the police and local authorities significantly shape the nature of the official response in an area. Some of the problems with this were witnessed in the police's response to indoor prostitution, which will be explored later.

The struggle with local politics in Area 2 resulted in ASBOs being used to deal with street sex workers alongside police operations (Rostron 2006). Anti-Social Behaviour Orders were used to 'effectively ban them from being in the area', because the 'enforcement side hasn't worked' (Malcolm, 36, white, Area 2 detective inspector). These views closely reflect the policy contained within the *Coordinated Strategy* document, in that:

> Unless very specific conditions are met, most individuals involved in prostitution are excluded from the category of 'victim', for 'victim' status is only conferred on those individuals: (i) for whom there is the presence of a third party coercer; (ii) who never return to prostitution after being offered help; and, (iii) who co-operate with the NGOs and authorities.
>
> (Phoenix and Oerton 2005: 90)

Those who do not choose to exit are therefore considered to be liable to prosecution. As Malcolm explained:

> One of the ways of dealing with them was getting them into treatment, getting them off the drugs so that they no longer had to commit crime.... That's through enforcement, treatment and going down the multi-agency

approach as well, bringing the city council on board and and getting antisocial behaviour orders against the most prolific offenders who have been given the help, but they won't accept it or they've been given the help and they've fallen off the wagon and gone back on to the drugs and gone back into the er, onto the streets and won't accept any more treatment.

(Malcolm, 36, Area 2 detective inspector)

Criticisms regarding taking a punitive approach towards dealing with sex workers have highlighted problems with punishments such as fines, which, some have argued, are a 'revolving door', as sex workers go back on the streets to be able to pay the fines that have been imposed upon them (Phoenix 2008a; Weitzer 1999).

Kerb-crawler re-education programmes

A rehabilitative approach to dealing with street sex buyers emerged in the early 2000s, following a pilot of the first 'John School' in the UK (Campbell and Storr 2001). Pioneered in the US and named after the slang word for kerb-crawler (Wainwright 2000), the idea behind such schemes focused on an attempt to re-educate or rehabilitate men out of their desire to pay for sex (Brooks-Gordon and Gelthorpe 2003a); increase men's awareness of the possible sexual health risks involved and their economic contribution to the drug market (Mower 2006); and 'to raise awareness about the impact street prostitution has on local communities and those involved in selling sex, and the potential criminal sanctions' (Home Office 2006: 34).

These schools provided men charged with kerb-crawling with an option. Once arrested by police, men charged with kerb-crawling offences were offered a choice between a court summons or completion of the kerb-crawler re-education programme. Its content was designed to explain 'the reality of street based prostitution' (Home Office 2007a: 1). This has been 'achieved' through providing a number of presentations from a range of individuals about legislation, sexual health, the effects of kerb-crawling on local communities, the impact of child prostitution on parents, the experiences of sex workers who had encountered coercion and violence and the drug use of those involved.

The first UK kerb-crawler re-education programme was piloted in Leeds, West Yorkshire, during 1998 to 1999 (Campbell and Storr 2001). The programme was set up by Leeds Metropolitan University's Research Centre for Violence, Abuse and Gender Relations, in conjunction with West Yorkshire Police. The pilot intended to shift the focus from sex workers to men who buy sex from women (Campbell and Storr 2001). This shift may be deemed indicative of a radical feminist-inspired response to dealing with prostitution, as many feminists have argued that the biased response to dealing with street prostitution has disproportionately concentrated on penalizing women that sell sex, rather than their clients. This ethos was incorporated into the formulation of the pilot, by identifying prostitution as a form of abuse and violence perpetrated against women (Campbell and Storr 2001). The two-day course involved the input of Fiona – an ex-prostitute, who was kidnapped by a client, driven to Oxford and raped violently for several hours (Thisisoxfordshire.co.uk 1999). Men who buy sex were to be reformed to understand that prostitution was a form of abuse.

The scheme was only piloted for one year in Leeds, which may appear a relatively short period of time in which to assess the effectiveness of a programme. Reconviction and re-offending rates cannot be fully ascertained after only a short period of time, and, although the funding for the programme ended, further funding could have been gained. Evidence suggests, however, that out of the eighty-one men who attended the pilot programme in Leeds, only one man was subsequently caught for kerb-crawling (Hamilton 2000a: 47WH). On the basis of these figures, it would appear that the programme was successful in re-educating and deterring kerb-crawlers. Yet the 'achievement' of 'educating' men who had been arrested and cautioned for kerb-crawling has, nonetheless, been questioned, due to its limited effectiveness (Campbell and Storr 2001; Sanders 2009). Rather than being reformed and no longer buying sex, men, it is argued, simply displace from one area to another or buy sex from indoor sex markets (Sanders 2009).

Scepticism

In this study, participants discussed the perceived ineffectiveness of kerb-crawler re-education programmes. Many participants believed that such programmes would not work, because the purchasers of sex cannot be re-educated. Malcolm believed that men's biological urges to purchase sex overrode any amount of re-education:

> Well I'm a man you see and when I get that feeling in my loin, regardless of what programmes I've been on, perhaps it might not be the deterrent ... I don't think they work.... What percentage of kerb-crawlers have actually re-offended, you know what are the chances of actually being caught for a second time as a kerb-crawler ... I think you'll find those statistics mean absolutely nothing.
> (Malcolm, 36, white, Area 2 detective inspector)

This 'male sex drive discourse' has been identified as evident in the narratives of men who pay for sex (Coy *et al.* 2007). Men are perceived as always willing to buy sex, because they are driven by their libido; thus, re-education is discounted. Rather than deterring men from purchasing sex, these courses, according to Ivor,

> [a]ctually would attract kerb-crawlers.... You know it sends the wrong message out. I mean the idea is fine ... but unfortunately the way in which it is delivered, that's got to be as impactive as that for me ... and if you really actually look at that closely you're actually encouraging people into that area.
> (Ivor, 40, white, Area 2 development officer)

The belief that was held was that male clients cannot be rehabilitated or re-educated, because they would not want to change their behaviour and wish to continue paying for sex. When discussing her interpretation of residents' responses to re-education programmes, Alarna suggested that:

> The opinion you might get off local people is that you can't, it won't work, you can't rehabilitate somebody ... I think the cynic in a lot of people might be well they'll just go on it to get out of being fined or to get out of being put on the record or something and they'll just do the day and not, it won't make any difference.
> (Alarna, 32, white, Area 2 community safety officer)

Nine residents expressed their scepticism that such courses or forms of rehabilitation programmes would be effective, arguing that such courses are 'a waste of money' (Linda, 62, Afro-Caribbean, Area 1 resident), because 'they'll never change' (Mary, 44, Afro-Caribbean, Area 1 resident), rather: 'They go onto those course because they've been caught and so they attend the course because they have to otherwise they're going to write this letter to my home and my wife may pick it up' (Paula, 42, Afro-Caribbean, Area 1 resident). Indeed, it was thought that clients may choose to go on such courses, in order to escape being fined or gaining a criminal record. It has been suggested that some sex buyers may opt for a court diversion scheme, rather than a court summons, in order to finalize the matter quickly and avoid getting a criminal record (Sanders 2009).

Due to these concerns, Malcolm (36, white, detective inspector) and Terry (53, white, police constable) both questioned the accuracy and validity of re-offending rates for men who attend kerb-crawler re-education courses. Studies that have demonstrated the ineffectiveness of such programmes have illustrated that, compared to a placebo group, no impact was recorded. According to Monto and Garcia (2001: 6), two of the ninety-one men who attended a course in Portland, Oregon, 're-offended', in comparison to one out of 100 men who did not attend the programme. The success of such courses were, therefore, deemed as

> [s]uccessful to a certain degree if you live on cloud cuckoo land and you think that that's worked, we haven't seen them again. Well of course you haven't seen them again, coz they haven't come back, coz they've been caught. 90 per cent of all kerb-crawlers who have been, who are caught will say it's my first time. Not so.... This is the ludicrous bit about these re-education programmes which doesn't address offender behaviour but only offender behaviour in that particular area where they've been caught.
> (Terry, 53, white, Area 1 police constable)

Despite this criticism, 'success' has been identified in the UK cities of Hull, Middlesbrough, Nottingham, Northamptonshire and Hampshire (BBC Inside Out 2007; BBC News 2005b; Mower 2006; Underwood and Doult 2006). Likewise, two US evaluation studies claimed that, following the attendance of an educational diversion programme, men changed their attitudes (Kennedy et al. 2005; Wortley et al. 2002). According to the evaluation of the Toronto (US) John School diversion programme, participants were 'more likely to accept responsibility for their actions, more likely to admit that they might have a sex addiction and are less likely to report favourable attitudes towards prostitution' (Wortley et al. 2002: 369). There was also evidence of 'significant' post-programme improvement in the respondents' knowledge of prostitution law and an 'increased awareness' of both the 'victims' and 'dangers' associated with the sex trade. According to the authors, the vast majority of John School participants indicated that they will never again attempt to purchase sexual services from a prostitute.

Yet, these claims must be viewed with caution. Men that attended the course, it could be argued, may say what is expected of them, rather than change their behaviour and attitude towards the sex industry. The apparent success of a scheme launched in Hull was a perception that I questioned at a conference, where a paper on this topic was given by police constable Mary Mower (2006). When asked why the scheme was deemed a success in Hull, police constable Mower suggested that the men who had attended such courses had not re-offended, despite recognizing that the men sent on the courses may not have been caught for their first offence. This suggests that apprehending kerb-crawlers is often opportunistic and that support for such programmes is more realistically based on non-apprehension of men who buy sex by the police. Rather than being caught, men who buy sex from women 'simply go elsewhere' and buy sex in other towns and cities (Sanders 2009: 6). Furthermore, an evaluation of San Francisco's John School showed no significant decline in the number of men who stated that they will no longer continue to pay for the sexual services of a prostitute (Shively et al. 2008). The perceived success of kerb-crawler re-education programmes has, therefore, been based on a 'flawed rationale' (Sanders 2009: 5).

Kerb-crawler typologies

Emerging from the discussions about kerb-crawler re-education programmes, specific categories of male clients were identified. According to some research participants, kerb-crawler re-education programmes would have been more effective with some types of street sex buyers than others. The relative effectiveness of such schemes was related to the type of client undertaking the programmes, in that re-education would 'work with some people, but not everyone' (Daniel, 62, white, Area 1 Labour councillor). The three types included:

> One of them was ... the regular kerb-crawler who is always out and about. One was one the contemplative kerb-crawler who was thinking about it but wasn't quite sure whether they were going to do it or not. One was ... a person ... who just does it on the odd occasion, but one that was thinking about it and thought it might be a good idea.
> (Kevin, age unknown, white, drug intervention worker)

136 *Responding to community concerns*

Table 7.1 Kerb-crawler typology

Types of kerb-crawlers	Local authority perceptions
Regular kerb-crawler	'Hardcore one'; 'always out and about'; 'dodgy geezers'
Infrequent	'done it on the odd occasion'; 'has a wife or partner'
Contemplator	'thinking about it, but wasn't quite sure whether they were going to do it or not'

These three types echo typologies of men who buy sex identified in international research – for instance, first timers, occasional and regular customers (Mansson 2004; Monto and McRee 2005). The following typologies were also identified by other participants.

These typologies were then utilized to explain the limited success of kerb-crawler re-education programmes. As Malcolm (36, white, Area 2 detective inspector) alluded to, re-education programmes:

> [M]ay have a very, very slight effect on those that maybe have a wife, or maybe have a partner. But the hardcore ones, who really don't care, if they get that feeling in their loin, they've got a propensity to use prostitutes regardless of what's happened to them previously.

Similarly, Kevin indicated that some types of purchasers may change their behaviour, but others will not:

> If it's a person who's a contemplator who's sent on one of those it would change their minds because they won't want to get caught. If you're a kerb-crawler and you've gone on that and you're a dedicated committed kerb-crawler and you've done that just to avoid going to court, you just change your area. And there was no evidence there was sustainable change in it really.
>
> (Kevin, age unknown, white, drug intervention worker)

Kevin further discussed the 'dedicated and committed' kerb-crawler, who, he suggested, were 'always out and about' and were more prolific purchasers of sex. Kevin engaged in what may be termed a 'pathologization' process, suggesting that kerb-crawlers are 'some real dodgy geezers', posing 'more of a threat to the community'. The level of threat posed by street clients was then contrasted against the perceived threat posed by sex workers. Stating the monetary reasons why women sell sex, Kevin questioned why men travel long distances for sexual pleasure. For Kevin, kerb-crawlers

> present a bigger threat than the women ... there are some dodgy geezers about to be fair who kind of kerb-crawl the area so and they come from a

long distance sometime and you have to wonder well what the hell are they doing over here, er if they not genuinely in Leeds for any other reason.

(Kevin, age unknown, white, drug intervention worker)

Geographical movements over long distances by men who buy sex from women on the street appear to cause some concern. However, geographical movements of kerb-crawlers are not uncommon. 'Zero tolerance' policing of street prostitution is frequently identified as the cause of geographical displacement of street prostitution (Hubbard 1998b; Hubbard and Sanders 2003; Kilvington et al. 2001).

Tolerance zones

Police forces often regard the visibility of street prostitution as more acceptable in some spaces than others (Hubbard 1998a). The spaces in which the police perceived street prostitution and those involved to be more acceptable may be described as 'zones of tolerance', 'managed areas' or 'official street walking zones'. 'Managed areas', 'tipple zones' or 'official street walking zones' are terms used to describe 'an official policy of allocating an area for street soliciting and the provision of a place where sexual services can be carried out, responsibility for the management of which is taken by the police and local responsible authorities' (Van Doorninck and Campbell 2006: 63). Although no such zones exist in the UK, 'official street walking zones' have existed in Utrecht, Rotterdam, Den Haagg, Amsterdam and Cologne (Matthews 2008; Van Doorninck and Campbell 2006).

In contrast, 'zones of tolerance' are areas within which street sex workers and their clients are 'tolerated' by the police under a no prosecution policy. Outside of these designated areas, a 'zero tolerance' approach is taken to prostitution that occurs outside the prescribed boundaries. Advocates of this approach argue that such zones provide safer working environments and minimize the public 'nuisance' caused by street prostitution on local communities (Clark et al. 2004). The attraction of establishing such zones is the removal of street prostitution from residential streets, where it causes most offence, coupled with a safe and controlled environment, where women can meet their clients (Matthews 2008).

This attraction may have led some local authorities in the UK to consider establishing some form of managed zone in their areas. This was observed in the 1990s, as managed zones were established in Bolton, Edinburgh, Northampton and Preston (Matthews 2005). Proposals to 'officially' establish 'England's first prostitution tolerance zone' in Liverpool was discussed in 2005 (BBC News 2005a). Following an indication by central government in 2004 that everything from overhauling legislation through to establishing managed zones was open for consideration (Home Office 2004b), Liverpool City Council examined alternative approaches to dealing with street prostitution (Bellis et al. 2007). Based on the success of a 'managed zone' (Tipplezone) in Utrecht, Holland, where sex workers are provided with a place to work, as well as sexual health and legal advice (Wagenaar and Altink 2009), Liverpool City Council sought to create one locally (BBC News 2005a), despite evidence that residential complaints had not reduced following its implementation in Utrecht (Van Doorninck and Campbell 2006).

In January 2005, Liverpool City Council voted to request approval from the Home Office to establish a 'managed zone' (BBC News 2005a). However, 'managed zones' were rejected in the final recommendations from the government's national consultation (Home Office 2006), despite 83 per cent of people who engaged in a consultation with John Moores University being in favour of a prostitution tolerance zone (BBC News 2005d). According to the Home Office:

> The creation of a managed area – even as a short-term arrangement – could give the impression that communities condone, or at least are forced to accept, street prostitution and the exploitation of women. While managed areas may offer some opportunity to improve the physical safety of those involved, there is no amount of protection that can keep women from harm in this inherently dangerous business. The majority of respondents shared this view.
>
> (Home Office 2006: 8)

This government stance towards official tolerance zones altered somewhat with a change in government office. When David Blunkett was Home Secretary, it was claimed that he was in support of managed zones and believed that the decision to establish managed zones should be in the hands of local authorities (The Guardian 2006; Travis 2004c). This support may have led to the identification of managed zones in the consultation document *Paying the Price*, despite opposition from Tim Brain – Gloucester's Chief Constable and author of the Association of Chief Police Officers' prostitution strategy (Travis 2004a, 2004b). Following Blunkett's resignation as Home Secretary in December 2004 (BBC News 2005c), five months after the publication of the consultation document *Paying the Price*, Home Office Minister Fiona MacTaggart confirmed that the government had dropped plans suggested by the former Home Secretary to allow for the establishment of managed zones (Travis 2006).

Despite the government's removal of plans to consider managed areas, the community in Liverpool supported the proposal to establish an official zone of tolerance (Bellis *et al.* 2007); support which was similarly found in a consultation with residents and sex workers in a study of five towns in England and Scotland (Pitcher *et al.* 2006). Consequently, because of the level of public support, many vice squads 'unofficially' recognize the existence of an area in which street prostitution is generally permissible. This 'unofficial recognition' was evident in Area 2 through the 'creation' of an 'unofficial zone of tolerance'. Such 'unofficial zones of tolerance' have been identified in Birmingham (Kinnell 2008), Nottingham (Goddard 2004), Glasgow, Edinburgh, Aberdeen (Scottish Parliament 2002), Plymouth and Preston (Bellis *et al.* 2007). There were also council-led discussions regarding creating zones of tolerance in Doncaster, Liverpool, Stoke-on-Trent (Cindi 2005), Manchester (Manchester Evening News 2002) and Leeds (Andrew 2005). What the creation of these 'unofficial zones of tolerance' suggests is that, despite official disapproval of such measures, the police, local authority officials and, to some extent, residents tolerate the sex industry in spatially prescribed areas.

Spatial tolerance on the street

It has been argued that the policing of prostitution have been 'fundamental in the creation of red-light districts, by effectively making it impossible for clients and prostitutes to meet elsewhere' (Lopez-Jones 1990: 658). This process was similarly identified by residents, councillors and the police, following the displacement of street prostitution from the city centre into an industrial site in Area 2. This area was identified and recognized as an 'unofficial' zone of tolerance by residents, councillors and the police. The existence and creation of a zone of tolerance in Area 1, according to Paul (56, white, Chief Superintendent), was a result of a lack of police enforcement. This lack of police intervention stemmed from the police's perception that street prostitution was more acceptable in an industrial site within Area 2, than in nearby residential streets. Such industrial sites have been identified as potential areas that could 'house' a zone of tolerance in the UK (BBC News 2001, 2005a).

Support for zoning was identified by Dean (30, white, police constable) and further supported by previous research, which has demonstrated that the majority of police constables in Area 1 of Leeds were in support of the introduction of tolerance zones (Scurlock 2005). Such support and acceptance of 'zones of tolerance' may have influenced the police forces decision to 'ignore' the industrial area of Area 2 as 'individual officers ... have always ... the ability to make decisions ... they'll set the priorities' (Paul, 56, white, Area 2 Chief Superintendent). According to Paul, the 'unofficial' zone of tolerance was short-lived, as businesses and residents began to occupy the area following redevelopment.

The regeneration of an industrial area used as a zone of tolerance has similarly been identified as a motivating factor in their demise in Edinburgh (Matthews 2008) and in Pitcher et al.'s study across five large cities in England, Wales and Scotland (2006). It is often when significant changes take place that prostitution is considered to be a problem, as was the case in Edinburgh, where an unofficial zone of tolerance operated for over ten years. It was only with the redevelopment of Leigh Docks, which took place in the 1990s, that complaints about the noise and nuisance associated with prostitution emerged. As a result of public pressure, the zone was closed, despite efforts to relocate it elsewhere, and street prostitution was displaced across the city (Hubbard et al. 2007).

Consequently, in Area 2, street prostitution dispersed into more heavily populated locations, which increased the visibility for those residents. This increased visibility led the community to prompt police intervention:

> I think we've had unofficial zones of tolerance if I'm perfectly honest ... we probably did create, by default a zone of tolerance, because we didn't enforce them. But of course it then all blew up when developers moved in ... created a twenty four hour situation in [the industrial area] and their activity itself dispersed further out into [Area 2], into a residential area and that's when the community got involved. And of course we react to the community.
>
> (Paul, 56, white, Area 2 Chief Superintendent)

With the regeneration of a previously rundown industrial site in Area 2, street prostitution was displaced into the ungentrified residential streets in the vicinity.

Yet, despite recognition that a zone of tolerance existed on the industrial site in Area 2, conflicting accounts came from two police officers. The claim that an unofficial zone of tolerance existed in the neighbourhood was disputed by Simon and Malcolm. According to Simon:

> There's nothing ever been discussed by the police about having a tolerance zone. I can firmly say prostitution is not tolerated ... the police do not tolerate prostitution ... we can prosecute, we do prosecute that being the people driving around to try and buy prostitutes for sex or the prostitutes ... hence why we have a vice team ... who's pure purpose is just to prosecute the men and the females as well. So there's nothing within [the Inner City Suburb] regarding any tolerance zone what so ever.
>
> (Simon, 33, white, Area 2 police sergeant)

Justifying the reasons why a 'tolerance zone' was not officially tolerated in the industrial site of Area 2, Simon and Malcolm proposed that such tolerance would have been 'condoning criminal behaviour' (Malcolm, 36, white, Area 2 detective inspector). Therefore, the suggestion was considered 'daft', as 'we can't say that there's going to be a "tolerance zone" when it's against the law' (Simon, 33, white, Area 1 police sergeant). In contrast, however, more senior officers, Paul (56, white, Area 1 Chief Superintendent) and Terry (53, white, Area 1 police constable) from Area 1, identified the existence of an unofficial zone of tolerance in Area 2. This was further supported by residents, business employees and local councillors that I spoke to.

Instead, it may be argued that claims that a tolerance zone existed were disputed by less senior officers, because such spatial tolerance of 'illegality' would be contrary to policy from central government and the Association of Chief Police Officers. It appears that Simon and Malcolm did not wish to admit that such a policy was operating in their policing division. As with O'Neill and Campbell's (2002) research, which discovered that police are guided by the Association of Chief Police Officers and wider police policies that did not support tolerance zones, similarly, these officers may be respecting force policy. Furthermore, the majority of officers in O'Neill and Campbell's (2002) study made it clear that they would be in support of such zoning, if there was a change in policy. These comments follow on from the Association of Chief Police Officers (2004: 7–8) prostitution policy guidance, in which it states that:

Although sensitive to the arguments in favour of 'zones of toleration', ultimately this policy and strategy does not support their introduction. Clearly if there is a change in the law which permits their introduction, then as always the police service will enforce the legislation of the day. However, at this stage their introduction is not supported. The first reason is that a change in the law would be necessary for such zones to operate lawfully. Chief constables do not currently possess the discretion as a matter of policy to dispense with an act of Parliament. The second reason is that the evidence that such zones work successfully in other jurisdictions is equivocal. Not only do such zones permit the continued exploitation of people through prostitution, there is evidence that illegal prostitution has been encouraged alongside the managed examples.

(Association of Chief Police Officers 2004: 7–8)

Arguably, then, the police may still continue to 'turn a blind eye' in certain spaces. 'Turning a blind eye' was similarly evident in police tolerance of indoor sex markets, where a lack of public complaints was identified as the reason for the police's non-intervention.

Tolerating indoor prostitution

Indoor sex workers and their clients have previously engaged in what has been termed a 'quasi-legal and semi-tolerated position' in the UK (Sanders 2005b: 321). This 'quasi-legal' position is identified as stemming from indoor sex markets being 'tolerated or ignored' by the police (Sanders 2004a: 560). Evidence of this tolerance can be seen in official statistics, which have shown that the number of convictions for brothel-keeping offences has plummeted from its peak in 1990, when 141 persons were found guilty of brothel-keeping, to only eight convictions in 2002 (Home Office 2004b: 93).

In recent years, however, evidence suggests that there has been an increase in the number of brothel raids across the UK. As a result of growing concerns over sex trafficking and reports of increasing numbers of foreign women and under-age girls working in brothels throughout the UK, Operation Pentameter was launched (Brain 2006). This policing operation involved all fifty-three police forces across the UK. In Leeds, this action came in the form of a joint police operation across South Yorkshire known as 'Operation Rampart' (Brain 2006).

In April 2004, more than 150 officers raided brothels across Yorkshire as part of 'Operation Rampart' (McTaggart 2007: 1). The eighteen-month operation was launched following intelligence that non-nationals were working in a brothel situated in Area 2 of Leeds and a Sheffield brothel (Matthews 2005; The Star 2007). Fifty-nine people were arrested following coordinated raids in both Leeds and Sheffield (BBC News 2004: 1), forty-eight of whom were in the UK unlawfully and one who was identified as a victim of trafficking (Coaker 2008: 1). Yet, despite the arrests made, no evidence of human trafficking was found, and, as a result, it was decided that the thirteen people apprehended would be charged with lesser offences (McTaggart 2007).

The case against the thirteen defendants charged with living off immoral earnings and immigration crimes took place three years after the execution of Operation Rampart in March 2007. Interestingly, the case was thrown out of court, after it was decided that there had been an abuse of court process (McTaggart 2007). It was found that the owner and staff of the raided brothels could not be prosecuted, because the police were well aware that sex was being sold on the premises and had chosen not to intervene. Judge Simon Lawler QC found that police had led sauna owners and staff to believe that they would not be prosecuted, if they abided by certain ground rules (Judge Simon Lawler QC 2007).

During the three-week hearing at the Sheffield Crown Court, many of South Yorkshire's most senior officers were called to give evidence and were questioned about the police's attitudes to prostitution. Judge Simon Lawler was informed that every officer was aware that sex was being sold on the premises, which were located 150 yards from the local police station. Despite such close proximity, the police, in effect, turned a blind eye to what was going on, either explicitly or by implication, through the actions of officers on the ground, while still making visits and informing staff that if they adhered to certain rules, they would not be prosecuted (Judge Simon Lawler QC 2007: 7). According to Judge Lawler:

> It must, at the very least, have created in the minds of the sauna operators over several years a reasonable and legitimate expectation that their activities were at best tolerated and they would not be prosecuted, providing they abided by the rules.
>
> (cited in the *Star* 2007: 1)

The case of *Regina* v *John Barrett* revealed a force-wide policy of brothels operating with consent. As the defense argued, during the court case following the raids on the Area 2 brothel in Leeds and a brothel in Sheffield, a lack of previous enforcement against the establishments was influenced by the individual attitudes of the police in Leeds and Sheffield, which 'shows tolerance, encouragement and therefore tacit endorsement' (Judge Simon Lawler QC 2007: 15). Within Judge Lawler's court judgement, it is apparent that police officers throughout West Yorkshire believed prostitution to be a low priority.

This limited use of brothel-keeping legislation has led some to suggest that such lack of police intervention is based upon informal agreements. For example, evidence from Sanders' (2005b) ten-month ethnographic study of indoor prostitution markets during 2000 to 2001 indicated that brothel owners and independent workers would strike up informal relationships with local police officers. In such instances, brothels were able to ply their trade undisrupted, on the basis that owners and workers provided information on other crimes.

Responding to Judge Simon Lawler's decision and the suggestion that the brothel in Area 1 was 'operating with consent', Paul suggested that his policing division exercised their discretion and

Responding to community concerns 143

[t]ook a policy decision that we would tackle the open market firstly, because in terms of its impact on local communities that was the one that was causing the most concern. That's not to say we ignore what's going on in the closed market because if issues come to light we'll deal with them. The reality is though, the local people are much more interested in what's happening, you know in their street, or round the back of their gardens or where they're working. And the anti-social behaviour, the drugs paraphernalia, the discarded condoms are all associated with the open market ... calls from the public to deal with brothels are virtually unreported.

(Paul, 56, white, Area 2 Chief Superintendent)

According to Paul, the lack of police intervention was a result of a lack of public complaints, as data had shown that the public were more tolerant of indoor prostitution than street prostitution. Other officers claimed that finite resources often dictated how they policed their districts:

It's the only one we can adopt, because we don't have the staff available to go down ... there are organizations that will condemn us because of what we're doing. But, we don't have the luxury to be able to sit down and muddy coddle people, you know. At the end of the day we're a police service and the community dictates what we do. We're there to listen. The government stance is that we will listen to the community. We work in cooperation, not with consent anymore, and according if we don't listen to them we're not doing our job, we're not delivering on that's sort of promise of doing what they want.

(Clive, 43, Area 1 chief inspector)

Similarly, many of the police officers that Matthews (2005) interviewed stated that they did not have the time or resources to engage proactively against off-street establishments. Instead, they stated that they were only prepared to respond if a problem arose or a complaint was made. Likewise, eight of the ten police interviewees stated that they had not received any complaints about indoor sex markets from residents or businesses in Leeds.

Less of a 'public nuisance'

The main reason why the police tolerated indoor sex markets stemmed from the belief that they caused less of a public nuisance than street prostitution. Seven police officers suggested that indoor prostitution caused little public nuisance in contrast to 'unorganized street prostitution which caused residents the greatest concern and anxiety' (Herbert, 53, white, Area 1 Chief Superintendent). Three indoor establishments were identified and utilized by police officers, in order to demonstrate the comparative levels of nuisance caused by off-street prostitution. One establishment discussed by police officers was a venue situated on a main road in Area 2, a few minutes' walk from the local police station. As Simon stated, the police received very few complaints about the establishment. This, he believes, is because the venue was situated in an industrial area of the suburb and its clients were not causing a public nuisance when attending it. As Simon argues:

> When you look at complaints we receive about [Area 2 brothel] its near enough zero because people attending coz it's not in a residential area, cars aren't coming through a residential area; people coming out on a night aren't causing the public problem and some people don't actually know what it is coz its operates under the heading of a sauna.... It's just at the top end of this street, opposite the fire station. It's not opposite houses, so people don't complain about it and locals use it as well. Coz it's in an industrial area, coz it's not in a housing estate where constant visitors would upset people, I think that's why we have such a low number, if any of complaints.
> (Simon, 33, white, Area 2 police sergeant)

According to the police, men who buy sex are 'going inside their own little building out of the way ... that's why ... places like [Area 2 brothel] ... go on for so long because they're out of the way and nobody can see what's going on' (Dean, 30, white, Area 2 police constable). Discussing the existence of a massage parlour in Area 1, Clive suggested that male clients became invisible and were assumed to be 'ordinary men' going in and out of a shop. The Area 1 brothel had

> [b]een there donkey's years.... But there's never an issue with the community about it.... There never ever have an issue because the guys come. They park their cars and go inside and I suppose it's out of sight out of mind really isn't it ... you've got a main road.... So they all park down here.... It doesn't affect any of these houses here. So it's not affecting the sort of life of individuals in there. I mean I can imagine the biggest thing being the parking. People park in front of their houses, would annoy them. But you've got men for, want of a better expression, going in and out of a shop. As simple as that, you know they're not, they're not propositioning anybody, they're not doing anything to anybody and so they're in and out.
> (Clive, 42, white, Area 1 chief inspector)

The perspective of the police, 'whether it's the official view or a private view ... prefer places like that because at least they know that the women are off the streets because they're not causing any nuisance to residents' (Peter, 35, white, Area 2 Labour councillor). Some police officers argued that even visible establishments caused little public nuisance in comparison to street prostitution. Two brothels were identified by police officers as visible establishments that were known to local residents in both Area 1 and Area 2. Residents in an adjacent part of Area 2 were aware of the motivations that men had for visiting a local brothel and were in support of the establishment. According to Sian (29, white, Area 2 PCSO): 'a lot of the community were quite in support of it because ... they're

Responding to community concerns 145

not on the streets ... people were saying you're not going to get rid of it so you may as well regulate it'. Rather than perceiving indoor prostitution as a public nuisance, 'people think of it as a bit of a joke ... nobody's fooled by what they're doing' (Sian, 29, white, Area 2 PCSO).

Similarly, Simon identified that local residents were in no way oblivious to a local brothel operating in Area 2. When explaining the reasons why residents did not complain about indoor sex work, he explained that:

> First one is that, the, the massage parlours within [Area 2] are historic, they're entrenched, been there a number of years and therefore, there's a tacit acceptance. Everybody knows about it and it's actually quite visible and blatant and therefore there's no problems with them. It was relatively well run. The main one, it's on a corner, just down from a pub, there's a lot of parking so it doesn't get in the way of the residents parking.... Secondly, I don't think the community are thick. I think they can see a direct correlation between prostitutes on the streets selling their body for money, for drugs.... And there's a number of individuals from the action group or the neighbourhood forum who actually live in those streets where they are and never mentioned, not bothered by it, no complaints about it, nothing. The only time that I've had any real dealings with the main premises, was the problems of bringing illegals over. Your classic scenario of Bosnian illegal's, this poor lass in Eastern Europe gets promised a job as a waitress, gets over here and suddenly she's enslaved in the sex trade ... a third point, is, as I say the public aren't daft and I think they accept that actually it's a far better solution and it's a long term solution with, it gets rid of my problem and rather than them being on the streets.
>
> (Simon, 33, white, Area 2 police sergeant)

Despite the lack of public nuisance caused by indoor sex venues evidenced here, amendments have been made to the Sexual Offences Act s153 in respect of Closure Orders through the Policing and Crime Act 2009, which has made it easier for the police to close brothels. Under s21 and Schedule 2 to the Policing and Crime Act 2009, a new Part 2A was inserted into the Sexual Offences Act 2003, which introduces powers that allow the police to seek a court order prohibiting access to premises associated with certain prostitution or pornography-related offences. Whether these powers will be used appropriately – if at all – will remain to be seen.

Support for legalization

Cusick and Berney (2005: 597) argue that 'trafficking, slavery, child abuse and problematic drug use have become particularly associated with sex work precisely because the sex industry is not regulated'. Legal establishments for indoor sex work are evident in places such as Germany, the Netherlands, Nevada (US) and New South Wales (Australia), where state-licensed brothels allow sex workers to sell sex. These workers are subject to health checks and must only work with state-licensed work permits. There are often strict legal regulations, which workers and proprietors of indoor sex venues must adhere to. In these places, indoor sex work is often tolerated by local communities. Interestingly, Brent and Hausbeck's explanation as to why legal brothels are accepted echoes much of the views expressed by my participants. As they explain:

> Legal brothel prostitution is justified by a discourse that maintains that (1) the sale of sex is one of the world's oldest professions and is unlikely to disappear (2) state and local government-regulated prostitution is superior to illegal prostitution insofar as it allows for limitations on what is sold, on the terms and conditions of sales, and on brothel ownership and employment practices; (3) such businesses are revenue generating; (4) legal prostitution provides a valuable service to certain individuals who have desires that cannot be easily fulfilled otherwise; and (5) limiting such activities to particular licensed venues curtails related criminal activities (drugs, pimping, violence) and helps control the spread of disease.
>
> (Brents and Hausbeck 2010: 259)

Legalization and regulation was supported by many of my participants. The rationale given for this support included the belief that prostitution can never be eradicated, so legalization was often considered to be the most appropriate approach:

> We're never going to eliminate prostitution. But what we can do is we can manage prostitution. We can licence prostitution. We can make it safe for the girls working in that particular environment. We can make it safe for the punters and an enjoyable experience and we can ensure that the due process of payments to society by way of income tax and everything else, licence fees and things.
>
> (Terry, 53, white, Area 1 police constable)

The support for licensing, Terry believed, would extend to 'eighty percent of this society would say let's have them licensed. Decriminalize it and license it, just as we license clubs and pubs and betting shops'. This belief shows the difference between UK Government policy and what some police officers believe is the best way to deal with prostitution.

Further reasons identified included the belief that legalization would increase sex worker safety and reduce levels of violence:

> Well you're never going to get rid of it so you might as well legalize it and regulate it seems to be the safest option.
>
> (Diane, 22, white, Area 2 resident)

> I reckon there'd be less attacks.
>
> (Pamela, 19, white, Area 2 resident)

These views were echoed in Brents and Hausbeck's (2010) research in Las Vegas, Nevada, where it was common among brothel owners and prostitutes to cite safety as a benefit of legalization. Intriguingly, for some, it was believed that this model would also increase the health and safety of the wider community, 'minimizing rape, sexual assault, extra-marital affairs and the spread of diseases' (Brents and Hausbeck 2010: 259). This was also somewhat mirrored in the views expressed by participants, who claimed that legalization would benefit the sexual health of prostitutes and their clients, which may prevent them from passing sexually transmitted infections (STI) on to their wives or partners:

> Less diseases spread about.
> (Diane, 22, white, Area 2 resident)

> Less chance of the men spreading the diseases all over the place.
> (Mary, 44, Afro-Caribbean, Area 1 resident)

The ability to control and manage prostitution in a structured way was also favoured by some – in particular, to manage sexual health and violence:

> If it was legalised like you said and controlled, we would never have all these things [violence and sexual infections] going on.
> (Liam, 54, Afro-Caribbean, Area 1 resident)

> Were we saying getting safe houses for them and legalising it and getting them regular checks and that, so that you know.
> (Tina, 31, Afro-Caribbean, Area 1 resident)

> At the end of the day the girls are human beings and they're crying out for help really. It would be nice if the government, you know, stepped in, make it legal, find them somewhere, give them the health care.
> (Mary, 44, Afro-Caribbean, Area 1 resident)

This belief was part of the reasoning behind Victoria's (Australia) moved towards legalization in 1984, as it was believed that legalization would reduce health risks –particularly, the risk of sexually transmitted diseases – for both prostitutes and their clients (Sullivan and Jeffreys 2002). In Nevada, regular health screening is an essential part of brothel management (Brents and Hausbeck 2010). Since 1985, the health department has imposed strict health requirements on brothels to control sexually transmitted infections. Each prostitute, before acquiring work in a brothel, is required to obtain a state health card, which indicates that they have been tested for STIs and that this test is negative. Once in employment, weekly testing for STIs by a registered doctor is undertaken, with monthly blood tests taken for HIV. If a prostitute is found to have contracted an STI, she is not legally permitted to work until the infection is treated and a doctor reinstates her health card. In addition, every brothel is required to provide information to clients on condom use, which is mandated by the state (Brents and Hausbeck 2010).

A small number of participants also believed that legalization would prevent forms of displacement to nearby streets, towns, cities and even other countries. It was felt that a more holistic approach was needed:

> Make it legal so you know where they are and they go one place. Make it legal rather than moving from area to area on the street.
>
> (James, 60, Afro-Caribbean, Area 1 resident)

> Because it's not legalized in this country people will take coach trips to Amsterdam where it is legalized and for me it needs to be something worldwide that's done about prostitution not just in this country.
>
> (Karen, 32, Afro-Caribbean, Area 1 resident)

Others expressed their views that legalization would remove prostitution from residential streets and move it indoors, which would appease residential anxieties. Control and containment were words often utilized to describe their support for legalization. This view, for some, was based upon their experiences and knowledge of the lack of concern of local brothels:

> I do think it should be off the streets. It should be in a, whether its brothels, you know what I mean, whatever you want to call these houses so that there's some kind of safety net for these women. That's what really it should be rather than having them on the streets. Get them off the streets fair enough. But get somewhere to put them.
>
> (Frank, 55, Afro-Caribbean, Area 1 resident)

> I think where there's some organization to it, I don't think people see it as an issues really coz I think people feel that as long as it's contained within an area and its properly controlled and obviously there are issues around [Area 2 brothel] and the workers they employ and they've been busted lots of times, but I don't think generally speaking I mean when we were working down [Area 2 road], in areas that were adjacent to [Area 2 brothel] there was no mention of issues around prostitution or [Area 2 brothel] or you know so in itself that maybe says something about where it's actually properly controlled and contained and organized you know it's not an issue to communities.
>
> (Vicky, 31, white, Area 2 researcher)

Yet, evidence indicates that, even in locations where prostitution is legal and regulated, illegal forms of prostitution occur. For example, in Las Vegas, there are estimates that up to 3500 illegal prostitutes work in underground economies at any given time (Hausbeck et al. 2006). Illegal independent prostitutes evade casino security and discreetly work the bars and/or advertise via weekly newspapers or the internet (Brents and Hausbeck 2007). As with other legal goods,

Responding to community concerns 149

such as the sale of cigarettes and alcohol, there is often always a black market, where people attempt to evade taxation and regulation.

The ability to tax prostitution was considered in these discussions, as it was felt that the income generated would be of benefit to wider society:

> Somewhere like Amsterdam, you know they've got it all set up, its regulated, they pay their taxes, erm and I tend to favour that as a model rather than tolerance zones.
> (Malcolm, 36, white, Area 2 detective inspector)

> You're never going to stop it, you are never going to stop prostitution it's what, the oldest profession in the world. Your never ever gona stop it, so why don't you try and tax it instead. I don't have a problem with it.
> (Daniel, 62, Area 1 Labour councillor)

Taxation can lead to high levels of income being generated from prostitution and other related activities. For example, in 2008, the Nevada Brothel Association estimated that the income gained by brothels in the US totalled 43 million dollars (cited in Brents and Hausbeck 2010). One brothel, the Moonlite Bunny Ranch in Las Vegas, paid US$353,800 in fees and taxes in 2007, which demonstrates the benefits that taxation of brothels can bring to a nation's economy.

For the minority of those who felt that prostitution should not exist, they, too, felt that legalization could be one method for tackling the perceived problem of prostitution:

> I think most people that work in brothels do it under cover in it. So if you legalize it, then I think it will be more, probably harder for them because they wouldn't want to.... Me personally if I worked in a brothel I wouldn't want no one to know that I did it.... So if you make it legal, you know what I mean it's like, to me it will be more open.
> (Naomi, 32, Afro-Caribbean, Area 1 resident)

It was very clear from my study that legalization was the approach most favoured as a means of dealing with community concerns, increasing levels of health and safety for sex workers, ensuring that prostitution is better managed, controlled and regulated and that any profits gained from the industry contribute to 'the nation's purse' through taxation and national insurance contributions. Evidently, given that the UK prostitution policy approach is to criminalize activities associated with prostitution, this would suggest that further consultation is required to address community needs. However, more recent research by Hubbard (2013) has highlighted public opposition to lap-dancing clubs in England and Wales, which has resulted in many local authorities in both England and Wales banning such clubs within their jurisdiction, through utilizing powers maintained within the Policing and Crime Act 2009. What this and my own research suggests is that further research is needed, as it is evident that differing priorities exist within both cities, as well as across nation states. A 'one size fits all' approach is clearly not always appropriate. Given the differences in communities' responses to, and attitudes towards, prostitution, it may be more reasonable to remove central government from strategic decision-making and allow for local solutions to local problems (Home Office 1998a). These local solutions should, however, engage those involved in prostitution and the agencies that support them. Excluding sex workers and their clients from consultation with local communities will often lead to its displacement to other areas.

Chapter summary

The police and local authorities are often torn between 'top down' and 'bottom up' requirements to deal with prostitution, as well as managing their own biases and interpretations of how best to deal with sex work. This chapter has highlighted how, even within the boundaries of one city, differing policing priorities can often work against each other and lead to the displacement of street sex work. In addition, approaches which go against UK Government strategy and law for tackling prostitution have been evidenced, as some police forces and local authorities have often ignored or discounted governmental direction. In these instances, the police have adopted tactics that they felt were best to deal with local concerns. Indeed, in light of the increasing pressure to take a localized approach to policing, some have felt greater pressure to respond to local complaints. Furthermore, it is apparent that the police and local authorities tolerated and accepted the existence of prostitution, both on the street and indoors, accepting an unofficial zone of tolerance in Area 2 and making informal arrangements with local brothels. This tolerance and acceptance was echoed by many residents, as support for legalization was profound in my research. In contrast, support for street prostitution remained absent. It will be argued in the next chapter that this lack of support stems from the continued stigmatization of street prostitution and the cultural norm that has suggested that sex and sexuality should be a practice maintained within a specific space – the private.

Notes

1 Schedule 8 of the Policing and Crime Act 2009 repealed the Sexual Offences Act 1985. This repealed the offences of kerb-crawling and persistent soliciting in that Act, replacing them with the single offence of soliciting (new section 51A of the Sexual Offences Act 2003).
2 The requirement for 'persistence' was removed by s53A The Policing and Crime Act 2009. In effect, people looking to buy sex on the street can now be arrested for their first offence. Police no longer need show that kerb-crawlers are persistent, in order to arrest them.
3 Civil injunctions obtained by local authorities using their powers under s222 of the Local Government Act 1972 were used in Leeds in 2005 as a way of prohibiting kerb-crawlers from a specified location.

8 Stigma management
The individual and the community

It has been suggested that the visibility or presence of street sex workers is hardly a sight that would cause a community great concern. Hubbard, for example, suggests that it is 'difficult to accept that the level of this nuisance alone would be sufficient to motivate the widespread community protests witnessed' (1998a: 281). As with Kantola and Squires' (2004: 77) research, residents in my study were concerned with the social stigma that prostitution brought to the local community and the impact that the presence of street prostitution had upon their local neighbourhoods.

In order to more fully understand the attitudes, action and resistance of the community, particularly in my research, notions of stigma and identity are important. These issues became key features and themes, which emerged in the narratives of participants and often were the underlying reasons why some people took action in their neighbourhoods. It became apparent that often residents, businesses employees, the police and local authority officials attempted to manage the stigma that was regularly associated with prostitution, in order to preserve, cleanse or maintain an identity that is not yet 'spoiled'. This was often achieved through employing, what Goffman (1963) termed, stigma management strategies, which were observed within my study as techniques that helped to create social and geographical distance. The intolerant and tolerant attitudes and action taken were often informed by people's attempts to manage the stigma that prostitution may have imposed on them. Thus, in order to displace or diffuse the possible stigma that may have become fused with them; they managed this stigma through creating distance, both socially and geographically, between their identity and that which is spoiled.

This chapter will begin by exploring the notion of 'identity', leading on to consider the concept of stigma and it is managed, in order to preserve an unspoiled identity. The chapter will then move on to examine how this management was evident in my participants' narratives, in order to demonstrate how some actions and reactions of the 'community' are informed by an attempt to manage stigma commonly associated with prostitution.

Identity

Many of the issues explored in the narratives of my participants related to notions of identity, both of an individual person (the self), but also of the community and neighbourhood. When discussing prostitution and those involved, it was apparent that these discussions were often fused and bound up with their own identities, as they often distinguished between 'I', 'us' and 'them'. Some of the attitudes expressed were often an attempt to 'other' male clients or prostitutes, in an attempt to create distance between themselves and those who are stigmatized.

Identity is a complex concept, but is generally understood as being

> [s]ocially produced, socially embedded and worked out in people's everyday social lives.... Far from identities being formed in opposition to the social world, they are ... formed by the social world ... formed between persons rather than within.... 'Without you I am nothing': without a nexus of others, none of us could be 'who we are'.
>
> (Lawler 2008: 6–8)

Thus, identity is not deemed to be fixed; people do not have a 'real' identity within themselves. What Foucault (1988) argues is that it is just a way of talking about the self – a discourse. Rather than a person having an inner and fixed 'essence', 'the self' is defined by a continuing discourse in a shifting communication of oneself to others. An 'identity' is communicated to others in their interactions with them and is a shifting, temporary construction. Building on Foucault, Judith Butler (1990) describes identity as a performance; it is what you do at particular times, rather than a universal 'who' that you are.

Central to the concept of identity, it is conceived of as a means of describing and conceptualizing the self, which may incorporate 'personal roles and attributes, membership in social groups or categories, and connections to geographical locations. It includes descriptions that are generated internally, as well as those that are imposed by others' (Devine-Wright and Clayton 2010: 267).

Yet, as Buckingham (2008) suggests, there is a paradox with the term, as it implies both similarity and difference:

> On the one hand, identity is something unique to each of us that we assume is more or less consistent (and hence the same) over time ... our identity is something we uniquely possess: it is what distinguishes us from other people. Yet on the other hand, identity also implies a relationship with a broader collective or social group of some kind ... we imply that our identity is partly a matter of what we share with other people ... whom we assume are similar to us.... On one level, I am the product of my unique personal biography. Yet who I am (or who I think I am) varies according to who I am with, the social situations in which I find myself, and the motivations I may have at the time, although I am by no means entirely free to choose how I am defined.
>
> (Buckingham 2008: 1)

Stigma management 153

In this sense, as Bauman (2000) suggests, identity is fluid and negotiable. As our everyday social interactions shift and change, so does our identity, albeit in minute ways. In contrast to earlier understandings of identity as fixed and immutable, identity is increasingly considered to be an evolving process (Peek 2005). Identity can shift over time, due to personal experiences and larger social changes (McMullen 2000). Goffman (1963) explored the presentation of multiple selves in multiple settings (such as in the family, school and community) and was particularly interested in the concept and ingredients of secrecy. As people became more individualized and less tied to neighbourhoods and pre-existing social groupings, it became easier for them to adopt an identity of choice and often chose to keep parts of 'the self' secret.

Identity is, therefore, identified as 'dynamic, contested, multiple and fluid [it] is not only a matter of will and strategy, but is enmeshed in the embodied, material ways in which we live' (Edensor 2002: vii). It is considered to be part of everyday social interactions and is not always something that is discussed or identified. As Bauman suggests, identity only becomes an issue when it is threatened or contested in some way and needs to be explicitly asserted. Stigma is one way in which identity can become threatened. For many of my participants, the stigma often associated with prostitution was seen as a threat to their own identity, by living or working in an area associated with prostitution, predominantly street prostitution. Although the boundaries of this area are not clearly drawn, whether geographical or symbolic, residents and business employees identified the presence of street prostitution on 'their' streets or in 'their' neighbourhoods as a problem.

Stigma

Stigma is a term used to describe 'an attribute that is deeply discrediting' (Goffman 1963: 13). A person with a discreditable attribute or, as Link and Phelan (2001) term, 'label' may be categorized as less desirable and reduced to a tainted or devalued individual with a 'spoiled identity'. Crocker *et al.* (1998: 505) indicate that 'stigmatized individuals possess (or are believed to possess) some attribute, or characteristic, that conveys a social identity that is devalued in a particular social context'. If the attribute or characteristic becomes known to others, the individual moves from discreditable to discredited. As Goffman explains:

> While the stranger is present before us, evidence can arise of his possessing an attribute that makes him different from others in the category of persons available for him to be, and of a less desirable kind – in the extreme, a person who is quite thoroughly bad, or dangerous, or weak. He is thus reduced in our minds from a whole and usual person to a tainted, discounted one. Such an attribute is a stigma, especially when its discrediting effect is very extensive ... it constitutes a special discrepancy between virtual and actual social identity ... not all undesirable attributes are at issue, but only

154 *Stigma management*

> those which are incongruous with our stereotype of what a given type of individual should be.
>
> (Goffman 1963: 12–13)

Once 'labelled', a person becomes associated with a set of undesirable characteristics that form the stereotype. This stereotype identifies the stigmatized person as different to 'normal' people:

> By definition, of course, we ['the normals'] believe the person with a stigma is not quite human. On this assumption we exercise varieties of discrimination, through which we effectively, if often unthinkingly, reduce his life chances.... We tend to impute a wide range of imperfections on the basis of the original one, and at the same time to impute some desirable but undesired attributes.
>
> (Goffman 1963: 15–16)

As a result, for example, 'the "mental patient" label linked the described person to stereotyped beliefs about the dangerousness of people with mental illness, which in turn led them to desire for social distance from the person' (Link and Phelan 2001: 369). This social distance is thereby created through identifying differences:

> Individuals are separated from other sources of identity, henceforward stigmatized and degraded by definition. Creation of alterity allows those in power to dehumanize, to scapegoat, to blame, and thus to avoid responsibility for sufferers [of HIV] ... other people who are assigned the status of 'dangerous others' in various times and places are believed to be morally contagious and often sexually polluting. The results are broadly similar: Such people may be consigned to limbo and to social or corporeal death.
>
> (Schoepf 2001: 339–340)

Yet, as Goffman explains, the stigmatized individual is also involved in the process – in the 'acceptance' of the stigmatized label – as they recognize that they possess an attribute that is discrediting:

> The central feature of the stigmatized individual's situation in life can now be stated. It is a question of what is often, if vaguely, called 'acceptance'. Those who have dealings with him fail to accord him the respect and regard which the un-contaminated aspects of his social identity have led them to anticipate extending, and have led him to anticipate receiving; he echoes this denial by finding that some of his own attributes warrant it.
>
> (Goffman 1963: 19)

Thus, the discreditable individual may attempt to manage knowledge of this characteristic. Goffman (1963) explores techniques that are used to conceal

Stigma management 155

behaviour and hide the 'truth' about discreditable attributes. If an individual is discreditable, but knowledge of their attribute is unknown, the person engages in 'the management of undisclosed discreditable information about the self' (Goffman 1963: 58). They do this through deciding whether 'to display or not to display; to tell or not to tell ... to lie or not to lie' (1963: 57). However, if the individual's attribute is known and the person is discredited, then they engage in covering up, in 'an effort to keep the stigma from looming large ... reduce tension ... ease matters for those in the know' (1963: 125).

Sanders (2005b, 2008a) explored how sex workers and their clients attempted to manage stigma that they often faced, because of their involvement in prostitution. Their behaviour and activities are generally thought to be immoral, antisocial and deviant (Sanders 2008b). Male clients are often seen as deviant and dangerous (Kinnell 2008; Sanders 2008b), whereas sex workers are 'defined as selling her honor' (Pheterson 1993: 43). Discourses evident in the media often construct 'clients as dehumanized, dirty and animalistic' (Campbell and Storr 2001: 98). They are often portrayed as a 'predator who needs to be guarded against, external to the community of "normal" men – an outsider who is untrustworthy and "dangerous"' (Cowburn and Dominelli 2001: 401). Sex workers, in contrast, are deemed as unfeminine, promiscuous, dirty and diseased. In managing this stigma, sex workers and their clients engage in a strategy that Goffman (1963: 58) defines as 'passing' – managing the disclosure of discreditable information, while still 'covering' and keeping the stigma from looming large. Sex workers often try to hide their work from family and friends in an attempt to intentionally and consciously control how they present themselves to others.

The stigma associated with prostitution was evident in many participants' narratives, as Terry explained:

> It was looked at that it's a disgusting trade.... Women involved in that are disgusting ... those men are coming, they're disgusting, money men, disgusting, women disgusting, prostitution disgusting full stop.
> (Terry, 63, white, Area 1 police constable)

Similarly, Clive (42, white, Area 1 chief inspector), explained how prostitution 'in this country it's seen as seedy isn't it'.

The stigma that sex workers and their clients often face was evidenced by many of the comments made by my participants about prostitution and those involved. It is this stigma that was perceived to pose a threat to participants, as they attempted to manage this stigma becoming fused with them.

The individual and the community: managing stigma

Techniques used to manage the stigma that is often associated with prostitution and thus may threaten an identity that is not yet 'spoiled' was evident throughout my research. As the following sections will explore, this stigma was managed through social and geographical distancing. It was clear that many participants were aware that the stigma associated with prostitution may be linked to them, their homes and families. Utilizing the research of Link and Phelan (2001), it was apparent that residents, for example, drew on dominant cultural beliefs or stereotypes about prostitution of dirt, danger and immorality, fearing that they, themselves, would become labelled with similar undesirable characteristics. Residents did not want to 'live within the world of one's stigmatized connexion' (Goffman 1963: 43). As Goffman explains: as with 'the loyal spouse of a mental patient, the daughter of an ex-con, the parent of the cripple, the friend of the blind, the family of the hangman' my participants believed they could be 'obliged to share some of the discredit of the stigmatized person to whom they are related' (Goffman 1963: 30). It was the process of being labelled as being in some way connected to prostitution that led them to 'distance' themselves, both socially and geographically, from 'a blemished person, ritually polluted, to be avoided, especially in public places' (Goffman 1963: ii). As Goffman (1963) suggests, those who are closely connected with a stigmatized person or group often experience the same social stigma.

As this chapter seeks to demonstrate, this close connection and subsequent desire to create distance between themselves and stigmatized groups was entwined with the degree to which this connected to 'the self' and their identity. As Devine-Wright and Clayton (2010: 267) explain, we are more likely to focus our attention and efforts on issues that are most relevant to our own lives and 'utilize interpretive biases in order to maintain and present a desired view of ourselves'. Sometimes, as they explain, 'we do this as individuals, responding to threats that are highly personal; in other circumstances, we respond as members of a group or collective, responding to a common threat to a shared identity'. Participants did this through creating distance, both socially and geographically.

Space, identity and place

The degree to which participants sought to create distance, because of the perceived threat of being stigmatized, was also linked to space, identity and place. Stedman (2002) explored how individuals who strongly identify themselves with a particular place may take action on behalf of that place, either to try to remedy problems that already exist or prevent problems occurring. This may explain why residents engaged in stigma management strategies to a greater degree than business employees, local authority officials or police officers. For residents, the streets and spaces that surround their homes are places that they strongly identify with. As police officer Clive explains, the importance of living in an area – in other words, the importance of place – is crucial to how he would respond to prostitution:

> Taking myself away from being a police officer, I wouldn't judge it. As a police officer and as a parent, living where I do, the idea of it coming on my street would appall me and would be one of those on [Area 1 Street] that would be demanding police action day in day out, because I would be one

of these where I wouldn't want it on my doorstep, because I've seen what comes with it and that's the issue ... So, bit of a difficult one really because you've got two hats on. There's the individual and ones the police officer.

(Clive, 42, Area 1 chief inspector)

Here, Clive distinguishes between his personal identity and social identity as a police officer, which feeds into Goffman's work on the presentation of the self and impression management. Goffman makes an important distinction between 'front stage' and 'back stage' behaviour. 'Front stage' actions are visible to the audience – in this case, being a police officer. 'Back stage' behaviours – when no audience is present – is often seen as 'the real me'. It is when prostitution is associated with his personal identity, home and the place where his personal identity is often symbolized – where he lives – that he recognizes that prostitution would become a problem. It is only when his true self and personal identity becomes threatened by associated stigma that his concerns arise.

The 'home' is, therefore, seen as symbolic. As Mahmoud and Martsin (2012: 732) argue: 'home is a personally relevant and significant place. It is an extension of the self, which starts to represent the self through the person's investment into the place.' This may help to explain why councillors, business employees and police officers do not express the same degree of concern that residents had, as it is only financial concerns, threats to a business reputation and, often, the concerns raised by residents that prompted their action. When prostitution and the potential threat of stigma are made to the 'front stage' or social identity (being a police officer), there is less concern than when it is linked to the 'true self', through associations with 'home' and where a person lives.

In order to manage and displace the potential stigma that may become transposed on to 'the self', participants engaged in stigma management strategies of social and geographical distancing. For those who did not live in the areas where prostitution was evident and visible – generally on the street – their desire to distance themselves geographically was not as pronounced. However, they often did engage in social distancing techniques, in order to disassociate themselves with prostitution, as social closeness was considered as much as a threat to the self.

Social distancing

The notion of 'social distance' has been drawn from Talmadge Wright's (1997) work on the homeless body and Elizabeth Coker's (2005) article on understanding psychiatric stigma in Egypt. According to Wright (1997: 69), words such as 'dirty', 'sick' and 'smelly' were used by the public to 'create social distance between housed and un-housed persons' when describing the homeless body. The use of these words and attempts to cast others as different is a means of creating social distance and demonstrating that they are not socially close. Similarly, Coker's (2005: 920) qualitative study of 'psychiatric stigma from the perspective of lay respondents' found that respondents attempted to create social

158 *Stigma management*

distance between themselves and people with specific mental or behavioural disorders. In this sense, social distancing may be described as 'the desire of those who feel threatened to distance themselves from defiled people and defiled places' (Sibley 1995: 49). Building on Weber's (1978: 342) notion of social closure, where 'usually one group of competitors takes some externally identifiable characteristic of another group of (actual or potential) competitors ... as a pretext for attempting their exclusion', participants may be understood as creating 'us' and 'them' through creating 'social distance'.

Social distance can be understood as the

> [e]xtent to which individuals share beliefs, customs, practices, appearances, and other characteristics that define their identity (Akerlof 1997). Socially distant individuals share few or none of these categories; they are heterogeneous. Individuals who are socially close, in contrast, share many or all of these categories. They are comparatively homogeneous.... For instance, two agents might share some of the same categories of belief, like religion or political persuasion. They may share appearance, such as the way they dress, or practices, like how they settle disputes. Individuals might also share customs, such as the way they greet strangers, the way they deal with colleagues, or other social rules that guide their behaviour.
>
> (Leeson 2008: 164)

Thus, creating social distance is an attempt to demonstrate that the creator and the person referred to do not share commonalities; they are not socially close. Through creating social distance, participants are highlighting that they do not share characteristics, common customs or practices – in other words, that they are strangers.

Words such as 'dirty', 'riddled' and 'perverts' were used by some of my participants, in order to distinguish themselves from sex workers and their clients. By suggesting that sex workers are to blame for any violence or abuse perpetrated against them – as explored in Chapter 4, for example – female residents attempted to create 'social distance' between themselves and sex workers. Distinguishing herself from sex workers, Gemma (46, Afro-Caribbean, Area 1 resident) explained how 'unfortunately, some women [not me] make it bad for the people who want to walk around and go about their daily ... business'. Similarly, Emma (27, Afro-Caribbean, Area 1 resident) identified her 'sexual purity' and distinguished herself from prostitutes, thereby employing a discourse of dirt and disease when she described how she would 'be sat there in the bath scrubbing myself'. Likewise, Diane (22, white, Area 2 resident) would 'rather scrub toilets than do that'. The use of these words and the ways that sex workers are described can be understood as an attempt to distance themselves from behaviour and actions considered to be 'bad' and that which is 'dirty'. Through creating 'social distance', female participants' are thereby demonstrating that they adhere to dominant forms of femininity, unlike female sex workers, who are stigmatized because they transgress moral boundaries regarding appropriate sexual behaviour. By 'other-ing' sex workers, female participants create 'social distance' between themselves and the deviant 'other', in order to distinguish between 'us' and 'them' and thereby deflect or neutralize any potential stigma.

The desire to distance the self from the immoral continued throughout residents' narratives. Male participants fed into cultural myths of the danger of strangers, by reinforcing their ideological basis and distinguishing themselves from sexual predators by, for example, telling family and friends to 'be careful' (Vernon, 57, Afro-Caribbean, Area 1 resident) when walking in red-light areas or getting into taxis and picking up their granddaughters, rather than allowing them to walk home from family and friends' homes (James, 60, Afro-Caribbean, Area 1 resident). I, similarly, experienced being told by male residents and councillors to take care when walking around Area 1 late in the evening. These views and actions directly mirror those witnessed in Pitcher *et al.*'s (2006) research, which identified how some men were concerned about female family members and friends and would often arrange to meet them in places known for prostitution, rather than allow them to walk home alone.

In a similar study by Hubbard (1998b), which highlighted the way in which moral narratives and discourses were deployed by protesters in their attempts to construct an idea of community predicated on the exclusion of 'immoral' sex workers, this notion of 'other-ing' was similarly explored. Hubbard (1998b) utilized the work of Kirby (1996) and Sibley (1995) to explain the boundary creation between 'the self' and others. Kirby (1996) argues that boundaries drawn between others and 'the self' maintain a purity of 'the self'. This attempt to create distance from the 'other' has been considered as a 'fundamental characteristic of socio-spatial relationships' (Sibley 1998: 120). Thus, through identifying men who buy sex from women as, for example, 'perverts' or 'big men in high places', resident participants attempted to identify boundaries between themselves and men who deviate from acceptable moral behaviour. Thus, through the act of 'other-ing', residents demonstrated their own adherence to social norms. Men who buy sex are, therefore, identified as the 'other'.

Race was also another means through which those who have devalued identities were othered. Many Afro-Caribbean Area 1 residents identified men who buy sex from women as from particular religious and/or ethnic backgrounds. White British, Asian and Eastern European men were identified and discussed by nine of the twenty research participants from the Afro-Caribbean Area 1 community. The two most commonly identified were Asian clients: 'I know a lot of them who buy it though, a lot of Asian men buy it I don't know why' (Craig, 45, Afro-Caribbean, Area 1 community worker); and white clients: 'A lot of the clients, two clients, mainly white men and Asian taxi men' (Brian, 47, Afro-Caribbean, Area 1 resident). According to the nine Afro-Caribbean residents, who identified Asian and white British men as men who buy sex from women, 'you don't really get a lot of black men looking for women' (Susan, 30, Afro-Caribbean, Area 1 resident).

The identification of the ethnic background of these men as characteristic of men who buy sex from women can be seen as a form of ethnic 'other-ing'.

Afro-Caribbean residents identify male clients as white or Asian, in order to create 'social distance' between themselves, their ethnic identity and men who buy sex. Through creating social distance between ethnic groups, Afro-Caribbean residents are suggesting that 'their men' do not engage in immoral behaviour, thus purifying and privileging their ethnic sexuality. Race and racism has been identified as a factor in explaining different perceptions about prostitution (Della Giusta et al. 2008; Farley and Kelly 2000). In Jakobsson and Kotsadam's research, racial othering was used as a means of justifying the purchase of sex. They argue that this justification could be because their participants tended to care less about or even legitimize the potentially deprived situations that prostitutes often find themselves in (Jakobsson and Kotsadam 2011).

Stigma-neutralizing techniques

Not all men who buy sex were, however, othered by participants. Although it was evident that many participants attempted to other sex workers and their clients, discussions changed somewhat when participants discussed men that they knew who had been on a stag party. Despite my own presumptions that some participants may admit their own biases in making judgements about all male sex buyers or show some sympathy for kerb-crawlers in their local area when reflecting on people they know, instead some participants engaged in what could be defined as stigma-neutralizing techniques. In other words, those designed to manage or displace any potential stigma associated with prostitution. As Goffman explains, if the individual is discredited, covering is sometimes put into action as 'an effort to keep the stigma from looming large ... reduce tension ... ease matters for those in the know' (1963: 125). For example, when discussing men that they knew, who had been on a stag party and visited a sex worker, one resident stated: 'People think its sex. But it's not all sex. The majority of them do not have sex' (Linda, 62, Afro-Caribbean, Area 1 resident). Similarly, Tina, (31, Afro-Caribbean, Area 1 resident) suggested that only a small percentage of those men who go on stag parties engage in 'sex': 'I think maybe a very, very small per cent have sex. I think a lot of them have simulated sex; a lot of them use whatever for the fun of it. I don't think a lot of them have sex a week before they get married.' This may be understood as de-stigmatising the behaviour of men on stag parties. By suggesting that men on stag parties do not buy sex, residents attempt to diffuse any potential criticism of men that they know – in other words, those who are socially close to 'the self'. Although research does support this statement, for some men who engage in the sex industry, the predominant motivating factor is the pursuit of genital sexual contact and oral sex (Freund et al. 1991, 1989).

Attempts to neutralize potential stigma afforded to people they knew and, thus, themselves was also observed, when some participants indicated that the men they knew who had been on stag parties were motivated by peer pressure. 'Peer pressure' (Wanda, 41, white, Area 2 resident) was identified by seven resident participants as a motive for men on stag parties who purchase 'sex'. The belief that was predominantly held was that men who go on stag parties and engage in sexual activities with sex workers did so because they felt pressurized by the stag party, thereby deflecting responsibility for purchasing sex onto 'others'. Resident participants identified men's motivations to engage in the sex industry on stag parties as stemming from situations where '[t]he lads will have been egging him on' (Liam, 54, Afro-Caribbean, Area 1 resident) and where men 'do it as a joke' (Rachel, 43, Afro-Caribbean, Area 1 resident). Peer pressure and group norms in female 'bachelorette' parties were also observed in Tye and Powers' (1998) research, whereby women engaged in the resistance of culturally constructed gender roles and values.

Although residents were able to identify and understand why men bought sex on stag parties, when residents discussed the behaviour of kerb-crawlers, they appeared to lack any understanding of the reasons why these men buy sex. These discussions are, therefore, a stark contrast to those made about the 'perverted' street sex buyer, who often visited the areas in which they lived to purchase sex. Excusing the behaviour on stag parties was, as shown, closely linked to knowing someone who had been to places such as the red-light district of Amsterdam on a stag party. Low social distance – in other words, knowing a man who had engaged in this sort of behaviour – meant that distinguishing and neutralizing strategies were adopted. In addition (and as will be explored more fully below), stag parties did not take place in the areas in which they lived and, thus, were not geographically close.

Further attempts were made by some participants to create distance between themselves, the men that they know and punters. For example, the quote below illustrates how recognition is paid to men purchasing sex on stag parties; however, in this context, this recognition is only afforded to the 'other':

> My husband, well [he] wasn't husband at the time, [he] went on his stag do in Blackpool and a few of the, blokes who had girlfriends went and paid for sex because they could and probably because it was an ego trip and that they.
>
> (Joanne, 25, white, Area 2 resident)

> God if my husband had of done that, I'd of battered him literally.
>
> (Ruby, 23, white, Area 2 resident)

> He went to bed, he rang me and said that they'd gone back out and, gone and paid for it.
>
> (Joanne, 25, Area 2 resident)

Similarly, when male participants talked about the purchase of sex, they often explained how they knew of men who had bought sex, but often no one who could be considered to be socially close, such as a relative or friend.

The geographical landscape and socio-spatial management

The desire to create social distance between prostitution and 'the self' was often fused with a desire for geographic distance. As Devine-Wright and Clayton explain:

> The physical environment has been shown to have strong connections to a sense of self.... Our identities are shaped by the experiences we have with both social and nonsocial stimuli, the people and places that we encounter, and these identities affect our responses to new events. Attention to, and interpretations of, *environmental threats are clearly filtered through a perspective based on the perceiver's identity.*
> (Devine-Wright and Clayton 2010: 267 [added emphasis])

Thus, the area in which a person's home or business is based, those 'bounded spatial units of self-identification' (Devine-Wright and Clayton 2010: 268), can impact upon a personal or business identity. In particular, the close proximity of prostitution to a person's home or business was considered to be a problem and often prompted activism, as residents and business employees attempted to change the area around them. As business employees and business owners explained in Chapter 5, the close proximity of street sex work to business premises could potentially taint the reputation of a business. The negative social attitude towards prostitution spreads out in waves and, thereby, could become associated with that business.

Geographical distance and the self

The importance of geographical distance was also observed when many participants discussed the reasons why men sometimes purchase sex while abroad. Some participants appeared to 'normalize' the purchase of sex abroad, through explaining that such behaviour was different to a person's general behaviour and a reflection of general holiday behaviour. Many expressed the view that men who buy sex abroad or on holiday do so in line with general holiday behaviour and accepted norms. This holiday behaviour was deemed as distinct and different to the way that people behaved in their home town or country. The purchase of sex abroad is accepted as general holiday behaviour and, thus, not out of the ordinary. In this sense, the purchase of sex was considered as reflecting a social trend to behave differently abroad. As Peter (35, white, Area 2 councillor) explains: 'you find that in holidays in general, you hear people say that they do stuff on holiday that they wouldn't do at home'.

The suggestion that 'when people are on holiday they act differently' (Malcolm, 36, white, Area 2 detective inspector) may be linked to the geographical distance of going on holiday abroad. The act of going abroad – 'that outside of England, holiday atmosphere and that escapism' – meant that, for Edward's (33, white, Area 2 police sergeant) friends, buying sex became *a* 'totally different story and suddenly its play time'. In contrast, 'if they said to their mates "oh I'm just popping down to [local brothel]" they'd be like ... seeing it as worse' than purchasing sex on holiday abroad (Darren, 36, white, Area 2 PCSO). This contrast illustrates the increasing intolerance and social disapproval of purchasing sex in geographical proximity to their 'own backyard'. By going abroad and engaging in prostitution, clients are thereby able to hide and conceal any sexual behaviour by managing information. In doing so, they are able to manage their spoiled identity and conceal knowledge of their deviant behaviour.

The geographical importance of purchasing sex abroad is further illustrated by Ivor (40, white, Area 2 development officer), who identified his own and his friends' experiences of stag parties and holidays abroad. Ivor explains that geographical distance is an important factor regarding his friends' sexual behaviour in general and not exclusive to men who buy sex from women. In the following comment, Ivor identifies his friends' experiences of one-night stands to support his claim that people generally act differently abroad:

> It's almost accepted that they do ... people tend to act, maybe it's a British thing ... but people tend to act differently when they go on holiday. I've got friends who don't do casual sex, we're not talking about prostitutes, they just don't do casual sex but they do when they go on holiday ... they're quite happy to go to Spain and have a one night stand ... but going out in Leeds or where ever else would dream of it.
> (Ivor, 40, white, Area 2 development officer)

According to Ivor, the importance of geographic distance is coupled with cultural context, which normalizes 'holiday behaviour'. As Ivor explains, the engagement in sexually promiscuous behaviour is part of the 'British character', which is 'sort of culturally ingrained' (Ivor, 40, white, Area 2 development officer). The purchase of sex abroad by British men is understood as part of British culture. To emphasize the cultural dimension, Ivor maintains that the 'Germans don't do that ... I bet they don't.'

There is limited evidence on British sexual behaviour abroad (Rogstad 2004). However, research has found that 35 per cent of people in one study had sex with new partners while on holiday (Batalla-Duran *et al.* 2003) and, as a result, were deemed at an increased risk of exposure to sexually transmitted diseases (Carter *et al.* 1997). This increased risk is considered to stem from '[t]he holiday atmosphere', which 'is geared towards sexual promiscuity, with excesses of alcohol, a perceived lack of consequences and holiday package companies positively encouraging sex' (Batalla-Duran *et al.* 2003: 494).

The cultural context of the place in which the purchase of sex occurs is also highlighted as an important factor informing the purchase of sex. Two police officers considered that the legality of prostitution abroad was an important factor that informed the decision regarding whether or not to purchase sex. According to Simon (33, white, Area 2 police sergeant): 'it's like people going to Amsterdam they'll go across and smoke Cannabis over there or eat cannabis cake but they wouldn't touch it over here because they know it's an offence and

I think that's the difference'. The importance of the cultural context is similarly identified by Dean (Dean, 30, white, Area 2 police constable), who suggests that 'it's a case of over here it's illegal and it's seen as perhaps dirty over there it's sort of semi, well it is legalized'.

This perception is supported by research that highlights that legality contributes to normalization, which, in turn, increases the likelihood of paying for sex. In their study of men who buy sex in East London, Coy *et al.* (2007) found that the three most popular destinations for men to purchase sex were Amsterdam, Germany and Spain, which are those in which prostitution is legal. Thus, it is argued that the socio-legal context in which the purchase of sex is made influences men's attitudes and behaviour.

Julia O'Connell Davidson argues that the purchase of sex in specific countries is not only motivated by the legality of a place, but also because the perceived legality is symbolic of a gendered hierarchy. According to O'Connell Davidson's (2001: 8) analysis of the perspectives of a group of white European and North American male heterosexual sex tourists and expatriates, 'hard core male heterosexual sex tourists travel to "Third World" countries as a means of release from the restraints that are supposedly placed on the white male's self-sovereignty in the "First World"'. This may explain the suggestion that locations such as Thailand, Amsterdam and Prague are increasingly becoming 'the lads destination hot-spots' (David, 62, Area 1 councillor), as men are able to 'reconcile themselves to the authority of a state which is overtly patriarchal and white supremacist', rather than just legal (O'Connell Davidson 2001: 12). The desire to engage in sexual relations with 'Others' while on holiday is considered to reflect 'not so much a wish to engage in any specific sexual practice as a desire for an extraordinarily high degree of control over the management of self and others as sexual, radicalized and engendered beings' (O'Connell Davidson and Sanchez-Taylor 1999: 37). The lack of disapproval and acceptance of this holiday behaviour by the research participants may stem from the belief that sex tourists and expatriates 'are certainly not alone in their disquiet, but they are distinguished by the fact that they attach such an immediate erotic significance to this sense of loss' (O'Connell Davidson 2001: 13). This sense of loss is identified as emanating from the existence of equality between men and women in their home nation. In this sense, the male research participants who 'normalize' male sexual behaviour abroad are voicing their sense of 'loss'.

Stigma, visibility and space

It would be naïve to suggest that distance alone can quell community concerns for the presence of prostitution in their local area. Visibility and containment can also impact on how prostitution is perceived and responded to by members of the local community. Often, some participants expressed an 'out of sight, out of mind' attitude towards prostitution that took place indoors. Many participants expressed a greater degree of tolerance towards indoor sex work. For instance, as Rachel explained:

Well it is a bit of harmless fun because the prostitutes are in the houses, they're not on the street, they're going to do it where ever they go aren't they and it is, it's like a day out at Blackpool, you go on the rides.
(Rachel, 43, Afro-Caribbean, Area 1 resident)

Similarly, in Area 2, Clive explains how although people know of a particular massage parlour's existence, its lack of visibility as a place where sexual transactions take place meant that the community did not complain:

There's the [name] which is a gay massage parlour ... it's been there donkeys years, but there's never an issue with the community about it. It's strange it's never, they've had a couple of robberies there but there's nothing. They [the community] never ever have an issue because the guys come, they park their cars and go inside and I suppose it's out of sight out of mind really isn't it.... So it's not affecting the sort of life of individuals.
(Clive, 42, Area 1 chief inspector)

For residents in this area, the main concern was that clients would often 'park in front of their houses' and this 'would annoy them'. As Clive goes on to explain:

But you've got men for, want of a better expression, going in and out of a shop. As simple as that ... they're not propositioning anybody ... they're in and out ... I can't remember that we've had many complaints ... [the] top ten residential or business [problems] where we've been called to continuously ... include drunkenness, mental health problems, anti-social behaviour problems and if there was a massage parlour where somebody was ringing continuously we'd hear about it. So I don't think that side of the sex trade affects er, the community as much.
(Clive, 42, Area 1 chief inspector)

What may be suggested is that sex workers, their clients and their visible presence represents 'uncleanness', which is 'out of place' when on the street (Douglas 2002: 50). The absence of a similar focus on indoor markets may suggest that they are 'out of place' on the street, but 'in the right place' when working in off-street prostitution settings. Beliefs that prostitution should not take place on the street, but may be tolerated indoors can be seen as far back as the *Wolfenden Report*. The report identified the problem of street prostitution as the visibility of women soliciting in public places, as such visibility was considered offensive to 'public decency'. Consequently, the report recommended that:

We are not charged to enter matters of private moral conduct, except in so far as they directly affect the public good.... It is not in our view, the function of the law to intervene in the private lives of citizens.
(Wolfenden 1957: 9–10)

The report made a crucial distinction between private actions and public order, proposing that it should not be the function of the law to regulate private behaviour, regardless of how distasteful it may seem to others (Weeks 2007). Within the report, prostitution 'is seen as a matter of private morality, except when it creates a public nuisance' (Kantola and Squires 2004: 78–79).

The cultural beliefs that sex and sexuality should be confined to the private sphere are not solely linked to prostitution and sex work. Kissing in public spaces is also often frowned upon. These cultural norms about acceptable and appropriate sexual behaviour clearly impact upon people's attitudes and actions. For those who transgress these moral and sexual boundaries, they may face criticism and be stigmatized for their behaviour.

Chapter summary

This chapter has highlighted how many views and attitudes held by some of my participants did not always represent intolerance towards prostitution. Instead, intolerant attitudes were more of an attempt to manage the stigma that prostitution may have posed to them and their personal identity. Prostitution and its close proximity to 'the self', either socially – through knowing someone who buys or sells sex – or geographically – through it taking place near a person's home or business premises – posed a threat and needed to be managed and neutralized. Participants did so through expressing views and making statements that attempted to distinguish themselves from stigmatized people and places – in other words, prostitutes and their clients. Moreover, attempts to manage the potential stigma that prostitution posed to the self was also manifested in a desire to create geographic distance, through displacing street prostitution to another area or engaging in sexual practices in another country.

Bibliography

Abreu, J. M., Ramirez, E., Kim, B. S. K. and Haddy, C. (2003). Automatic activation of yellow peril Asian American stereotypes: Effects on social impression formation. *The Journal of Social Psychology, 143*(6), 691–706.

Abu-Lughob, L. (1995). A community of secrets: The separate world of Bedoin women. In Penny A. Weiss and M. Friedman (eds), *Feminism and Community*. Philadelphia: Temple University Press, 21–44.

Adams, L. (2008). The kerb crawlers: middle class and married *The Herald* 28 February. Online. Available at: www.theherald.co.uk/news/news/display.var.2078546.0.The_kerb_crawlers_middle_class_and_married.php (accessed 29 February 2008).

Agar, M. (1980). *The Professional Stranger: An Informal Introduction to Ethnography*. San Diego: Academic Press.

Agustín, L. M. (2005). New research directions: The cultural study of commercial sex. *Sexualities, 8*(5), 618–631.

Alcock, P. (2010). Building the big society: A new policy environment for the third sector in England. *Voluntary Sector Review, 1*(3), 379–389.

Alexander, C. (2000a). *The Asian Gang: Ethnicity, Identity, Masculinity*. Oxford: Berg Publishers.

Alexander, C. (2000b). (Dis)entangling the 'Asian gang': Ethnicity, identity, masculinity. In H. Barnor (ed.), *Un/Settled Multiculturalisms: Diasporas, Entanglements, Transruptions*. London: Zed Books, 123–147.

Andrew, R. (2005). Red-light tolerance zone may be set up in city. *Yorkshire Post*, 17 February. Online. Available at: www.yorkshiretoday.co.uk/ViewArticle.aspx?SectionID=55&ArticleID=947821 (accessed 22 February 2007).

Asian News (2005). Three weeks to 'clean' streets. *Asian News*, 30 March. Online. Available at: www.theasiannews.co.uk/news/index/11637.html (accessed 17 February 2006).

Association of Chief Police Officers (2004). *Policing Prostitution: ACPO's Policy, Strategy and Operational Guidelines for Dealing with Exploitation and Abuse through Prostitution*. London: ACPO. 1 October. Online. Available at: www.acpo.police.uk/documents/crime/2011/20111102%20CBA%20Policing%20Prostitution%20and%20%20Sexual%20Exploitation%20Strategy_Website_October%202011.pdf (accessed 20 June 2013).

Augustin, L. (2007). *Sex at the Margins: Migration, Labour Markets and the Rescue Industry*. London: Zed Books.

Baeva, N. (2005). Cologne leads the way in safe prostitution. *Dw-world.de*, 7 July. Online. Available at: www.dw-world.de/dw/article/0,,1641575,00.html (accessed 23 August 2011).

168 Bibliography

Baker, L. M. (2007). Undercover as sex workers: The attitudes and experiences of female vice officers. *Women & Criminal Justice, 16*(4), 25–41.

Baldock, L. (2009). Operation Pinehurst tackling prostitution in Sheil Road area of Kensington and Fairfield. In L. Baldock (ed.), *Louise Baldock Blogspot*. Online. Available at: http://louisebaldock.blogspot.com/2009/03/operation-pinehurst-tackling.html (accessed 23 August 2009).

Banks, M. (2001). *Visual Methods in Social Research*. London: Sage.

Bao, J. (2004). *Marital Acts: Gender, Sexuality, and Identity among the Chinese Thai Diaspora*. Honolulu: University of Hawaii Press.

Barlow, C. (2008). Lap dancing and sexual violence. *Newstatesman*, 2 April. Online. Available at: www.newstatesman.com/life-and-society/2008/04/lap-dancing-clubs-local (accessed 6 January 2009).

Barnard, M. and McKeganey, N. (1992). Risk behaviours among male clients of female prostitutes. *International Conference AIDS, 8*, 19–24.

Barnard, M., McKeganey, N. and Leyland, A. H. (1993). Risk behaviours among male clients of female prostitutes. *British Medical Journal, 307*(6900), 361–362.

Barry, K. (1984). *Female Sexual Slavery*. New York: New York University Press.

Barter, C. and Renold, E. (1999). The use of vignettes in qualitative research. *Social Research Update* (25). Online. Available at: http://sru.soc.surrey.ac.uk/SRU25.html (accessed 20 June 2013).

Bartley, P. (2000). *Prostitution: Prevention and Reform in England 1860–1914*. London: Routledge.

Barton, B. C. (2006). *Stripped: Inside the Lives of Exotic Dancers*. New York: New York University Press.

Bassermann, L. (1967). *The Oldest Profession*. London: Arthur Barker Ltd.

Batalla-Duran, E., Oakeshott, P. and Hay, P. (2003). Sun, sea and sex? Sexual behaviour of people on holiday in Tenerife. *Family Practice, 20*(4), 493–494.

Bauman, Z. (2000). *Liquid Modernity*. Cambridge: Polity Press.

Bayley, D. and Shearing, C. (1996). The future of policing. *Law and Society Review, 30*(3), 585–606.

BBC Inside Out (2007). Kerb crawler rehab: Inside Out East visits Northamptonshire to look at a new approach to tackle prostitution … a rehabilitation course for men who are caught kerb crawling. *BBC Inside Out*, 4 December. Online. Available at: www.bbc.co.uk/insideout/content/articles/2007/10/09/east_kerb_crawl_s12_w4_feature.shtml (accessed 29 November 2007).

BBC News (2001). Talks over prostitution zone. *BBC News*, 15 November. Online. Available at: http://news.bbc.co.uk/1/hi/scotland/1656885.stm (accessed 23 June 2008).

BBC News (2004). Man released after parlour raids. *BBC News*, 18 March. Online. Available at: http://news.bbc.co.uk/1/hi/england/west_yorkshire/3634309.stm (accessed 16 June 2008).

BBC News (2005a). Approval for first red light zone: England's first prostitution tolerance zone could be set up within months after councillors in Liverpool approved the move. *BBC News*, 26 January. Online. Available at: http://news.bbc.co.uk/1/hi/england/merseyside/4207391.stm (accessed 11 June 2008).

BBC News (2005b). Kerb-crawler rehab 'is working': A tough rehabilitation course for men caught kerb crawling has proved very successful, according to Notts police. *BBC News*, 4 February. Online. Available at: http://news.bbc.co.uk/1/hi/england/nottinghamshire/4261835.stm (accessed 14 February 2005).

BBC News (2005c). Profile: David Blunkett. *BBC News*, 6 May. Online. Available at: http://news.bbc.co.uk/1/hi/uk_politics/vote_2005/frontpage/4521577.stm (accessed 23 June 2008).

BBC News (2005d). Residents support prostitute plan: Research in Liverpool revealed that more than 80% of people are in favour of a prostitution tolerance zone. *BBC News*, 26 January. Online. Available at: http://news.bbc.co.uk/1/hi/england/merseyside/4208729.stm (accessed 28 January 2005).

BBC News (2006). Kerb-crawlers caught in the act: Police in Leeds have charged 28 men with kerb crawling following a major operation in the city. *BBC News*, 14 June. Online. Available at: http://news.bbc.co.uk/1/hi/england/west_yorkshire/5078784.stm (accessed 17 July 2007).

Bearwood Blog (2010). Police step up operations against prostitution in Bearwood. Abbey Ward Labour Councillors. *Bearwood Blog*, 6 September. Online. Available at: http://bearwoodblog.wordpress.com/2010/09/06/police-step-up-operations-against-prositution-in-bearwood/ (accessed 23 August 2011).

Beck, U. (1992). *Risk Society*. London: Sage.

Begum, S. (2008a). Red light fight. *Oldham Advertiser*. Online. Available at: www.oldhamadvertiser.co.uk/news/s/1062351_red_light_fight (accessed 17 June 2009).

Begum, S. (2008b). Residents will name and shame drug dealers. *The Asian News*, 31 July. Online. Available at: www.theasiannews.co.uk/news/s/1060697_residents_will_name_and_shame_drug_dealers (accessed 17 June 2009).

Bellah, R. N., Madsen, R., Sullivan, W. M., Swidler, A. and Tipton, S. M. (1985). *Habits of the Heart: Individualism and Commitment in American Life*. New York: Harper and Row.

Bellis, M. A., Watson, F. L. D., Hughes, S., Cook, P. A., Downing, J., Clark, P. and Thomson, R. (2007). Comparative views of the public, sex workers, businesses and residents on establishing managed zones for prostitution: Analysis of a consultation in Liverpool. *Health and Place, 13*(3), 603–616.

Belza, M. J., de la Fuente, L., Suarez, M., Vallejo, F., Garcia, M., Lopez, M., Barrio, G. and Bolea, A. (2008). Men who pay for sex in Spain and condom use: Prevalence and correlates in a representative sample of the general population. *Sexually Transmitted Infections, 84*(3), 207–211.

Benson, C. and Matthews, R. (1995). Street prostitution: Ten facts in search of a policy. *International Journal of the Sociology of Law, 23*(4), 395–415.

Bentley, T., McCathy, H. and Mean, M. (2003). *Inside Out: Rethinking Inclusive Communities*. London: Demos/Barrow Cadbury Trust. 24 February. Online. Available at: www.demos.co.uk/insideout (accessed 21 March 2006).

Berman, J. (2003). (Un)popular strangers and crises (un)bounded: Discourses of sex-trafficking, the European political community and the panicked state of the modern state. *European Journal of International Relations, 9*(1), 37–86.

Bernardo, F. M. and Vera, H. (1981). The groomal shower: A variation of the American bridal shower. *Family Relations, 30*(3), 395–401.

Bernstein, E. (2001). The meaning of the purchase: Desire, demand and the commerce of sex. *Ethnography, 2*(3), 389–420.

Bernstein, E. (2007). Sex work for the middle classes. *Sexualities, 10*(4), 473–488.

Berrington, E. and Jones, H. (2002). Reality vs. myth: Constructions of women's insecurity. *Feminist Media Studies, 2*(3), 307–323.

Birmingham Mail (2007). ASBOs issued in kerb-crawling crackdown. *Birmingham Mail*, 13 August 2007.

Blaikie, N. (2000). *Designing Social Research*. Cambridge: Polity Press.
Bloor, M. J., McKeganey, N. P., Finlay, A. and Barnard, M. A. (1992). The inappropriateness of psycho-social models of risk behaviour for understanding HIV-related risk practices among Glasgow male prostitutes. *AIDS Care, 4*(2), 131–137.
Blunkett, D. (2004). Foreword. In Home Office (eds), *Paying the Price: A Consultation Paper*. London: HMSO, 5–6.
Bourdieu, P. (1989). Social space and symbolic power. *Sociological Theory, 7*(1), 14–25.
Bourdieu, P. (1992). *The Logic of Practice*. Cambridge: Polity.
Boxer, P. and Tisak, M. (2003). Adolescents' attributions about aggression: An initial investigation. *Journal of Adolescence, 26*(5), 561–575.
Brain, T. (2006). Operational overview. *Crown Prosecution Service*. Online. Available at: www.cps.gov.uk/publications/docs/pentameter_0706.pdf (accessed 17 December 2008).
Brehman, B. (2010). *Factors Influencing Attitudes towards Prostitution*. University of Las Vegas Theses/Dissertations/Professional Papers/Capstones. Online. Available at: http://digitalcommons.library.unlv.edu/thesesdissertations/217 (accessed 30 May 2011).
Brents, B. G. and Hausbeck, K. (2007). Marketing sex: US legal brothels and late capitalist consumption. *Sexualities, 10*(4), 425–439.
Brents, B. and Hausbeck, K. (2010). Sex work matter: What the blurring of boundaries around the sex industry means for sex work, research and activism. In M. H. Ditmore, A. Levy and A. Willman (eds), *Sex Work Matters*. New York: Zed Books, 9–22.
Brock, D. R. (1998). *Making Work, Making Trouble: Prostitution as a Social Problem*. London: University of Toronto Press.
Brooks-Gordon, B. (2006a). *Government Strategy on Sex Work: A Comedy of Errors or Attack on Civil Liberties?* Paper presented at the British Psychological Society, 30 March–1 April, Cardiff.
Brooks-Gordon, B. (2006b). *The Price of Sex: Prostitution, Policy and Society*. Cullompton: Willan Publishing.
Brooks-Gordon, B. and Gelthorpe, L. (2003a). Prostitutes' clients, Ken Livingstone and a new Trojan horse. *The Howard Journal, 42*(5), 437–451.
Brooks-Gordon, B. and Gelthorpe, L. (2003b). What men say when apprehended for kerb crawling: A model of prostitutes clients' talk. *Psychology, Crime & Law, 9*(2), 145–171.
Brown, A. and Barratt, D. (2002). *Knowledge of Evil: Child Prostitution and Sexual Abuse in Twentieth-Century England*. Cullompton: Willan Publishing.
Brown, L. (2007). Performance, status and hybridity in a Pakistani red-light district: The cultural production of the courtesan. *Sexualities, 10*(4), 409–423.
Browne, K., Cull, M. and Hubbard, P. (2010). The diverse vulnerabilities of lesbian, gay, bisexual and trans sex workers in the UK. In K. Hardy, S. Kingston and T. Sanders (eds), *New Sociologies of Sex Work*. Surrey: Ashgate, 197–212.
Bruce, S. (1999). *Sociology: A Very Short Introduction*. Oxford: Oxford University Press.
Buckingham, D. (2008). Introducing identity. In D. Buckingham (ed.), *The John D. and Catherine T. MacArthur Foundation Series on Digital Media and Learning*. Cambridge: The MIT Press, 1–24.
Buckley, T. (2009). Locals sweep sex workers off streets. *Sunday News*, 19 April. Online. Available at: www.stuff.co.nz/national/2345076/Locals-sweep-sex-workers-off-streets#share (accessed 3 August 2009).
Butler, J. (1990). *Gender Trouble: Feminism and the Subversion of Identity*. London: Routledge.

Cabezas, A. L. (2004). Between love and money: Sex, tourism, and citizenship in Cuba and the Dominican Republic. *Signs: Journal of Women in Culture and Society, 29*(4), 987–1015.

Calder, G. (2005). Communitarianism and New Labour. *White Horse Bulletin*. Online. Available at: http://whb.co.uk/socialissues/vol.2gc.htm (accessed 23 December 2005).

Campbell, C. (1998). Invisible men: Making visible male clients of female prostitutes in Merseyside. In J. Elias, V. Bullough, V. Elis, G. Brewer and J. Elders (eds), *Prostitution: On Whores, Hustlers and Johns*. New York: Prometheus Books, 155–171.

Campbell, R. (1997). 'It's just business, its' just sex': Male clients of female prostitutes in Merseyside. *Journal of Contemporary Health, 5*, 47–51.

Campbell, R. (2011). *Treating Crimes against Sex Workers as Hate Crime in Merseyside*. Paper presented at the Rethinking Hate Crime: Bringing Theory and Practice Together, University of Bradford, 25 July 2011, Bradford.

Campbell, R. and Storr, M. (2001). Challenging the kerb crawler rehabilitation programme. *Feminist Review, 67*(1), 94–108.

Carey, L. and Smith-Miles, C. (2008). Fighting prostitution takes community effort, expert says. *Independentmail.com*, 25 August. Online. Available at: www.independentmail.com/news/2008/aug/25/fighting-prostitution-takes-community-effort-exper/ (accessed 23 August 2011).

Carpenter, B. (1998). The prostitute and the client: Challenging the dualisms. *Women's Studies. International Forum, 4*(8), 387–399.

Carroll, B. E. (2003). *American Masculinities*. London: Sage.

Carter, S. P., Carter, S. L. and Dannenberg, A. L. (2003). Zoning out crime and improving community health in Sarasota, Florida: 'Crime prevention through environmental design'. *American Journal of Public Health, 93*(9), 1442–1445.

Carter, S., Horn, K., Hart, G., Dunbar, M., Scoular, A. and Macintyre, S. (1997). The sexual behaviour of international travellers at two Glasgow GUM clinics. *International Journal for STD and AIDS, 8*(5), 336–338.

CBC News (2009). Montreal residents fight prostitution online. *CBC News*, 8 December. Online. Available at: www.cbc.ca/canada/montreal/story/2009/12/08/montreal-prostitutes-hochelaga-maisonneuve.html (accessed 10 December 2009).

Chambers, C. T. and Craig, K. (1998). An intrusive impact of anchors in childrens' faces pain scales. *Pain, 78*, 27–37.

Chan, W. (2001). *Women, Murder and Justice*. Basingstoke: Palgrave.

Charon, J. M. (2009). *Symbolic Interactionism: An Introduction, an Interpretation, an Integration*. Cambridge: Pearson.

Cheryl, S. and Henry Jay, B. (1978). The use of vignettes in survey research. *The Public Opinion Quarterly, 42*(1), 93–104.

Cindi, J. (2005). Tackling prostitution around the UK. *BBC News*, 27 January. Online. Available at: http://news.bbc.co.uk/1/hi/uk/4212115.stm (accessed 28 January 2005).

City News (2006). West End residents complain about prostitutes at town hall meeting. *City News*, 27 September. Online. Available at: www.citytv.com/toronto/citynews/news/local/article/23522–west-end-residents-complain-about-prostitutes-at-town-hall-meeting (accessed 17 June 2009).

Clark, P., Bellis, M. A., Cook, P. A. and Tocque, K. (2004). *Consultation on a Managed Zone for Sex Trade Workers in Liverpool: Views from Residents, Businesses and Sex Trade Workers in the City of Liverpool: Executive Summary*. Liverpool: Centre for Public Health, Faculty of Health and Applied Social Sciences, Liverpool John Moores University.

Clarke, J. (2004). New Labour's citizens: Activated, empowered, responsibilized, abandoned? *Critical Social Policy, 25*(4), 447–463.

Clarke, R. (2002). Closing streets and alleys to reduce crime: Should you go down this road? Problem-orientated guides for police, response guide no. 2. *Community Orientated Policing Services*. Online. Available at: www.cops.usdoj.gov/mime/open.pdf?Item=1346 (accessed 24 January 2011).

Clarke, R. (2005). Seven misconceptions of situational crime prevention. In N. Tilley (ed.), *Handbook of Crime Prevention and Community Safety*. Cullumpton: Willan, 39–70.

Clarkson, A. (1939). History of prostitution. *The Canadian Medical Association Journal, 41*(3), 296–301.

Coaker, V. (2008). Immigration House of Commons Hansard written answers for 29 January 2008 (pt. 0006). Column 210W. *United Kingdom Parliament*, 29 January. Online. Available at: www.publications.parliament.uk/pa/cm200708/cmhansrd/cm080129/text/80129w0006.htm (accessed 30 January 2008).

Cohen, A. (1985). *The Symbolic Construction of Community*. London: Routledge.

Cohen, D. and Strayer, J. (1996). Empathy in conduct-disordered and comparison youth. *Developmental Psychology, 32*, 988–998.

Coker, E. M. (2005). Selfhood and social distance: Toward a cultural understanding of psychiatric stigma in Egypt. *Social Science & Medicine, 61*(5), 920–930.

Collier, J. and Collier, M. (1986). *Visual Anthropology: Photography as a Research Method*. Albuquerque: University of New Mexico Press.

Colosi, R. (2010). 'Just get pissed and enjoy yourself': Understanding lap-dancing as 'anti-work'. In K. Hardy, S. Kingston and T. Sanders (eds), *New Sociologies of Sex Work*. Surrey: Ashgate, 181–198.

Cotton, A., Farley, M. and Barton, R. (2000). Attitudes toward prostitution and acceptance of rape myths. *Journal of Applied Social Psychology, 32*(9), 1790–1796.

Cowburn, M. and Dominelli, L. (2001). Masking hegemonic masculinity: Reconstructing the paedophile as the dangerous stranger. *British Journal of Social Work Research, 31*(3), 399–415.

Coy, M., Horvath, M. and Kelly, L. (2007). *'It's Just Like Going to the Supermarket': Men Buying Sex in East London*. London: Child & Women Abuse Studies Unit and Centre for Independent Research, Training, Consultancy and Networking, London Metropolitan University.

Crawford, A. (1994). The partnership approach to community crime prevention: Corporatism at the local level. *Social & Legal Studies, 3*(4), 497–519.

Crawford, A. (1997). *The Local Governance of Crime: Appeals to Community and Partnerships*. Oxford: Clarendon Press.

Crawford, A. (1998). *Crime Prevention and Community Safety: Politics, Policies and Practices*. London: Longman.

Crawford, A. (2003). The pattern of policing in the UK: Policing beyond the police. In T. Newburn (ed.), *The Handbook of Policing*. Devon: Willan Publishing, 136–168.

Cresswell, T. (1997). Weeds, plagues and bodily secretions: A geographic interpretation of metaphors of displacement. *Annals of the Association of American Geographers, 87*, 336–345.

Crime Stoppers (2006). Dodgy punters. *Crime Stoppers*, 22 August. Online. Available at: www.crimestoppers-uk.org/solving/campaignsandinitiatives/dodgypunters/ (accessed 12 April 2007).

Crime Stoppers (2008). Walk in a punter: Walk out a rapist. *Crime Stoppers*, 6 May.

Online. Available at: www.crimestoppers-uk.org/media-centre/crime-in-the-news/may-2008–crime-in-the-news/walk-in-a-punter-walk-out-a-rapist (accessed 4 October 2008).

Crocker, J., Major, B. and Steele, C. (1998). Social stigma. In L. Gardner, D. Gilbert and S. T. Fiske (eds), *The Handbook of Social Psychology: Volume II* (4th edition). New York: Oxford University Press, 504–553.

Croucher, S. (2003). *Globalization and Belonging: The Politics of Identity in a Changing World*. New York: Rowman and Littlefield Publishers.

Curry, T. J. (2002). Fraternal bonding in the locker room: A profeminist analysis of talk about competition and women. In S. Scraton and A. Flintoff (eds), *Gender and Sport: A Reader*. London: Routledge, 169–187.

Cusick, L. and Berney, L. (2005). Prioritizing punitive responses over public health: Commentary on the Home Office consultation document *Paying the Price*. *Critical Social Policy*, 25(4), 596–606.

Dahles, H. and Bras, K. (1999). Entrepreneurs in romance tourism in Indonesia. *Annals of Tourism Research*, 26(2), 267–293.

Daily Echo (2006). Putting a stop to kerb crawling. *Daily Echo*, 18 January. Online. Available at: http://archive.dailyecho.co.uk/2006/1/18/97813.html (accessed 15 June 2008).

de Albuquerque, K. (1998). Sex, beach boys, and female tourists in the Caribbean. *Sexuality and Culture*, 2(1), 87–112.

de Bruxelles, S. (2007). Punter escapes kerb-crawling charge because he had a bike. *The Times*, 1 March. Online. Available at: www.timesonline.co.uk/tol/news/uk/crime/article1454673.ece (accessed 21 May 2008).

Della Giusta, M., Di Tommaso, M. and Strøm, S. (2008). *Sex Markets: The Denied Industry*. London: Routledge.

Devine-Wright, P. and Clayton, S. (2010). Introduction to the special issue: Place, identity and environmental behaviour. *Journal of Environmental Psychology*, 30(3), 267–270.

Dodge, M., Starr-Gimeno, D. and Williams, T. (2005). Puttin' on the sting: Women police officers' perspectives on reverse prostitution assignments. *International Journal of Police Science and Management*, 7(2), 71–85.

Douglas, M. (2002). *Purity and Danger: An Analysis of Concept of Pollution and Taboo*. London: Routledge.

Dovkants, K. (2009). Soho brothel to re-open after judge throws out police case. *London Evening Standard*, 18 February. Online. Available at: www.thisislondon.co.uk/standard/article-23646265-soho-brothel-to-re-open-after-judge-throws-out-police-case.d (accessed 3 December 2009).

Duncan, N. (1996). Introduction: (Re)placings. In N. Duncan (ed.), *Body Space: Destabilizing Geographies of Gender and Sexuality*. London: Routledge, 1–12.

Durkheim, E. (1893). *The Division of Labor in Society*. Cambridge: The Free Press; Reprint edition (25 August 1997).

Dynes, W. R. (1990). Prostitution. In Wayne R. Dynes (ed.), *Encyclopedia of Homosexuality (Vol. 2)*. Chicago: St. James Press, 1054–1058.

Eagleton, T. (1994). *Ideology: An Introduction*. London: Verso Books.

Earle, S. and Sharp, K. (2008). Intimacy, pleasure and the men who pay for sex. In G. Letherby, K. Williams, P. Birch and M. Cain (eds), *Sex as Crime*. Cullumpton: Willan Publishing, 63–79.

Echo (2001a). Southend: Kerb crawlers charged after police crackdown. *The Echo*,

11 June. Online. Available at: http://archive.echo-news.co.uk/2001/6/11/180392.html (accessed 15 June 2008).
Echo (2001b). Southend: Vice girls arrested in police operation. *The Echo*, 9 September. Online. Available at: http://archive.echo-news.co.uk/2001/9/9/174669.html (accessed 15 June 2008).
Edelstein, J. (1988). In the massage parlor. In F. Delacoste and P. Alexander (eds), *Sex Work: Writings by Women in the Sex Industry*. London: Virago, 62–69.
Edelstein, J. (2007). Why second-wave feminism has gone soft. *Public Policy Research*, 14(3), 164–167.
Edensor, T. (2002). *National Identity, Popular Culture and Everyday Life*. Oxford: Berg Publishers.
Edwards, A. and Hughes, G. (2002). Introduction: The community governance of crime control. In A. Edwards and G. Hughes (eds), *Crime Control and Community: The New Politics of Public Safety*. Cullompton: Willan Publishing, 1–19.
Edwards, R. (2005). Street legal: City's shock plan for official red light zone. *Yorkshire Evening Post*, 17 February 2005.
Edwards, R. (2006). Is this the Ripper's fourth victim? *London Evening Standard*, 31 July 2006.
Edwards, S. M. (1991). Prostitution, whose problem? *Final Report to Wolverhampton Safer Cities Project*. Buckingham: University of Buckingham.
Elifson, K. W., Boles, J. and Sweat, M. (1993a). Risk factors associated with HIV infection among male prostitutes. *American Journal of Public Health*, 83(1), 79–83.
Elifson, K. W., Boles, J., Posey, E., Sweat, M., Darrow, W. and Elsea, W. (1993b). Male transvestite prostitutes and HIV risk. *American Journal of Public Health*, 83(2), 260–262.
Etzioni, A. (1995). *The Spirit of Community: Rights, Responsibilities and the Communitarian Agenda*. London: Fontana Press.
Evening Star (2007). Ipswich left out of kerb crawling scheme. *Evening Star*, 15 May. Online. Available at: www.eveningstar.co.uk/content/eveningstar/news/story.aspx?brand=ESTOnline&category=murders&tBrand=ESTOnline&tCategory=murders&itemid=IPED14%20May%202007%2014%3A39%3A36%3A657 (accessed 18 May 2007).
Farley, M. (2001). Prostitution: The business of sexual exploitation. In J. Worell (ed.), *Encyclopaedia of Women and Gender: Sex Similarities and Differences and the Impact of Society and Gender*. San Diego: Academic Press, 879–892.
Farley, M. and Kelly, V. (2000). Prostitution: A critical review of the medical and social sciences literature. *Women and Criminal Justice*, 11(4), 29–64.
Favell, A. (1999). To belong or not to belong: The postnational question. In A. Geddes and A. Favell (eds), *The Politics of Belonging: Migrants and Minorities in Contemporary Europe*. Aldershot: Ashgate, 209–227.
Field, J. (2009). Some Burton residents still unhappy over prostitutes roaming South Dort Highway. *The Flint Journal*, 27 June. Online. Available at: www.mlive.com/news/flint/index.ssf/2009/06/some_burton_residents_still_un.html (accessed 3 August 2009).
Fielding, N. (2005). Concepts and theory in community policing. *The Howard Journal*, 44(5), 460–472.
Flick, U. (2002). *An Introduction to Qualitative Research*. London: Sage.
Flint, J. and Nixon, J. (2006). Governing neighbours: Anti-social behaviour orders and new forms of regulating conduct in the UK. *Urban Studies*, 43(5), 939–955.
Ford, K., Wirawan, N. and Fajans, P. (1993). AIDS knowledge, condom beliefs and sexual behaviour among male sex workers and male tourist clients in Bali, Indonesia. *Health Transition Review*, 3(2), 191–204.

Fotiou, R. D., MacKinnon, R., Muntu, G., O'Neill, L., Pickering, J., Ponsonby, A., Smitheman, M., Edwards, S., Williment, S. and Ward, J. (2007). Religious mapping of Chapeltown 2007. Online. Available: www.google.co.uk/url?sa=t&rct=j&q=&esrc=s&source=web&cd=1&ved=0CC8QFjAA&url=http%3A%2F%2Fwww.leeds.ac.uk%2Farts%2Fdownload%2F823%2Freligious_mapping-chapeltown&ei=cvPCUdOtOcSM4ATq2oCQAg&usg=AFQjCNFk9Cp3H6RKpNRX4MHi79niJkjrdQ&bvm=bv.48175248,d.bGE (accessed 20 June 2013).

Foucault, M. (1972). *The Archaeology of Knowledge*. New York: Vintage Books.

Foucault, M. (1977). *Discipline and Punish: The Birth of the Prison*. Harmondsworth: Penguin.

Foucault, M. (1978). *The History of Sexuality, Vol. 1: An Introduction*. New York: Vintage Books.

Foucault, M. (1988). What is an author? In P. Rabinow (ed.), *Aesthetics, Method, and Epistemology*. New York: The New Press, 113–138.

Fox, J., Tideman, R. L., Gilmour, S., Marks, C., van Beek, I. and Mindel, A. (2006). Sex work practices and condom use in female sex workers in Sydney. *International Journal of STD & AIDS, 17*(5), 319–323.

Fremeaux, I. (2005). New Labour's appropriation of the concept of community: a critique. *Community Development Journal, 40*(3), 265–274.

Freund, M., Lee, N. and Leonard, T. (1991). Sexual behaviour of clients with street prostitutes in Camden, New Jersey. *The Journal of Sex Research, 28*(4), 579–591.

Freund, M., Leonard, T. and Lee, N. (1989). Sexual behavior of resident street prostitutes with their clients in Camden, New Jersey. *The Journal of Sex Research, 26*(4), 460–478.

Friedman, M. (1995). Feminism and modern friendship: Dislocating the community. In Penny A. Weiss and M. Friedman (eds), *Feminism and Community*. Philadelphia: Temple University Press, 187–208.

Gabor, T. (1981). The crime displacement hypothesis: An empirical examination. *Crime and Deliquency, 27*(3), 390–404.

Garland, D. (2001). *The Culture of Control: Crime and Social Order in Contemporary Society*. Oxford: Oxford University Press.

Gates, J. (2008). Prostitution 'on the way back' despite closure of brothel. *Ealing Gazette*, 29 August. Online. Available at: www.ealinggazette.co.uk/ealing-news/local-ealing-news/2008/08/29/prostitution-on-the-way-back-despite-closure-of-brothel-64767-21628319/ (accessed 17 June 2009).

Gemme, R. (1993). Prostitution: A legal, criminological, and sexological perspective. *Canadian Journal of Human Sexuality, 1*(4), 217–220.

Gibbens, T. C. N. and Silverman, M. (1960). The clients of prostitutes. *British Journal of Veneral Disease, 36*(2), 113–117.

Gibbs, A. (1997). Focus groups. *Social Research Update, 19*(Winter). Online. Available at: www.soc.surrey.ac.uk/sru/SRU19.html (accessed 30 June 2005).

Giddens, A. (1992). *The Transformation of Intimacy*. Cambridge: Polity.

Giobbe, E. (1993). An analysis of individual, institutional, and cultural pimping. *Michigan Journal of Gender and Law, 1*(1), 33–57.

Goddard, L. (2004). Midlands: prostitution. *BBC News*, 18 November. Online. Available at: http://news.bbc.co.uk/1/hi/programmes/politics_show/4022055.stm (accessed 20 October 2008).

Goffman, E. (1963). *Stigma: Notes on the Management of Spoiled Identity*. New Jersey: Prentice-Hall.

176 Bibliography

Goodyear, M. D. E. and Cusick, L. (2007). Protection of sex workers: Decriminalisation could restore public health priorities and human rights. *British Medical Journal*, 334, 52–53.

Government News Network (2007). The Real Price of Sex. *Government News Network*, 14 May. Online. Available at: www.gnn.gov.uk/Content/Detail.asp?ReleaseID=284016&NewsAreaID=2 (accessed 12 May 2007).

Gräbener, J., Jing, L., Mukerjee, M. and Varin, V. (2010) Fostering dialogue: Addressing community tensions towards prostitution in Lyon. *Humanity in Action*. Online. Available at: www.humanityinaction.org/knowledgebase/327-fostering-dialogue-addressing-community-tensions-towards-prostitution-in-lyon (accessed 20 June 2013).

Greer, C. and Jewkes, Y. (2004). Extremes of otherness: Media images of social exclusion. *Social Justice: A Journal of Crime, Conflict and World Order*, 32(1), 20–31.

Groom, T. M. and Nandwani, R. (2006). Characteristics of men who pay for sex: A UK sexual health clinic survey. *Sexually Transmitted Infections*, 82(5), 364–367.

Guardian (2006). Tolerance zones plan in tatters. *Guardian*, 14 December. Online. Available at: www.guardian.co.uk/uk/2006/dec/14/suffolkmurders (accessed 14 December 2006).

Gülçür, Leyla and İlkkaracan, Pinar. (2002). The 'Natasha' experience: Migrant sex workers from the former Soviet Union and Eastern Europe in Turkey. *Women's Studies International Forum*, 25(4), 411–421.

Gutierrez, J. P., Molina-Yepz, D., Samuels, F. and Bertozzi, S. M. (2006). Inconsistent condom use among sexual workers in Ecuador: Results from a behavior survey. *Salud Publica de Mexico*, 48(2), 104–122.

Hale, S. (2006). *Blair's Community: Communitarian Thought and New Labour*. Manchester: Manchester University Press.

Hall, Stuart. (1980). Reformism and the legislation of consent. In J. Clarke and M. Fitzgeralds (eds), *Permissiveness and Control: The Fate of the Sixties Legislation*. London: Macmillan, 1–43.

Hamilton, F. (2000a). Crime and prostitution (Leeds). *Hansard Committee Debate*, 19 December 2000 vol 360 cc47–54WH.

Hamilton, F. (2000b). HANSARD 1804–2004 Westminster Hall Sitting: Crime and Prostitution (Leeds) London: 12.30pm. 19 December. Online. Available at: http://hansard.millbanksystems.com/westminster_hall/2000/dec/19/crime-and-prostitution-leeds (accessed 17 June 2008).

Hamilton, P. (1985). Editor's foreword. In P. Hamilton (ed.), *The Symbolic Construction of Community*. London: Routledge, 7–9.

Hammond, N. (2010a). *Paying for Sex: A Socio-Cultural Exploration of Sexual Commerce*. Unpublished doctoral thesis, University of Sheffield, Sheffield.

Hammond, N. (2010b). Tackling taboos: Men who pay for sex and the emotional researcher. In K. Hardy, S. Kingston and T. Sanders (eds), *New Sociologies of Sex Work*. Surrey: Ashgate, 59–74.

Hammond, N. and Kingston, S. (Forthcoming). Experiencing stigma as sex work researchers in professional and personal lives. *Sexualities*.

Hamnett, C. (1984). Gentrification and residential locational theory: A review and assessment. In D. T. Herbert and R. J. Johnston (eds), *Geography and the Urban Environment. Progress in Research and Applications*. London: John Wiley, 283–320.

Hancock, L. (2001). *Communities, Crime and Disorder: Safety and Regeneration in Urban Neighbourhoods*. Basingstoke: Palgrave.

Harcourt, C. and Donovan, B. (2005). The many faces of sex work. *Sexually Transmitted Infections*, *81*(3), 201–206.

Harcourt, C., Beek, I., Heslop, J., McMahon, M. and Donovan, B. (2001). The health and welfare needs of female and transgender street sex workers in New South Wales. *Australian and New Zealand Journal of Public Health*, *25*(1), 84–89.

Hardy, K. (2010). 'If you shut up, they will kill you': Sex work resistance in Argentina. In K. Hardy, S. Kingston and T. Sanders (ed.), *New Sociologies of Sex Work*. Surrey: Ashgate Publishing Limited, 167–180.

Hare, B. (2006). A life in brown and white. *The Guardian*, 25 January 2006.

Harman, H. (2007). Harman on outlawing sex trade. *BBC News, Radio Four*, 20 December.

Harrison, S. (2010). Sex workers win certain unfair dismissal rights. *International Law Office*, 16 June. Online. Available at: www.internationallawoffice.com/newsletters/detail.aspx?g=a1293fda-9b88-4891-95a5-c5fe94c55292 (accessed 5 August 2011).

Harvey, P. (2001). Doctor caught kerb crawling. *Liverpool Echo*, 6 March. Online. Available at: www.liverpoolecho.co.uk/liverpool-news/local-news/2001/03/06/doctor-caught-kerb-crawling-100252-7554583/ (accessed 15 June 2008).

Haslam, D. (2004). Action plan all set to clean up streets. *Rochdale Observer*, 3 August. Online. Available at: www.rochdaleobserver.co.uk/news/index/articles/article-id=20988.html (accessed 23 July 2006).

Hausbeck, K., Brents, B. G. and Jackson, C. (2006). Sex industry and sex workers in Nevada. In D. Shalin (ed.), *Social Health of Nevada: Leading Indicators and Quality of Life*. University of Nevada, Las Vegas: Center for Democratic Culture Publications. Online. Available at: http://cdclv.unlv.edu//mission/index2.html (accessed 12 June 2012).

Hawtin, M., Hughes, G. and Percy-Smith, J. (1994). *Community Profiling: Auditing Social Needs*. Buckingham: Open University Press.

Hay, C. (1995). Mobilization through interpellation: James Bulger, juvenile crime and the construction of a moral panic. *Social & Legal Studies*, *6*(4), 197–223.

Hazel, N. (1995). Elicitation techniques with young people. *Social Research Update*, *12*(Winter), 105–114. Online. Available at: http://sru.soc.surrey.ac.uk/SRU12.html (accessed 20 June 2013).

Heater, D. (1991). Citizenship: A remarkable case of sudden interest. *Parliamentary Affairs*, *44*(2), 140–156.

Helmore, Edward. (1995). Prostitute delivers a blow to Hugh Grant's image. *Independent*, 28 June. Online. Available at: www.independent.co.uk/news/uk/prostitute-delivers-a-blow-to-hugh-grants-image-1588621.html (accessed 21 May 2009).

Helsingin Sanomat (2000). Street prostitution clearly disturbed Helsinki residents before clean-up. *Helsingin Sanomat, International Edition*, 1 November. Online. Available at: www2.hs.fi/english/archive/news.asp?id=20001101IE5 (accessed 17 June 2009).

Her Majesty's Crown Prosecution Service Inspectorate (2007). Without consent: A report on the joint review of the investigation and prosecution of rape offences. *HMIC*, 31 December 2006. Online. Available at: http://inspectorates.homeoffice.gov.uk/hmic/inspections/thematic/wc-thematic/them07-wc.pdf?view=Binary (accessed 4 February 2008).

Herbert, S. (2001). Policing the contemporary city: Fixing broken windows or shoring up neo-liberalism? *Theoretical Criminology*, *5*(4), 445–466.

Herold, E., Garcia, R. and DeMoya, T. (2001). Female tourists and beach boys: Romance or Sex Tourism? *Annals of Tourism Research*, *28*(4), 978–997.

Bibliography

Heslett, C. (2006). Banned From vice zone: Court slaps Asbo on man who is accused of ferrying prostitutes into city's red light area. *Yorkshire Evening Post*, 27 April. Online. Available at: www.leedstoday.net/ViewArticle2.aspx?SectionID=39&ArticleID=1469 146 (accessed 18 May 2007).

Hester, M. and Westmarland, N. (2004). *Tackling Street Prostitution: Towards an holistic approach*. London: Home Office.

Hill, M. (1997). Research review: Participatory research with children, child and family social work. *Family Social Work, 2*, 171–183.

Hirst, P. (2000). Statism, pluralism and social control. In D. Garland and R. Sparks (eds), *Criminology and Social Theory*. Oxford: Oxford University Press, 127–148.

Hiscock, John. (1995). Hugh Grant on prostitute charge. *The Telegraph*, 28 June. Online. Available at: www.telegraph.co.uk/news/1471976/Hugh-Grant-on-prostitute-charge.htm (accessed 21 May 2009).

Holloway, W. and Jefferson, T. (1997). The risk society in an age of anxiety: Situating the fear of crime. *British Journal of Sociology, 48*(2), 255–266.

Home Office (1959). *Street Offences Act 1959*. London: HMSO. Online. Available at: www.opsi.gov.uk/RevisedStatutes/Acts/ukpga/1959/cukpga_19590057_en_1 (accessed 12 May 2006).

Home Office (1972). *Local Government Act 1972*. London: HMSO.

Home Office (1984). *The Police and Criminal Evidence Act*. London: HMSO. Online. Available at: www.legislation.gov.uk/ukpga/1984/60/contents (accessed 2 June 2012).

Home Office (1985). *Sexual Offences Act 1985*. London: HMSO. Online. Available at: www.together.gov.uk/article.asp?aid=1812&c=121 (accessed 17 June 2006).

Home Office (1998a). *Crime and Disorder Act*. London: The Stationary Office. Online. Available at: http://opsi.gov.uk/acts/acts1998/19980037.html (accessed 4 May 2006).

Home Office (1998b). *Home Office Leaflet, A Review of Sex Offences*. London: HMSO, The Stationary Office Group Ltd.

Home Office (2000). *Setting the Boundaries: Reforming the Law on Sex Offences*. London: HMSO.

Home Office (2001). *The Cantle Report – Community Cohesion: A Report of the Independent Review Team*. London: HMSO. Online. Available at: http://resources.cohesioninstitute.org.uk/Publications/Documents/Document/Default.aspx?recordId=96 (accessed 3 May 2012).

Home Office (2002). *Nationality, Immigration and Asylum Act*. London: HMSO. Online. Available at: www.opsi.gov.uk/Acts/acts2002/ukpga_20020041_en_1 (accessed 21 November 2008).

Home Office (2003). *Sexual Offences Act*. London: HMSO. Online. Available at: www.opsi.gov.uk/ACTS/acts2003/20030042.htm (accessed 7 September 2007).

Home Office (2004a). *Asylum and Immigration Act*. London: HMSO. Online. Available at: www.opsi.gov.uk/ACTS/acts2004/ukpga_20040019_en_1 (accessed 22 November 2008).

Home Office (2004b). *Paying the Price: A Consultation Paper on Prostitution: Home Office Communication Directorate. July 2004*. London: HMSO.

Home Office (2004c). Unique scheme to crack drug-crime is launched in Bradford. *Home Office*. Online. Available at: http://press.homeoffice.gov.uk/press-releases/Unique_Scheme_To_Crack_Drug-Crim?version=1 (accessed 10 December 2007).

Home Office (2006). *A Coordinated Prostitution Strategy and a Summary of Responses to Paying the Price*. London: HMSO.

Home Office (2007a). Campaign to deter kerb crawling. *Home Office*. Online. Available

Bibliography 179

at: www.homeoffice.gov.uk/documents/kerb-crawling-marketing-material/ (accessed 5 January 2008).

Home Office (2007b). *Forced Marriage (Civil Protection) Act 2007*. London: HMSO. Online. Available at: www.legislation.gov.uk/ukpga/2007/20/contents (accessed 2 June 2012).

Home Office (2007c). The new Home Office: Protecting the public, securing our future. *Home Office*. Online. Available at: www.homeoffice.gov.uk/about-us/news/new-home-office (accessed 19 December 2007).

Home Office (2007d). Tackling Kerb Crawlers. Online. Available at: www.respect.gov.uk/members/article.aspx?id=7666 (accessed 11 June 2008).

Home Office (2007e). *UK Action Plan on Tackling Human Trafficking*. London: HMSO.

Home Office (2008a). Impact assessment of removing requirements of persistence from the offences of kerb-crawling and persistent soliciting. *Home Office*. Online. Available at: www.homeoffice.gov.uk/documents/ia-police-crime-bill-08/ia-kerb-crawling?view=Binary (accessed 3 May 2009).

Home Office (2008b). Tackling demand For prostitution review begins with Sweden visit. *Home Office*. Online. Available at: http://press.homeoffice.gov.uk/press-releases/Tackling-Demand-For-Prostitution (accessed 30 September 2008).

Home Office (2008c). *Tackling Demand For Prostitution: A Review*. London: HMSO.

Home Office (2009a). Equality impact assessment: Provisions to tackle the demand for prostitution in the Policing and Crime Bill. *Home Office*. Online. Available at: www.homeoffice.gov.uk/documents/ia-police-crime-bill-08/ia-prostitution-tackling-demand?view=Binary (accessed 3 May 2009).

Home Office (2009b). *Policing and Crime Act 2009*. London: HMSO.

Howell, P., Beckingham, D. and Moore, F. (2008). Managed zones for sex workers in Liverpool: Contemporary proposals, Victorian parallels. *Transactions of the Institute of British Geographers, 33*(2), 233–250.

Hubbard, P. (1997). Red-light districts and toleration zones: Geographies of female street prostitution in England and Wales. *Area, 29*(2), 129–140.

Hubbard, P. (1998a). Community action and the displacement of street prostitution: Evidence from British cities. *Geoforum, 29*(3), 269–286.

Hubbard, P. (1998b). Sexuality, immorality and the city: Red-light districts and the marginalisation of female street prostitutes. *Gender, Place and Culture – A Journal of Feminist Geography, 5*(1), 55–76.

Hubbard, P. (2001). Sex zones: Intimacy, citizenship and public space. *Sexualities, 4*(1), 51–71.

Hubbard, P. (2004). Revenge and injustice in the neoliberal city: Uncovering masculinist agendas. *Antipode, 36*(4), 665–686.

Hubbard, P. (2006a). Cleansing the Metropolis: sex work and the politics of zero tolerance. In A. Collins (ed.), *Cities of Pleasure*. London: Routledge, 57–72.

Hubbard, P. (2006b). *City*. London: Sage.

Hubbard, P. (2006c). Out of touch and out of time? The contemporary policing of sex work. In R. Campbell and M. O'Neill (eds), *Sex Work Now*. Cullompton: Willan Publishing, 1–32.

Hubbard, P. (2011). *Cities and Sexualities*. London: Routledge.

Hubbard, P. (2012). Initial findings: sexual entertainment venues and managing risk. *Economic and Social Research Council*. Online. Available at: www.esrc.ac.uk/my-esrc/grants/ES.J002755.1/outputs/read/228e6fd6-bfd4-4866-b0c5-bca112752a6d (accessed 10 January 2013).

Bibliography

Hubbard, P. (2013). *Lap Dancing Study*. Paper presented at the Social Sciences Seminar Series, Leeds Metropolitan University, 14 May 2013, Leeds.

Hubbard, P. and Sanders, T. (2003). Making space for sex work: Female street prostitution and the production of urban space. *International Journal of Urban and Regional Research, 27*(1), 73–87.

Hubbard, P., Campbell, R., O'Neill, M. and Scoular, J. (2007). Prostitution, gentrification, and the limits of neighbourhood space. In R. Atkinson and G. Helms (eds), *Securing an Urban Renaissance: Crime, Community, and British Urban Policy*. Bristol: Policy Press, 203–218.

Hughes, G. (1998). *Understanding Crime Prevention: Social Control, Risk and Late Modernity*. Buckingham: Open University Press.

Hughes, G. (2008). Bolton responds to public demand for tough action on street sex trade. *Bolton Community Safety Services*. Online. Available at: http://webarchive.nationalarchives.gov.uk/20100413151430/asb.homeoffice.gov.uk/members/case-studies/article.aspx?id=12482 (accessed 23 August 2011).

Hughes, R. and Huby, M. (2004). The construction and interpretation of vignettes in social research. *Social Work & Social Sciences Review, 11*(1), 36–51.

Hussain, Y. and Bagguley, P. (2005). Citizenship, ethnicity and identity: British Pakistanis after the 2001 'riots'. *Sociology, 39*(3), 407–425.

Hylton, C. (1999). *African-Caribbean Community Organisations: The Search for Individual and Group Identity*. Stoke-on-Trent: Trentham books.

Imrie, R. and Raco, M. (2003). New Labour and the turn to community regeneration. In R. Imrie and M. Raco (eds), *Urban Renaissance? New Labour, Community and Urban Policy*. London: Polity Press, 3–36.

India eNews (2009). Local residents bust prostitution racket in Delhi. *India e News*, 29 October. Online. Available at: www.indiaenews.com/print/?id=228735 (accessed 23 June 2010).

Jaccarino, M. (2009). City Island residents push cops to make prostitution busts. *New York Daily News*, 14 July. Online. Available at: www.nydailynews.com/ny_local/bronx/2009/07/14/2009-07-14_city_island_residents_push_cops_to_make_prostitution_busts.html (accessed 17 June 2009).

Jacobs, J. (1961). *The Death and Life of Great American Cities*. New York: Vintage.

Jakobsson, N. and Kotsadam, A. (2011). Gender equity and prostitution: An investigation of attitudes in Norway and Sweden. *Feminist Economics, 17*(1), 31–58.

Jansson, K. (2006). Black and minority ethnic groups' experiences and perceptions of crime, racially motivated crime and the police: findings from the 2004/05 *British Crime Survey*. *Home Office*. Online. Available at: www.homeoffice.gov.uk/rds/pdfs06/rdsolr2506.pdf (accessed 4 January 2007).

Jansson, K., Budd, S., Lovbakke, J., Moley, S. and Thorpe, K. (2007). *Home Office Statistical Bulletin: Attitudes, Perceptions and Risks of Crime: Supplementary Volume 1 to Crime in England and Wales 2006/07*. London: The Stationary Office.

Jeffreys, S. (1997). *The Idea of Prostitution*. Melbourne: Sphinifex Press.

Jeffreys, S. (2009). *The Industrial Vagina: The Political Economy of the Global Sex Trade*. London: Routledge.

Jenness, V. (1993). *Making it Work*. New York: Aldine Transaction.

Johnson, A. M., Mercer, C. H., Erens, B., Copas, A., McManus, S., Wellings, K., Fenton, K. A., Korovessis, C., Macdowall, W., Nanchahal, K., Purdon, S. and Field, J. (2001). Sexual behaviour in Britain: Partnerships, practices, and HIV risk behaviours. *Lancet, 358*, 1835–1842.

Johnson, A., Wadsworth, J., Wellings, K. and Field, J. (1994). *Sexual Attitudes and Lifestyles*. London: Blackwell.

Johnston, J. (1988). Out in the cold. In F. Delacoste and P. Alexander (eds), *Sex Work: Writings by Women in the Sex Industry*. London: Virago Press, 29–31.

Johnston, L. (1996). What is Vigilantism? *British Journal of Criminology, 36*(2), 220–236.

Jones, J. (2009). Street sex: Islington residents may sue. *The Herald*, 5 March. Online. Available at: www.theherald.com.au/news/local/news/general/street-sex-islington-residents-may-sue/1450516.aspx (accessed 17 June 2009).

Jones, P., Shears, P. and Hillier, D. (2003). Retailing and the regulatory state: A case study of lap dancing clubs in the UK. *International Journal of Retail & Distribution Management, 31*(4), 214–219.

Jones, T. (2009). Policing. In C. Hale, K. Hayward, A. Wahidin and E. Wincup (eds), *Criminology* (2nd edn). Oxford: Oxford University Press.

Jones, T. and Newburn, T. (1998). *Private Security and Public Policing*. Oxford: Clarendon Press.

Jones, T. and Newburn, T. (2002). The transformation of policing?: Understanding current trends in policing systems. *British Journal of Criminology, 42*(1), 129–146.

Jordan, J. (1997). User pays: Why men buy sex. *Australian and New Zealand Journal of Criminology, 30*(1), 55–71.

Judge Simon Lawler QC (2007). *Judgement: Regina v John Barrett and Others*. Sheffield Crown Court. 23 February. Sheffield.

Justice System – Public Attitudes and Perceptions. London: Home Office Research and Statistics Directorate, 65–73.

Kaminer, W. (1990). *A Fearful Freedom: Women's Flight from Equality*. Reading: Addison Wesley Longman Publishing Co.

Kantola, J. and Squires, J. (2004). Discourses surrounding prostitution policies in the UK. *European Journal of Women's Studies, 11*(1), 77–101.

Kearns, A. (1995). Active citizenship and local governance: Political and geographical dimensions. *Political Geography, 14*(2), 155–175.

Kelly, L., Coy, M. and Davenport, R. (2009). Shifting sands: A comparison of prostitution regimes across nine countries. *Child and Women's Abuse Study Unit*. Online. Available at: www.uknswp.org/resources%5Chomeoffshiftingsandscoyetal09.pdf (accessed 5 August 2011).

Kennedy, M. A., Klein, C., Gorzalka, B. B. and Yuille, J. C. (2005). Attitude change following a diversion program for men who solicit sex. *Journal of Offender Rehabilitation, 40*(1–2), 41–60.

Kesler, K. (2002). Is a feminist stance in support of prostitution possible? An exploration of current trends. *Sexualities, 5*(2), 219–235.

Kilvington, J., Day, S. and Ward, H. (2001). Prostitution policy in Europe: A time of change? *Feminist Review, 67*(1), 78–93.

Kimmel, M. S. (1994). Masculinity as homophobia: Fear, shame, and silence in the construction of gender identity. In H. Brod and M. Kaufman (eds), *Theorizing Masculinities*. London: Sage, 119–141.

Kingston, S. (2010). Intent to criminalise: Men who buy sex and prostitution policy in the UK. In K. Hardy, S. Kingston and T. Sanders (eds), *New Sociologies of Sex Work*. Surrey: Ashgate, 23–38.

Kingston, S. and Sanders, T. (2010). Introduction: New sociologies of sex work in perspective. In K. Hardy, S. Kingston and T. Sanders (eds), *New Sociologies of Sex Work*. Surrey: Ashgate, 1–8.

Bibliography

Kinnell, H. (1989). *Prostitutes, their Clients and Risks of HIV Infection in Birmingham.* Birmingham: Department of Public Health Medicine, Central Birmingham Health Authority.

Kinnell, H. (2008). *Violence and Sex Work in Britain.* Cullumpton: Willan Publishing.

Kinsey, R., Lea, J. and Young, J. (1986). *Losing the Fight against Crime.* Oxford: Basil Blackwell.

Kirby, K. (1996). *Indifferent Boundaries: Spatial Concepts of Human Subjectivity.* London: Guilford Press.

Kitzinger, J. (1994). Focus groups: Methods or madness? In M. Boulton (ed.), *Research Methods.* London: Taylor and Francis, 159–175.

Koskela, H. and Tani, S. (2005). 'Sold out!' Women's practices of resistance against prostitution related sexual harassment. *Women's Studies International Forum, 28*(5), 418–429.

Kulick, D. (1998). *Travesti: Sex, Gender, and Culture among Brazilian Transgendered Prostitutes.* Chicago: University of Chicago Press.

Kurtz, S. P., Surratt, H. L., Inciardi, J. A. and Kiley, M. C. (2004). Sex work and 'date' violence. *Violence against Women, 10*(4), 357–385.

Lancashire Evening Post (2008). Cleaning up after the sex workers. *Lancashire Evening Post*, 7 May. Online. Available at: www.lep.co.uk/features/Cleaning-up-after-the-sex.4057303.jp (accessed 3 August 2009).

Langer, G., Arnedt, C. and Sussman, D. (2004). Poll: American sex survey: A peek beneath the sheets. *ABC News*, 21 October. Online. Available at: http://abcnews.go.com/Primetime/PollVault/Story?id=156921&page=1 (accessed 20 December 2008).

Lapadat, J. and Lindsay, A. (1999). Transcription in research and practice: From standardization of technique to interpretive positionings. *Qualitative Inquiry, 5*(1), 64–86.

Lawler, Steph. (2008). *Identity: Sociological Perspectives.* Cambridge: Polity.

Lawrence, J. and Aral, S. (2005). *The Dynamic Topology of Sex Work in Tallinn, Estonia: A Report of the Findings from a Rapid Assessment Conducted May 22–29 2005.* Atlanta: Division of Sexually Transmitted Diseases, Centers for Disease Control and Prevention.

Lazaridis, G. and Wickens, E. (1999). 'Us' and the 'others': Ethnic minorities in Greece. *Annals of Tourism Research, 26*(3), 632–655.

Leahey, E. (2004). The role of status in evaluating research: The case of data editing. *Social Science Research, 33*(3), 521–537.

Leahey, E., Entwisle, B. and Einaudi, P. (2003). Diversity in everyday research practice: The case of data editing. *Sociological Methods Research, 32*(1), 64–89.

Lee, A. K. and Craig-Henderson, K. M. (2005). Interethnic aggression and willingness to help: Judgements of black and white victims and perpetrators. *Social Behavior and Personality: An International Journal, 33*(5), 513–522.

Lee, R. (1993). *Doing Research on Sensitive Topics.* London: Sage.

Leeds City Council (2004). Area Statistics. Online. Available at: http://statistics.leeds.gov.uk/PDF_Downloads/Files/AKV05_PD_ALL.PDF (accessed 12 September 2006).

Leeds City Council (2005). Village crime fears allayed. *Holbeck Urban Village Newsletter*, January 2004. Online. Available at: www.leeds.gov.uk/files/2005/week17/inter__B10AE66D51AD874580256DFF0054F390_5414f1f3-a585–4331-a94f-12044c0f78bc.pdf (accessed 12 September 2006).

Leeds City Council (2007). *Prostitution Strategy for Leeds.* Online. Available at: www.leeds.gov.uk/moderngov/Published/C00000465/M00001109/AI00005882/$4hannahPROSTITUTIONSTRATEGYFORLEEDS.docA.ps.pdf (accessed 10 December 2007).

Leeds Community Safety Partnership Board (2004). Minutes of the meeting held on 19th August 2004. Online. Available at: www.leeds-csp.org.uk/files/Minutes19august04(1).doc. (accessed 12 September 2006).

Leeds Net (2004). Prostitution meeting a 'great success'. *Leeds Net*, 7 September. Online. Available at: www.leedsnet.com/gl/article.php?story=20040907131955229 (accessed 12 September 2006).

Leeson, P. T. (2008). Social distance and self-enforcing exchange. *Journal of Legal Studies*, *37*(1), 161–188.

Lewis, P. (2006). Police warn prostitutes to stay off the streets. *Guardian*, 12 December. Online. Available at: www.guardian.co.uk/uk/2006/dec/12/ukcrime.suffolkmurders1 (accessed 12 December 2006).

Lim, L. L. (1998). *The Sex Sector: The Economic and Social Bases of Prostitution in Southeast Asia*. Geneva: International Labour Office.

Link, B. G. and Phelan, J. C. (2001). Conceptualizing stigma. *Annual Review of Sociology*, *27*(1), 363–385.

Linnane, F. (2003). *A Thousand Years of Vice in the Capital: London the Wicked City*. London: Robson Books.

Liska, A., Lawrence, J. and Sanchirico, A. (1982). Fear of crime as a social fact. *Social Forces*, *60*(3), 760–770.

Lister, Billie M. (2012). Precarious labour and disposable bodies: The effects of cultural and economic change upon sexualised labour in lap-dancing venues in Scotland. Stirling: University of Stirling.

Loader, I. (2000). Plural policing and democratic governance. *Social & Legal Studies*, *9*(3), 323–345.

Lonsway, K. and Fitzgerald, L. (1994). Rape myths: In review. *Psychology of Women Quarterly*, *18*, 133–164.

Lopez-Jones, N. (1990). Guilty until proven innocent. *New Law Journal*, *140*, 658–659.

Lord Williams of Mostyn (1999). Sex offences: Review. *Hansard, House of Lords Debates, 25 January 1999, Volume 596, cc127–8WA*. Online. Available at: http://hansard.millbanksystems.com/written_answers/1999/jan/25/sex-offences-review (accessed 4 April 2008).

Lorway, R., Reza-Paul, S. and Pasha, A. (2009). On becoming a male sex worker in Mysore. *Medical Anthropology Quarterly*, *23*(2), 142–160.

Lowman, J. (2000). Violence and the outlaw status of (street) prostitution in Canada. *Violence against Women*, *6*(9), 987–1011.

Luken, J. N., Dobbs, R. R. and del Carmen, A. (2006). Vehicle cues and perceptions of driver characteristics: A comparative analysis of police officers and college students. *The Southwest Journal of Criminal Justice*, *3*(2), 127–147.

MacKinnon, C. (1989). *Towards a Feminist Theory of the State*. London: Harvard University Press.

MacQueen, K. M., McLellan, E., Metzger, D. S., Kegeles, S., Strauss, R. P., Scotti, R., Blanchard, L. and Trotter R. T. (2001). What is community? An evidence-based definition for participatory public health. *American Journal of Public Health*, *91*(12), 1929–1938.

Mahmoud, H. and Martsin, M. (2012). Never 'at-home': Migrants between societies. In J. Valsiner (ed.), *The Oxford Handbook of Culture and Psychology*. Oxford: Oxford University Press, 730–748.

Mail Online. (2005). Hugh to be hung for prostitute shame. *Mail Online*, 29 June. Online. Available at: www.dailymail.co.uk/tvshowbiz/article-353900/Hugh-hung-prostitute-shame.html (accessed 21 May 2009).

Bibliography

Manchester Evening News (2002). Bid for 'red light haven'. *Manchester Evening News*, 14 January. Online. Available at: www.manchestereveningnews.co.uk/news/s/40/40602_bid_for_red_light_haven.html (accessed 23 June 2008).

Mansson, S. (2004). Men's practices in prostitution and their implications for social work. In S. Mansson and C. Proveyer (eds), *Social Work in Cuba and Sweden: Achievements and Prospects*. Goteborg/Havanna: Department of Social Work/Department of Sociology. Online. Available at: www.aretusa.net/.../centro%20documentazione/.../c-05Men_practices.doc (accessed 13 November 2008).

Marina, A. B. (1993). Violence and vulnerability: Conditions of work for streetworking prostitutes. *Sociology of Health & Illness*, 15(5), 683–705.

Marino, R., Minichello, V. and Disogra, C. (2004). A profile of clients of male sex workers in Cordoba, Argentina. *International Journal of STD & AIDS*, 15(4), 266–272.

Marshall, G. (1994). *The Concise Oxford Dictionary of Sociology*. Oxford: Oxford University Press.

Mason, J. (2002). *Qualitative Researching*. London: Sage.

Matthews, R. (1986). Beyond Wolfenden? Prostitution, politics and the law. In R. Mathews and J. Young (eds), *Confronting Crime*. London: Sage, 188–210.

Matthews, R. (2005). Policing prostitution: Ten years on. *British Journal of Criminology*, 45(6), 877–895.

Matthews, R. (2008). *Prostitution, Politics and Policy*. Oxon: Routledge-Cavendish.

May, T. (1997). *Social Research: Issues, Methods and Process* (2nd edn). Buckingham: Open University Press.

McGuire, J. (2011). End Prostitution Now campaign backed by thousands of Glaswegians. *TheGlaswegian.co.uk*, 10 March. Online. Available at: www.theglaswegian.co.uk/glasgow-news/news/2011/03/10/end-prostitution-now-campaign-backed-by-thousands-of-glaswegians-102692-22979667/ (accessed 23 August 2011).

McGurran, A. (2006). Ripper: 2 more missing. *Daily Mirror*, 12 December.

McKeganey, N. (1994). Why do men buy sex and what are their assessments of the HIV-related risks when they do? *AIDS Care*, 6(3), 289–301.

McKeganey, N. and Barnard, M. (1996). *Sex Work on the Streets: Prostitutes and their Clients*. Buckingham: Open University Press.

McKewon, E. (2003). The historical geography of prostitution in Perth, Western Australia. *Australian Geographer*, 34(3), 297–310.

McKinstry, B. (2000). Do patients wish to be involved in decision making in the consultation? A cross sectional survey with video vignettes. *British Medical Journal*, 321, 867–871.

McLaughlin, E., Munice, J. and Hughes, G. (2001). The permanent revolution: New Labour, new public management and the modernization of criminal justice. *Criminal Justice*, 1(3), 301–318.

McLella, E., MacQueen, K. and Neidig, J. (2003). Beyond the qualitative interview: Data preparation and transcription. *Field methods*, 15(1), 63–84.

McLeod, E. (1982). *Working Women: Prostitution Now*. London: Croom Helm.

McMillan, D. W. and Chavis, D. M. (1986). Sense of community: A definition and theory. *Journal of Community Psychology*, 14(1), 6–23.

McMullen, M. (2000). *The Baha'i: The Religious Construction of a Global Identity*. New Brunswick: Rutgers University Press.

McNichol, T. (2011). One city takes on a plague of prostitution. *Time U.S.*, 29 March. Online. Available at: www.time.com/time/nation/article/0,8599,2060969,00.html (accessed 23 August 2011).

McTaggart, S. (2007). £4m price tag as sex-trade case collapses. *Yorkshire Evening Post*, 30 March. Online. Available at: www.yorkshireeveningpost.co.uk/news/4m-price-tag-as-sextrade.2192333.jp (accessed 12 September 2008).

Mead, G. H. (1967). *Mind, Self, & Society: From the Standpoint of a Social Behaviorist*. Chicago: University of Chicago Press.

Meher, D. S. (2002). Opportunities and identities: Bridge-building in the study of social movements. In D. Meher, S. N. Whittier and I. Robnett (eds), *Social Movements: Identity, Culture, and the State*. Oxford: Oxford University Press, 3–21.

Melrose, M. (2002). Labour pains: Some considerations on the difficulties of researching juvenile prostitution. *International Journal of Social Research Methodology*, 5(4), 333–351.

Milbourne, L., Macrae, S. and Maguire, M. (2003). Collaborative solutions or new policy problems: Exploring multi-agency partnerships in education and health work. *Journal of Education Policy*, 18(1), 19–35.

Miller, D. (2001). Behind closed doors. In D. Miller (ed.), *Home Possessions: Material Culture Behind Closed Doors*. Oxford: Berg, 1–19.

Milman, B. (1980). New rules for the oldest profession: Should we change our prostitution laws? *Harvard Women's Law Journal*, 3, 1–82.

Mittelmann, L. (2008). 'Help us protect our streets,' petition begs local officials. *TheVillager.com*, 6 August. Online. Available at: www.thevillager.com/villager_275/helpus-protect.html (accessed 17 June 2009).

Moffat, P. and Peters, S. (2004). Pricing personal services: An empirical study of earnings in the UK prostitution industry. *Scottish Journal of Political Economy*, 51(5), 675–690.

Monto, M. (2000). Why men seek out prostitutes. In R. Weitzer (ed.), *Sex for Sale: Prostitution, Pornography and the Sex Industry*. London: Routledge, 67–84.

Monto, M. (2001). Prostitution and fellatio. *The Journal of Sex Research*, 38(2), 140–145.

Monto, M. (2004). Female Prostitution, Customers, and Violence. *Violence against Women*, 10(2), 160–188.

Monto, M. A. (2010). Prostitutes' customers: Motives and misconceptions. In R. Weitzer (ed.), *Sex for Sale: Prostitution, Pornography and the Sex Industry* (2nd edn). New York: Routledge, 233–254.

Monto, M. A. and Garcia, S. (2001). Recidivism among the customers of female street prostitutes: Do intervention programs help? *Western Criminology Review*, 3(2). Online. Available at: http://wcr.sonoma.edu/v3n2/monto.html (accessed 20 June 2013).

Monto, M. A. and McRee, N. (2005). A comparison of the male customers of female street prostitutes with national samples of men. *International Journal of Offender Therapy and Comparative Criminology*, 49(5), 505–529.

Moore, N. (2004). Pop star admits 'kerb crawling'. *Telegraph*, 4 June. Online. Available at: www.telegraph.co.uk/news/1463594/Eighties-pop-star-admits-kerb-crawling.html (accessed 15 June 2008).

Morgan, P. (1988). Living on the edge. In F. Delacoste and P. Alexander (eds), *Sex Work: Writings by Women in the Sex Industry*. London: Virago Press, 21–28.

Mower, M. (2006). *The Way Out Project: The Hull Kerb-Crawler Re-Education Programme Sex as Crime*. The Conservatoire: University of Central England: British Society of Criminology and British Sociological Association Joint Workshop. 5 April 2006. Preston.

Mullan, F., Phillips, R. L. and Kinman, E. L. (2004). Geographic retrofitting: A method of community definition in community-oriented primary care practices. *Family Medicine,* 36(6), 440–446.

Navarro, Z. (2006). In search of a cultural interpretation of power: The contribution of Pierre Bourdieu. *IDS Bulletin,* 37(6), 11–22.

Neuwirth, J. (2005). Inequality before the law: Holding states accountable for sex discriminatory laws under the convention on the elimination of all forms of discrimination against women and through the Beijing platform for action. *Harvard Human Rights Journal, 18*. Online. Available at: www.law.harvard.edu/students/orgs/hrj/iss18/neuwirth.shtml (accessed 22 November 2008).

Newman, O. (1972). *Defensible Space: People and Design in the Violent City.* London: Architectural Press.

New Zealand Herald (2009). Community group squares off with street prostitutes. *New Zealand Herald.* 19 April. Online. Available at: www.nzherald.co.nz/prostitution/news/article.cfm?c_id=612&objectid=10567403&pnum=1 (accessed 3 August 2009).

New Zealand Ministry of Justice (2008). *Report of the Prostitution Law Review Committee on the Operation of the Prostitution Reform Act 2003.* Online. Available at: www.justice.govt.nz/policy-and-consultation/legislation/prostitution-law-review-committee/publications/plrc-report (accessed 21 June 2009).

Nicholson, P. (2007). Operation targets sex trade. *West Yorkshire Police,* 20 March. Online. Available at: www.westyorkshire.police.uk/section-item.asp?sid=12&iid=3252 (accessed 20 March 2007).

Nixon, K., Tutty, L., Downe, P., Gorkoff, K. and Ursel, J. (2002). The everyday occurrence: Violence in the lives of girls exploited through prostitution. *Violence against Women,* 8(9), 1016–1043.

Northern Echo (1998). Kerb-crawling charges. *Northern Echo,* 23 December 2008.

Nuttavuthisit, K. (2007). Branding Thailand: Correcting the negative image of sex tourism. *Place Branding and Public Diplomacy,* 3, 21–30.

O'Connell Davidson, J. (1995). British sex tourists in Thailand. In M. Maynard and J. Purvis (eds), *(Hetero)sexual Politics.* London: Taylor & Francis, 42–64.

O'Connell Davidson, J. (1998). *Prostitution, Power and Freedom.* Cambridge: Polity Press.

O'Connell Davidson, J. (2001). The sex tourist, the expatriate, his ex-wife and her 'other': The politics of loss, difference and desire. *Sexualities,* 4(1), 5–24.

O'Connell Davidson, J. (2003). 'Sleeping with the enemy'? Some problems with feminist abolitionist calls to penalise those who buy commercial sex. *Social Policy and Society,* 2(1), 55–63.

O'Connell Davidson, J. (2007). Sex slaves and the reality of prostitution. *Guardian,* 28 December. Online. Available at: www.guardian.co.uk/politics/2007/dec/28/ukcrime.uk (accessed 29 December 2007).

O'Connell Davidson, J. and Sanchez-Taylor, J. (1999). Exploring the demand for sex tourism. In K. Kempadoo (ed.), *Sun, Sex, and Gold: Tourism and Sex Work in the Caribbean.* Oxford: Rowman & Littlefield Publishers, 37–54.

O'Dell, R. (2003). Police to move forward with naming prostitutes', Hohns. *North County Times,* 15 October. Online. Available at: www.nctimes.com/news/local/article_4b6ea138-77a1-5153-aceb-570b391279d1.html (accessed 16 October 2011).

O'Kane, M. (2002). Mean streets. *Guardian,* 16 September. Online. Available at: www.guardian.co.uk/media/2002/sep/16/crime.comment (accessed 16 March 2005).

O'Neill, M. (1996). *Prostitution and Feminism: Towards a Politics of Feeling.* Cambridge: Polity Press.

O'Neill, M. (1997). Prostitute women now. In G. Scrambler and S. Scrambler (eds), *Rethinking Prostitution: Purchasing Sex in the 1990's*. London: Routledge, 3–28.

O'Neill, M. and Campbell, R. (2002). *Working Together to Create Change: Walsall Prostitution Consultation Research*. Staffordshire and Liverpool: Staffordshire University and Liverpool Hope University.

O'Neill, M. and Campbell, R. (2006). Street sex work and local communities: Creating discursive spaces for genuine consultation and inclusion. In R. Campbell and M. O'Neill (eds), *Sex Work Now*. Cullompton: Willan Publishing, 33–61.

O'Neill, M., Campbell, R., Hubbard, P., Pitcher, J. and Scoular, J. (2008). Living with the other: Street sex work, contingent communities and degrees of tolerance. *Crime, Media, Culture, 4*(1), 73–93.

Okazaki, S. (2002). Influences of culture on Asian Americans' sexuality – Statistical data included. *Journal of Sex Research, 39*(1), 34–41.

Oliver, D., Serovich, J. and Mason, T. (2005). Constraints and opportunities with interview transcription: Towards reflection in qualitative research. *Social Forces, 84*(2), 1273–1290.

One News (2011). Community debates pros and cons of prostitution bill. *One News*, 28 January. Online. Available at: http://tvnz.co.nz/national-news/community-debates-pros-and-cons-prostitution-bill-4009374 (accessed 23 August 2011).

Outshoorn, J. (2005). The political debates on prostitution and trafficking of women. *Social Politics, 12*(1), 141–155.

Overall, C. (1992). What's wrong with prostitution? Evaluating sex work. *Signs, 17*(4), 705–724.

Parliamentary Counsel Office (1981). Summary Offences Act 1981. *New Zealand Legislation*. Online. Available at: www.legislation.govt.nz/act/public/1981/0113/latest/DLM53348.html (accessed 6 June 2012).

Parsons, J. T. (2005). Researching the world's oldest profession: Introduction to the special issue on sex-work research. *Journal of Psychology and Human Sexuality, 17*, 1–3.

Partington, K. (2005). What do we mean by our community? *Journal of Intellectual Disabilities 9*(3), 241–251.

Pateman, C. (1988). *The Sexual Contract*. Cambridge: Polity Press.

Peek, L. (2005). Becoming Muslim: The development of a religious identity. *Sociology of Religion, 66*(3), 215–242.

Penfold, C., Hunter, G., Campbell, R. and Barham, L. (2004). Tackling client violence in female street prostitution: Inter-agency working between outreach agencies and the police. *Policing and Society, 14*(4), 365–379.

Peterson, D. L. and Pfost, K. S. (1989). Influence of rock videos on attitudes of violence against women. *Psychological Reports, 64*, 35–47.

Pheterson, G. (1993). The whore stigma: Female dishonor and male unworthiness. *Social Text, 37*(4), 39–64.

Phoenix, J. (2006). Regulating prostitution: Controlling women's lives. In F. Heidensohn (ed.), *Gender and Justice: New Concepts and Approaches*. Cullompton: Willan Publishing, 76–95.

Phoenix, J. (2008a). ASBOs and working women: A new revolving door? In P. Squires (ed.), *ASBO Nation: The Criminalisation of Nuisance*. Bristol: Policy Press, 289–303.

Phoenix, J. (2008b). Be helped or else! Economic exploitation, male violence and prostitution policy in the UK. In V. Munro and M. D. Giusta (eds), *Demanding Sex*. Surrey: Ashgate, 33–50.

Bibliography

Phoenix, J. and Oerton, S. (2005). *Illicit and Illegal: Sex, Regulation and Social Control*. Cullompton: Willan Publishing.

Pickering, H., Todd, J., Dunn, D., Pepin, J. and Williams, A. (1992). Prostitutes and their clients: A Gambien survey. *Social Science and Medicine, 34*(1), 75–88.

Pitcher, J. and Aris, R. (2003). *Women and Street Sex Work: Issues Arising from an Evaluation of an Arrest Referral Scheme*. London: Nacro.

Pitcher, J., Campbell, R., Hubbard, P., O'Neill, M. and Scoular, J. (2006). *Living and Working in Areas of Street Sex Work: From Conflict to Coexistence*. York: Joseph Rowntree Foundation.

Pitts, M. K., Smith, A. M. A., Grierson, J., O'Brien, M. and Misson, S. (2004). Who pays for sex and why? An analysis of social and motivational factors associated with male clients of sex workers. *Archives of Sexual Behaviour, 33*(4), 353–358.

Plumbrige, L. (2001). Rhetoric, reality and risk outcomes in sex work. *Health, Risk and Society, 3*(2), 199–215.

Plumbrige, E., Chetwynd, S. J., Reed, A. and Gifford, S. J. (1997). Discourses of emotionality in commerical sex: The missing client voice. *Feminism & Psychology, 7*(2), 165–181.

Posner, E. (2002). *Law and Social Norms*. Cambridge: Harvard University Press.

Potterat, J. J., Rothenberg, R. B., Muth, S. Q., Darrow, W. W. and Phillips-Plummer, L. (1998). Pathways to prostitution: The chronology of sexual and drug abuse milestones. *Journal of Sex Research, 35*(4), 333–340.

Prasad, M. (1999). The morality of market exchange: Love, money, and contractual justice. *Sociological Perspectives, 42*(2), 181–213.

Press Association (2007). New crackdown targets kerb-crawlers. *Guardian*, 12 May. Online. Available at: www.guardian.co.uk/uklatest/story/0,,-6627732,00.html (accessed 12 May 2007).

Prideaux, S. (2005). *Not so New Labour: A Sociological Critique of New Labour's Policy and Practice*. Bristol: The Policy Press.

Pruitt, D. and LaFont, S. (1995). For love and money: Romance tourism in Jamaica. *Gender in Tourism, 22*(2), 422–440.

Raphael, J. and Shapiro, D. L. (2004). Violence in indoor and outdoor prostitution venues. *Violence against Women, 10*(2), 126–139.

Rayburn, N. R., Mendoza, M. and Davidson, G. C. (2003). Bystanders' perceptions of perpetrators and victims of hate crime: An investigation using the person perception paradigm. *Journal of Interpersonal Violence, 18*(9), 1055–1074.

Rehle, T., Brinkmann, U., Siraprapasiri, T., Coplan, P., Aiemsukawat, C. and Ungchusak, K. (1992). Risk factors of HIV-1 infection among female prostitutes in Khon Kaen, Northeast Thailand. *Infection, 20*(6), 328–331.

Reimann, A. and Preuss, M. (2007). Influx of prostitutes: Berlin district concerned about sex trade. *Spiegal Online*, 11 January. Online. Available at: www.spiegel.de/international/germany/0,1518,514696,00.html (accessed 17 June 2009).

Rhodes, R. A. W. (1996). The new governance: Governing without government. *Political Studies, 44*(4), 652–667.

Robinson, D. (2005). The search for community cohesion: Key themes and dominant concepts of the public policy agenda. *Urban Studies, 42*(8), 1411–1427.

Robson, T. (2000). *The State and Community Action*. London: Pluto Press.

Rogstad, K. E. (2004). Sex, sun, sea, and STIs: Sexually transmitted infections acquired on holiday. *British Medical Journal, 329*(7459), 214–217.

Romero-Daza, N. and Freidus, A. (2008). Female tourists, casual sex, and HIV risk in Costa Rica. *Qualitative Sociology, 31*(2), 169–187.

Rose, N. (1999). *Powers of Freedom: Reframing Political Thought*. Cambridge: Cambridge University Press.
Ross, B. L. (2010). Sex and (evacuation from) the city: The moral and legal regulation of sex workers in Vancouver's West End, 1975–1985. *Sexualities, 13*(2), 197–218.
Rostron, J. (2006). Vice girl gets ban from city red light zone. *Yorkshire Evening Post*, 29 June. Online. Available at: www.encyclopedia.com/doc/1G1-182321968.html (accessed 21 August 2007).
Rostron, J. (2007). Police sting traps 18 kerb crawlers. *Yorkshire Evening Post*, 24 March 2007.
Rovai, A. P. (2002). Building sense of community at a distance. *The International Review of Research in Open and Distance Learning, 3*(1). Online. Available at: www.irrodl.org/index.php/irrodl/article/view/79/153 (accessed 20 June 2013).
Safer Leeds (2005). Safer Leeds Strategy 2005–2008. *Safer Leeds*. Online. Available at: www.leeds.gov.uk/residents/Pages/Safer-Leeds.aspx (accessed 15 December 2008).
Sagar, T. (2005). Street watch: Concept and practice: Civilian participation in street prostitution control. *British Journal of Criminology, 45*(1), 98–112.
Salfati, C. G., James, A. R. and Ferguson, L. (2008). Prostitute homicides: A descriptive study. *Journal of Interpersonal Violence, 23*(4), 505–543.
Sánchez-Taylor, J. (2001). Dollars are a girl's best friend? Female tourists' sexual behaviour in the Caribbean. *Sociology, 35*(3), 749–764.
Sanders, T. (2004a). A continuum of risk? The management of health, physical and emotional risks by female sex workers. *Sociology of Health & Illness, 26*(5), 557–574.
Sanders, T. (2004b). The risks of street prostitution: Punters, policy and protesters. *Urban Studies, 41*(9), 1703–1717.
Sanders, T. (2005a). 'It's just acting': Sex workers' strategies for capitalizing on sexuality. *Gender, Work and Organization, 12*(4), 319–342.
Sanders, T. (2005b). *Sex Work: A Risky Business*. Devon: Willan Publishing.
Sanders, T. (2005c). The impact of new UK legislation on street-based sex workers: Anti-social behaviour orders. *Research for Sex Work: Sex Work and Law Enforcement, 8*(June), 23–24.
Sanders, T. (2006a). Behind the personal ads: Indoor sex markets in Britain. In R. Campbell and M. O'Neill (eds), *Sex Work Now*. Cullumpton: Willan Publishing, 92–115.
Sanders, T. (2006b). Sexing up the subject: Methodological nuances in researching the female sex industry. *Sexualities, 9*(4), 449–468.
Sanders, T. (2007). The politics of sexual citizenship: Commercial sex and disability. *Disability and Society, 22*(5), 439–455.
Sanders, T. (2008a). Male sexual scripts: Intimacy, sexuality and pleasure in the purchase of commercial sex. *Sociology, 42*(3), 400–417.
Sanders, T. (2008b). *Paying for Pleasure: Men Who Buy sex*. Cullompton: Willan Publishing.
Sanders, T. (2009). Kerbcrawler rehabilitation programmes: Curing the 'deviant' male and reinforcing the 'respectable' moral order. *Critical Social Policy, 29*(1), 77–99.
Sanders, T. and Campbell, R. (2007). Designing out vulnerability, building in respect: Violence, safety and sex work policy. *The British Journal of Sociology, 58*(1), 1–19.
Sanders, T. and Hardy, K. (2010). Research on lap dancing in England: Preliminary findings. *University of Leeds*. Online. Available at: www.sociology.leeds.ac.uk/assets/files/research/events/PreliminaryMediaAug2010.pdf (accessed 10 December 2012).
Sanders, T., O'Neill, M. and Pitcher, J. (2009). *Prostitution: Sex Work, Policy & Politics*. London: Sage.

Sanger, W. (1858). *History of Prostitution: Its Extent, Causes, and Effects throughout the World*. New York: Harper and Brothers Publishers.

Schoepf, B. G. (2001). International AIDS research in anthropology: Taking a critical perspective on the crisis. *Annual Review of Anthropology*, 30(1), 335–361.

Schumacher, M., Corrigan, P. and Dejong, T. (2003). Examining cues that signal mental illness stigma. *Journal of Social and Clinical Psychology*, 22(5), 467–476.

Schwandt, T. A. (1997). *Qualitative Inquiry: A Dictionary of Terms*. London: Sage.

Scott, H. (2003). Stranger danger: Explaining women's fear of crime. *Western Criminology Review*, 4(3), 203–214.

Scott, J., Minichiello, V., Marião, R., Harvey, G. P., Jamieson, M. and Browne, J. (2005). Understanding the new context of the male sex work industry. *Journal of Interpersonal Violence*, 20(3), 320–342.

Scottish Parliament (2002). Prostitution Tolerance Zones (Scotland) Bill, Policy Memorandum, SP Bill 67 – PM (Vol. SP Bill 67 as introduced in the Scottish Parliament on 28 October 2002, Session 1 (2002)). Online. Available at: www.scottish.parliament.uk/business/bills/billsPassed/b67s1pm.pdf (accessed 3 May 2007).

Scoular, J. (2004). The 'subject' of prostitution: Interpreting the discursive, symbolic and material position of sex/work in feminist theory. *Feminist Theory*, 5(3), 343–355.

Scoular, J. and O'Neill, M. (2007). Regulating prostitution: Social inclusion, responsibilization and the politics of prostitution reform. *British Journal of Criminology*, 47(5), 764–778.

Scurlock, B. (2005). *Individual Attitudes towards the Policing of Street Sex Workers within the Chapeltown Policing Division, Leeds: Is the Flesh Willing but the Mind Weak?* Foundation degree in Police Studies: Professional Practice in Policing project module.

Segal, L. (1994). *Straight Sex*. London: Virago.

Seidler, V. J. (1989). *Rediscovering Masculinity: Reason, Language and Sexuality*. London: Routledge.

Self, H. (2003). *Prostitution, Women, and Misuse of the Law: The Fallen Daughters of Eve*. London: Routledge.

Semilong Northampton Residents Group (2009). Prostitution and kerb crawling in Semilong Northampton. *Semilong.org*. Online. Available at: http://semilong.org/prostitution.html (accessed 23 August 2011).

Shapland, J. and Vagg, J. (1988). *Policing by the Public*. London: Routledge.

Sharp, K. and Earle, S. (2002). Cyberpunters and cyberwhores: Prostitution on the internet. In Y. Jenkins (ed.), *Dot. Cons: Crime, Deviance, and Identity on the Internet*. Cullumpton: Willan Publishing, 36–52.

Shaver, F. M. (2005). Sex work research: Methodological and ethical challenges. *Journal of Interpersonal Violence*, 20(3), 296–319.

Shead, K. and Hamilton, J. (2002). Protest over prostitutes hits streets. *Edinburgh Evening News*, 14 November. Online. Available at: http://edinburghnews.scotsman.com/index.cfm?id=1267712002 (accessed 3 May 2006).

Sheptycki, J. (2000). *Issues in Transnational Policing*. London: Routledge.

Shively, M., Jalbert, S. K., Kling, R., Rhodes, W., Finn, P., Flygare, C., Tierne, L., Hunt, D., Squires, D., Dyous, C. and Wheeler, K. (2008). *Final Report on the Evaluation of the First Offender Prostitution Program*. Washington: US Department of Justice.

Shrage, L. (1999). Do lesbian prostitutes have sex with their clients? A Clintonesque reply. *Sexualities*, 2(2), 259–261.

Shumsky, N. and Springer, L. (1981). San Francisco's zone of prostitution, 1880–1934. *Journal of Historical Geography*, 7(1), 71–89.

Sibley, D. (1995). *Geographies of Exclusion: Society and Difference in the West*. London: Routledge.

Sibley, D. (1998). The problematic nature of exclusion. *Geoforum*, 29(2), 119–121.

Sidhu, H. (2009). Local residents bust prostitution racket in Delhi. *Top News in Dehli*, 29 October. Online. Available at: www.topnews.in/local-residents-bust-prostitution-racket-delhi-2230169 (accessed 29 October 2009).

Simmel, G. (2000). The metropolis and mental life. In J. Farganis (ed.), *Readings in Social Theory: The Classic Tradition to Post-Modernism* (3rd edn). New York: McGraw Hill, 149–157.

Smith, J. (1989). *Misogynies*. London: Faber.

Smith, J. (2006). Why British men are rapists. *New Statesman*, 23 January. Online. Available at: www.newstatesman.com/print/200601230006 (accessed 23 January 2006).

Smith, O. and Skinner, T. (2012). Observing court responses to victims of rape and sexual assault. *Feminist Criminology*, 7(4), 298–326.

Snell, J. G. (1994). Mandatory HIV testing and prostitution: The world's oldest profession and the world's newest deadly disease. *Hastings Law Journal*, 45(6), 1565–1592.

Spanier, G. (2008). Stringfellow's laps up profits. *Evening Standard*, 6 August. Online. Available at: www.thisismoney.co.uk/markets/article.html?in_article_id=449128&in_page_id=3&ito=1565 (accessed 3 May 2008).

Spice, W. (2007). Management of sex workers and other high-risk groups. *Occupational Medicine*, 57(5), 322–328.

Spratt, T. (2001). The influence of child protection orientation on child welfare practice. *British Journal of Social Work*, 31(6), 933–954.

Stanton, S. (2011). Community activist concerned motel's sign promotes prostitution on Biscayne Blvd. *The Miami Herald*, 20 June. Online. Available at: www.miamiherald.com/2011/06/20/2275369/community-activist-concerned-motels.html#ixzz1c4NdZkBT (accessed 23 August 2011).

Stedman, R. C. (2002). Toward a social psychology of place: Predicting behavior from place-based cognitions, attitude and identity. *Environment and Behavior*, 34(5), 561–581.

Stoker, G. E. (2000). *The New Politics of Brtish Local Governance*. Bassingstoke: Macmillan.

Stolte, J. F. (1994). The context of satisficing in vignette research. *Journal of Social Psychology*, 134, 727–733.

Suarez, E. and Gadalla, T. M. (2010). Stop blaming the victim: A meta-analysis on rape myths. *Journal of Interpersonal Violence*, 25(11), 2010–2035.

Sullivan, B. (1997). *The Politics of Sex: Prostitution and Pornography in Australia since 1945*. Cambridge: Cambridge University Press.

Sullivan, M. L. and Jeffreys, S. (2002). Legalization: The Australian experience. *Violence Against Women*, 8(9), 1140–1148.

Surratt, H. L., Inciardi, J. A., Kurtz, S. P. and Kiley, M. C. (2004). Sex work and drug use in a subculture of violence. *Crime & Delinquency*, 50(1), 43–59.

Swanson, I. (2010). Prostitute-plagued residents say new Bill fails community. *Edinburgh Evening News*, 25 October. Online. Available at: http://edinburghnews.scotsman.com/edinburgh/Prostituteplagued-residents-say-new-Bill.2821437.jp (accessed 1 December 2010).

Bibliography

Tapaleao, V. (2009a). Renewed call to outlaw street prostitution. *New Zealand Herald*, 15 April. Online. Available at: www.nzherald.co.nz/prostitution/news/article.cfm?c_id=612&objectid=10566667&pnum=1 (accessed 3 August 2009).

Tapaleao, V. (2009b). Sex workers given one month's grace. *New Zealand Herald*, 22 April. Online. Available at: www.nzherald.co.nz/prostitution/news/article.cfm?c_id=612&objectid=10567874&pnum=1 (accessed 3 August 2009).

Tarvainen, S. (2007). The sex worker trade in Spain turns over an estimated 40 billion euros annually, earning it the nickname the 'brothel of Europe'. *Samilia Foundation*. Online. Available at: www.samilia.org/userfiles/files/prostitution,%20Spain.pdf (accessed 12 May 2010).

Taylor, M. (2007). Community participation in the real world: Opportunities and pitfalls in new governance spaces. *Urban Studies, 44*(2), 297–317.

Telegraph. (2004). Rooney admits to having sex with prostitutes. *Telegraph*, 22 August. Online. Available at: www.telegraph.co.uk/news/1469950/Rooney-admits-to-having-sex-with-prostitutes.html (accessed 21 May 2009).

The Christian Institute (2001). Residents win battle to remove 'prostitute zone' from their streets. *The Christian Institute Update, 1*. Online. Available at: www.christian.org.uk/issues/archive_html/Update%20Magazines/art8.htm (accessed 17 June 2009).

The Crown Prosecution Service (2008). Violence against Women Strategy and Action Plans. Online. Available at: www.cps.gov.uk/publications/equality/vaw/vaw_strategy_annex_b.html (accessed 15 June 2008).

The Daily Mail (2006). Prostitutes to get shoe stickers in crime crackdown. *Daily Mail*, 21 August. Online. Available at: www.dailymail.co.uk/pages/live/articles/news/news.html?in_article_id=401609&in_page_id=1770 (accessed 30 February 2007).

The Evening Press (2005). Sex is always going to be sold. *The Evening Press*, 23 February. Online. Available at: http://archive.thisisyork.co.uk/2005/2/23/228882.html (accessed 3 July 2005).

The International Committee on the Rights of Sex Workers in Europe (2005). The Declaration of the Rights of Sex Workers in Europe. Online. Available at: www.scot-pep.org.uk/declaration.pdf (accessed 5 August 2011).

The Leeds Initiative (2006). Going up a league executive: Minutes of the meeting held on 8 March 2006. Online. Available at: www.leedsinitiative.org/initiativeDocuments/2006215_97060794.pdf (accessed 3 June 2006).

The Lord Archbishop of Canterbury (1957). Homosexual offences and prostitution House of Lords debate. HL Deb 04 December 1957 vol 206 cc753–832. Online. Available at: http://hansard.millbanksystems.com/lords/1957/dec/04/homosexual-offences-and-prostitution-1 (accessed 30 May 2009).

The Portugal News Online (2008). Lisbon residents concerned by prostitution. *The Portugal News Online*, 12 July. Online. Available at: www.the-news.net/cgi-bin/article.pl?id=967–25 (accessed 17 June 2009).

The Star (2007). Legal victory for brothel owner. *The Star*, 30 March. Online. Available at: www.thestar.co.uk/news/Legal-victory-for-brothel-owner.2193921.j (accessed 3 December 2007).

The Swish Project (2008). The Swish Project (Sex Workers into Sexual Health) Terrence Higgins Trust. Online. Available at: www.compassunit.com/docs/SWISHproject.doc (accessed 17June 2009).

This is Bristol.co.uk (2011). Community bid to curb prostitution. *This is Bristol*, 25 April. Online. Available at: www.thisisbristol.co.uk/Community-bid-curb-prostitution/story-11239049-detail/story.html (accessed 23 August 2011).

This is Walsall Online (2009). Caldmore residents in call to rid streets of crime. *This is Waslsall Online*, 20 August. Online. Available at: www.thisiswalsallonline.co.uk/news/Caldmore-residents-rid-streets-crime/article-1271258-detail/article.html (accessed 28 August 2009).

Thisisoxfordshire.co.uk (1999). Ex-hooker Fiona teaches kerb-crawlers a lesson. *Thisisoxfordshire.co.uk*, 30 January. Online. Available at: http://archive.thisisoxfordshire.co.uk/1999/1/30/83166.html (accessed 11 June 2008).

Thorpe, K. and Wood, M. (2004). Attitudes to anti-social behaviour. In S. Nicholas and A. Walker (eds), *Crime in England and Wales 2002/2003 Supplementary Volume 2: Crime, Disorder and the Criminal Justice System – Public Attitudes and Perceptions, Home Office, Statistical Bulletin 02/04*. London: Home Office, 41–54.

Tilley, S. A. (2003). 'Challenging' research practices: Turning a critical lens on the work of transcription. *Qualitative Inquiry, 9*(5), 750–773.

Tonnies, F. (1955). *Community and Association (Gemeinschaft und Gesellschaft)/Translated and Supplemented by Charles P. Loomis*. London: Routledge & Kegan Paul.

Travis, A. (2004a). Police chiefs say no to red light 'toleration zones'. *Guardian*, 11 December. Online. Available at: www.guardian.co.uk/uk/2004/dec/11/ukcrime.prisonsandprobation2 (accessed 31 December 2004).

Travis, A. (2004b). Tread warily on vice reform, say police. *Guardian*, 17 July. Online. Available at: www.guardian.co.uk/uk/2004/jul/17/ukcrime.prisonsandprobation (accessed 14 February 2007).

Travis, A. (2004c). Wary Blunkett back prostitution zones. *Guardian*, 16 July.

Travis, A. (2005). New crackdown on prostitution: Plan for licensed 'red light' zones ditched in favour of zero-tolerance strategy. *Guardian*, 28 December. Online. Available at: www.guardian.co.uk/uk/2005/dec/28/ukcrime.immigrationpolicy (accessed 4 January 2006).

Travis, A. (2006). Small worker-run brothels proposed to deter exploitation of prostitutes. *Guardian*, 18 January. Online. Available at: www.guardian.co.uk/uk/2006/jan/18/ukcrime.immigrationpolicy (accessed 20 January 2006).

Traynor, L. (2007). Don't turn a blind eye to our plight over brothels. *Liverpool Echo*.

Troup, J. (2006). How many more are dead? *The Sun*, 12 December.

Tye, D. and Powers, A. M. (1998). Gender, resistance and play: Bachelorette parties in Atlantic Canada. *Women's Studies International Forum, 21*(5), 551–561.

Underwood, M. (2003). Thirty face charge of kerb crawling. *Evening Gazette*, 7 January. Online. Available at: http://icteesside.icnetwork.co.uk/0100news/0001head/kerbthecrawlers/2003/01/07/thirty-face-charge-of-kerb-crawling-50080-12678089/ (accessed 15 June 2008).

Underwood, M. and Doult, B. (2006). Nation follows Tees lead. *Evening Gazette*, 17 January. Online. Available at: http://icteesside.icnetwork.co.uk/0100news/newsarchives/tm_headline=nation-follows-tees-lead&method=full&objectid=16594694&siteid=50080-name_page.html (accessed 2 February 2009).

Valleroy, L. A., MacKellar, D. A., Karon, J. M., Rosen, D. H., McFarland, W., Shehan, D. A., Stoyanoff, S. R., LaLota, M., Celentano, D. D., Koblin, B. A., Thiede, H., Katz, M. H., Torian, L. V. and Janssen, R. S. (2000). HIV prevalence and associated risks in young men who have sex with men. *The Journal of American Medical Association, 284*(2), 198–204.

Van Doorninck, M. and Campbell, R. (2006). 'Zoning' street sex work: The way forward? In R. Campbell and M. O'Neill (eds), *Sex Work Now*. Cullompton: Willan Publishing, 62–91.

Vanwesenbeeck, I., de Graf, R., van Zessesn, G., Straver, C. J. and Visser, J. H. (1993). Protection styles of prostitutes' clients: Interventions, behaviour, and considerations in relation to AIDS. *Journal of Sex Education and Therapy, 19*(2), 79–92.

Wagenaar, H. and Altink, S. (2009). To toe the line: Streetwalking as contested space. In D. Canter (ed.), *Safer Sex in the City: The Experience and Management of Street Prostitution.* Chichester: Ashgate, 155–168.

Wahab, S. (2002). 'For their own good?': Sex work, social control and social workers, a historical perspective. *Journal of Sociology and Social Welfare, 29*(4), 39–57.

Wainwright, M. (2000). Kerb-crawler schools runs short of clients. *Guardian Unlimited. Guardian,* 24 January. Online. Available at: www.guardian.co.uk/uk_news/story/0,,237229,00.html (accessed 9 July 2007).

Walkowitz, J. (1980). *Prostitution and Victorian Society.* Cambridge: Cambridge University Press.

Walsh, C. (2003). Spearmint's bottom line? £2.3m profit. *Observer,* 2 March. Online. Available at: www.guardian.co.uk/business/2003/mar/02/theobserver.observerbusiness (accessed 3 May 2008).

Walzer, M. (2002). The concept of civil society. In M. Walzer (ed.), *Toward a Global Civil Society.* Oxford: Berghahn Books, 7–28.

Ward, H., Mercer, C. H., Wellings, K., Fenton, K., Erens, B., Copas, A. and Johnson, A. M. (2005). Who pays for sex? An analysis of the increasing prevalence of female commercial sex contacts among men in Britain. *Sexually Transmitted Infections, 81*(6), 467–471.

Waugh, R. (2006). Despair of girl thrown on to the streets. *Yorkshire Evening Post,* 21 January. Online. Available at: www.yorkshiretoday.co.uk/ViewArticle2.aspx?SectionID=55&ArticleID=1423930 (accessed 7 July 2007).

Weber, M. (1978). Economy and society. In G. Roth and C. Wittich (eds), *An Outline of Interpretive Sociology.* Berkeley: University of California, 212–299.

Websdale, N. (1999). The social construction of 'stranger danger' in Washington State as a form of patriarchal ideology. In J. Ferrell and N. Websdale (eds), *Making Trouble: Cultural Constructions of Crime, Deviance and Control.* New York: Aldine De Gruyter, 91–114.

Weeks, J. (1981). *Sex, Politics and Society: The Regulation of Sexuality since 1800.* Harlow: Longman.

Weeks, J. (2007). *The World we have Won: The Remaking of Erotic and Intimate Life.* London: Routledge.

Weitzer, R. (1999). Prostitution control in America: Rethinking public policy. *Crime, Law and Social Change, 32*(1), 83–102.

Weitzer, R. (2005). New directions in research on prostitution. *Crime, Law and Social Change, 43*(4–5), 211–235.

Weitzer, R. (2007a). Prostitution as a form of work. *Sociology Compass, 1*(1), 143–155.

Weitzer, R. (2007b). The social construction of sex trafficking: Ideology and institutionalization of a moral crusade. *Politics Society, 35*(3), 447–475.

Weitzer, R. (2009). *Sex for Sale: Prostitution, Pornography, and the Sex Industry* (2nd edn). New York: Routledge.

Wellman, B. (1999). The network community: An introduction to networks in the global village. In B. Wellman (ed.), *Networks in the Global Village: Life in Contemporary Communities.* Oxford: Westview Press, 1–48.

Wesley, J. K. (2002). Growing up sexualized. *Violence Against Women, 8*(10), 1182–1207.

Bibliography 195

West Yorkshire Police (2005). First ASBO tackling prostitution in Leeds. *West Yorkshire Police*, 20 April. Online. Available at: www.westyorkshirepolice.uk/section-item.asp?sid=12&iid=1448 (accessed 30 May 2006).

West Yorkshire Police (2006). Twenty eight charged following vice operation. *West Yorkshire Police*, 13 June. Online. Available at: www.westyorkshire.police.uk/section-item.asp?sid=12&iid=2350 (accessed 13 June 2006).

West Yorkshire Police (2007a). News: Holbeck urban village. *West Yorkshire Police*, 21 December. Online. Available at: http://wypnpt.org/NPT.asp?id=58 (accessed 5 April 2007).

West Yorkshire Police (2007b). Operation targets sex trade. *West Yorkshire Police*, 20 March. Online. Available at: www.westyorkshire.police.uk/section-item.asp?sid=12&iid=3252 (accessed 5 April 2007).

Westheimer, J. (1998). Conceptualizing community: Problems and possibilities for research on teachers' work. *Journal of Research in Education, 8*(1), 9–15.

Wheeler, R. (2009). Prostitute patrols launched by locals in Berkshire town. *The Mirror*, 27 October.

Whowell, M. (2010). Male sex work: Exploring regulation in England and Wales. *Journal of Law and Society, 37*(1), 125–144.

Williams, F. (2005a). New Labour's family policy. In M. Powell, L. Bauld and K. Clarke (eds), *Social Policy Review 17: Analysis and Debate in Social Policy on Behalf of the Social Policy Association*. Bristol: Polity Press, 289–302.

Williams, K. (2005b). 'Caught between a rock and a hard place': Police experiences with the legitimacy of street watch partnerships. *The Howard Journal, 44*(5), 527–537.

Wilson, A. (2011). Residents' anger at prostitutes and drugs in Peddie Street, Dundee. *The Courier*, 26 November. Online. Available at: www.thecourier.co.uk/News/Dundee/article/12230/residents-anger-at-prostitutes-and-drugs-in-peddie-street-dundee.html (accessed 23 August 2011).

Wilson, J. Q. and Kelling, G. (1982). Broken windows: The police and neighbourhood safety. *Atlantic Monthly, 249*(3), 29–38.

Winchester, H. P. M. and White, P. E. (1988). The location of marginalised groups in the inner city. *Environment and Planning D: Society and Space, 6*(1), 37–54.

Wintour, P. (2008). Harman: Poll shows public support for ban on buying sex. *Guardian*, 4 September. Online. Available at: www.guardian.co.uk/politics/2008/sep/04/harrietharman.socialcare?gusrc=rss&feed=networkfront (accessed 9 September 2008).

WMUR (2007). Manchester residents complain of prostitution problem: Neighbors record names, license plates. *WMUR New Hampshire*, 7 May. Online. Available at: www.wmur.com/news/13272426/detail.html (accessed 17 June 2009).

Wolfenden, J. S. (1957). *Report of the Committee on Homosexual Offences and Prostitution*. London: HMSO.

Wong, M. L., Chan, R. K. W., Koh, D., Barrett, M. E., Chew, S. K. and Wee, S. S. H. (2005). A comparative study of condom use and self-reported sexually transmitted infections between foreign Asian and local clients of sex workers in Singapore. *Sexually Transmitted Diseases, 32*(7), 439–445.

Woodward, W. (2007). Harman calls for prostitution ban to tackle trafficking. *Guardian*, 21 December. Online. Available at: www.guardian.co.uk/politics/2007/dec/21/uk.ukcrime (accessed 21 December 2007).

Worley, C. (2005). 'It's not about race. It's about the community': New Labour and 'community cohesion'. *Critical Social Policy, 25*(4), 483–496.

Wortley, S., Fischer, B. and Webster, C. (2002). Vice lessons: A survey of prostitution offenders enrolled in the Toronto John School diversion program. *Canadian Journal of Criminology, 44*(4), 369–402.

Wright, S., Sims, P. and Rayner, G. (2006). How many more has he killed? *Daily Mail*, 12 December.

Wright, T. (1997). *Out of Place: Homeless Mobilization, Subcities and Contested Landscapes*. New York: State University of New York Press.

Xantidis, L. and McCabe, M. P. (2000). Personality characteristics of male clients of female commercial sex workers in Australia. *Archives of Sexual Behaviour, 29*(2), 165–176.

Xu, Y., Fiedler, M. L. and Flaming, K. H. (2005). Discovering the impact of community policing?: The broken windows thesis, collective efficacy, and citizens' judgement. *Journal of Research in Crime and Delinquency, 42*(2), 147–186.

Yamin, K. (1999). Jakarta's brothel closedown sends industry underground. *Asia Times Online*, 24 December. Online. Available at: www.atimes.com/se-asia/AL24Ae01.html (accessed 17 June 2009).

Young, I. M. (1995). *The Ideal of Community and the Politics of Difference*. Philadelphia: Temple University Press.

Yuval-Davis, N. (2011). *The Politics of Belonging: Intersectional Contestations*. London: Sage.

Zhou, J. (2006). Chinese prostitution: Consequences and solutions in the post-Mao era. *China: An International Journal, 4*(02), 238–262.

Index

Aberdeen 138
abolitionist approach 10–11
Abreu, J. M. 46
Abu-Lughob, L. 5
abuse of young women 58
action and resistance 12–13
action groups 99–101; Action Group on Prostitution, Leeds 40; Islington Action Group, New Zealand 117
active citizenship 21, 22, 120–1
activism, implications 21, 119–22; accountability and legitimacy 119–20; active citizenship and belonging 120–1; NIMBYISM and displacement 121–2
Adams, L. 110
Afro-Caribbean residents 42, 43, 76, 160
Agar, M. 50
Agustin, L. M. 15
Akerlof, G. A. 158
Alcock, P. 22
Alexander, C. 76
Altink, S. 138
AMMAR, Argentina 56
Ancient Greece/Ancient Rome, brothels in 57
Ancient Rome, brothels in 57
Andrew, R. 139
anti-prostitution protests 97, 98, 99, 106, 107
Anti-Social Behaviour Orders (ASBOs) 125, 126, 130, 131
Aral, S. 73
Argentina 56, 57
Aris, R. 121
ASBOs *see* Anti-Social Behaviour Orders (ASBOs)
Asian men, perceptions of 75–6
Association of Chief Police Officers 129, 140–1

Asylum and Immigration Act 2004 35
attitudes, community 9–12, 43, 54–77; towards clients 66–76; divided 38; towards prostitutes 57–66; prostitution as oldest profession 54–7; *see also* clients, perceptions of; prostitutes, perceptions of
audio research 46, 50–1
Augustin, L. 58–9
Australia: employment rights for sex workers 56–7; indoor prostitution 145–6, 147

Baeva, N. 102
Bagguley, P. 76
Baker, L. M. 125
Baldock, L. 58, 108
Balsall Heath, Birmingham 82; community action 102, 108, 120
Band of Gold (TV series) 28
Banks, M. 46
Bao, J. 74
Barlow, C. 29
Barnard, M. 46, 64, 66, 70, 71, 72, 126
Barratt, D. 25
Barry, K. 10
Barter, C. 45
Bartley, P. 55, 57
Barton, B. C. 28
Bassermann, L. 55, 77n1
Batalla-Duran, E. 163
bathhouses 23
Bauman, Z. 9, 153
Bayley, D. 13
Beck, U. 3, 26, 61
Begum, S. 75, 108
Bellah, R. N. 5
Bellis, M. A. 10, 38, 54, 137, 138
belonging 120–1

Belza, M. J. 66
Benson, C. 125
Bentley, T. 5
Berkshire 88
Berlin 81
Berman, J. 94
Bernardo, F. M. 73
Berney, L. 121, 145–6
Bernstein, E. 29, 110, 112
Berrington, E. 64
Bible, existence of prostitution in 55, 57
'Big Society' (David Cameron) 22
Birmingham 82, 83, 88, 98, 102, 138
black market 149
Black privilege, perception of 21
Blaikie, N. 47
Blair, E. 27
Bloor, M. J. 2, 16, 67
Blunkett, D. 30, 138
Bolton, 104, 137
bondage 71
'bottom-up' social movement-based strategy 20
Bourdieu, P. 116
Bournemouth 33
Boxer, P. 46
Bradford 97, 98
Bradford Freedom Charity 12
Brain, T. 138, 141
Bras, K. 67
Brehman, B. 15, 19, 38, 43, 54
Brents, B. G. 2, 29, 146, 147, 148, 149
Bristol 32, 104
British Crime Survey 42
British National Party (BNP) 21
Brixton, London 20
Brock, D. R. 82
'broken windows' theory 82
Brooks-Gordon, B. 23, 24, 26, 27, 36n1, 45, 122, 125, 132
brothels 16, 23, 28, 29, 56, 57, 75; action against 102, 116, 141; closing of 145; licensed 30, 145, 146; offence of brothel-keeping 141, 142; owners of as crime prevention source 95–6
Brown, A. 25
Brown, L. 19, 73
Browne, K. 57
Bruce, S. 38
Buckingham, D. 152
Buckley, T. 84, 109
Burnley riot (2001) 21
business representatives, local 38, 49–52; socio-demographics 50

Butler, J. 152

Cabezas, A. L. 67
Calder, G. 3, 7, 18n3
Cameron, D. 22
Campbell, C. 69, 72
Campbell, R. 14, 62, 70, 71, 78, 90–1, 103, 124, 126, 132, 133, 137, 138, 140, 155
Cantle, T./*Cantle Report* 21
Cardiff 4, 97, 120
Carey, L. 102
Carpenter, B. 71
Carroll, B. E. 23, 26
Carter, S. 163
Carter, S. P. 1
Chambers, C. T. 46
Chan, W. 63
Charon, J. M. 9
Chavis, D. M. 5
Cheryl, S. 45
Cindi, J. 139
cities, revitalization 3
citizenship, active 21, 22, 120–1
City Island (US) 81
Clark, P. 137
Clarke, J. 7
Clarke, R. 107, 122
Clarkson, A. 55
Clayton, S. 152, 156, 162
clients, perceptions of: 'genuine' vs. violent 38; as hypocritical Muslim men 75–6; as main 'problem' 124–5; as men 23, 66–7, 75–6; motivations *see* motivations of client, perceptions; as sexual deviants 26; as threat 26, 31; as weak and powerless 23
Closure Orders, Policing and Crime Act 2009 145
Coaker, V. 33, 34, 141
Coalition government, UK 22
Cohen, A. 5, 53n1
Cohen, D. 46
Coker, E. M. 157–8
cold-calling technique 42, 47
Coleman, A. 107
Collier, J. and M. 46
Colosi, R. 60
'common prostitute,' term 35
communitarianism 7
community: action *see* community action; attitudes 9–12, 54–77; common characteristics 6; concept, as problematic 103–4, 107; crime prevention programmes 21, 37–8;

definitions 5–6, 8, 9; engagement, and prostitution policy 19–22; exploring 2–5; geographically based notions 41; group leaders 42; impact of prostitution on 78–96; locating 5–7; non-participant observation of meetings 46; and prostitution policy 19–36; researching 37–53; social obligations 7–9; and stigma management 155–6; traditional communities 8

community action: action groups 99–101; anti-prostitution protests 97, 98, 99, 106, 107; characteristics of activists 110–12; concern for female residents 112–13; implications of activism 119–22; naming and shaming 75, 107–9; and police 4, 102, 107–8, 109; rationale for 109–19; removing the problem 113–16; and resistance 12–13; responding to state and police inaction 116–19; and social class 106, 110–12; street marches 100–1; types 98–109; violence and vigilantism 101–3

Community and Association (Tonnies) 8–9
computer sex 16, 27
condom use 64, 148; environmental waste, residential concerns 79, 83, 84
Contagious Diseases Acts 1864, 1866 and 1869 64
Coordinated Prostitution Strategy, A (Home Office, 2006) 3, 4, 10, 30, 31–2, 33, 131
Cotton, A. 43, 63
Cowburn, M. 155
Coy, M. 72, 125, 133, 164
Craig, K. 46
Craig-Henderson, K. M. 46
Crawford, A. 2, 3–4, 13, 19–20, 22, 98, 107, 122
Cresswell, T. 82
crime displacement 121–2
crime prevention: community programmes 21, 37–8; Crime Reduction Partnerships 7; situational 122; and street prostitution 95–6
Crime Reduction Partnerships 7
crime reduction strategy 21
criminal gangs and networks 58
Crocker, J. 153
Croucher, S. 95
CROWE (Concerned Residents of the West End), Vancouver 99
cultural context 163–4; and social order 13–15

Curry, T. J. 73
Cusick, L. 62, 121, 145–6
cycle of decline, street prostitution seen as encouraging 81–3

Dahles, H. 67
de Albuqurque, K. 67
de Bruxelles, S. 127
Declaration of Human Rights for Sex Workers initiative 56
decline, cycle of 81–3
decoy officers 125, 129, 130
Delhi, violent action against brothel 101–2, 116
Della Giusta, M. 160
dependency and sexual needs, perceived motivations of client 70–1
Desiree Alliance, US 56
Development and Planning department, Leeds 47
Devine-Wright, P. 152, 156, 162
direct sex work 16
dirt and disease, associations of sex work with 64–5; stigma 155, 158
disabled residents, propositioning of 86–7
disadvantaged communities 21
displacement, and NIMBYISM 121–2
Dodge, M. 125
dominatrix services 2, 16
Dominelli, L. 155
Doncaster 130, 139
Donovan, B. 16
Douglas, M. 165
Doult, B. 134
Dovkants, K. 119
drug addiction, and prostitution 59–60, 83–4, 131
Duncan, N. 63
Dundee, street prostitution and residential concerns 79
Durkheim, E. 8
Dynes, W. R. 57

Eagleton, T. 36n2
Earle, S. 11, 68
Edelstein, J. 45, 92
Edensor, T. 153
Edinburgh 84, 106, 137; police and local government responses 137, 138, 139
Edwards, A. 20, 21, 22
Edwards, R. 40
Edwards, S. M. 78
Elifson, K. W. 2, 16, 67

employment rights, sex workers 56–7
enforcement-led approach 124–7
English Collective of Prostitutes 34, 56, 102
entertainment, prostitution viewed as 95
environmental debris, and street prostitution 78, 83
escort agencies 16, 27, 66
ethnic background: Afro-Caribbean residents 42, 43, 76, 160; Muslim background, perceptions of clients as having 75–6; of pimps 93–4; stigma 159–60
ethnographic research 142
Etzioni, A. 7
excitement and fun, perceived motivations of client 69–70
experimentation, sexual 70

Facebook groups 99
family values 25, 26, 76
fantasies 71
Farley, M. 27, 28, 160
Favell, A. 121
female sex buyers 67
female sex-worker, male client stereotype 57–8, 67
feminism 10, 12, 26, 27, 58
fetish work 2, 16
Field, J. 79, 81
Fielding, N. 5
Fitzgerald, L. 63
Flick, U. 45
Flint, J. 106
focus groups 43, *44*, 45–6; audio research 46; group norms and shared values 45; transcription 50–1; vignettes, use of 45–6
Forced Marriage (Civil Protection) Act 2007 12
Ford, K. 57
For Your Eyes Only (lap-dance club), west London 27–8
Fotiou, R. D. 76
Foucault, M. 116, 152
Fox, J. 64
Freidus, A. 67
Fremeaux, I. 7
Freund, M. 160
Friedman, M. 6
frustration, sexual 70
Fyle, D. M. 24

Gabor, T. 121

Gabriel, A. 40
Gadalla, T. M. 63
Garcia, S. 134
Garland, D. 21
Gates, J. 81, 85
Gelthorpe, L. 23, 24, 26, 27, 125, 132
Gemeinschaft (Community) 8–9; *see also* community; community action
Gemme, R. 71
gender bias, in 1950s 25
gentlemen's clubs 29
gentrification 105–6
geographical distance and the self 162–4
Germany 57, 137, 145
Gesellschaft (Society of Individuals and Association) 8–9
Gibbens, T. C. N. 70, 72
Gibbs, A. 45
Giddens, A. 26
Gilmore, D. 119
Giobbe, E. 93
Glasgow 97, 138
Goddard, L. 138
Goffman, E. 14, 18, 52, 79, 151, 153–5, 156, 157, 160
Goody, J. 27
Goodyear, M. D. E. 62
governance 120–1
Gräbener, J. 104–5
Grant, H. 31
gratification, sexual 71
Greer, C. 33
Groom, T. M. 66
Gülçür, L. 58
Gutierrez, J. P. 72

habitus 116
Hale, S. 18n2
Hall, S. 25
Hamilton, F. 39, 133
Hamilton, J. 93
Hamilton, P. 41
Hammond, N. 2, 52, 53, 67
Hamnett, C. 106
Hampshire 134
Hancock, L. 21, 111
Harcourt, C. 2, 16
Hardy, K. 2, 56
Hare, B. 40
Harman, H. 34
Harrison, S. 57
Harvey, P. 130
Haslam, D. 6
'hate crime' 62

Hausbeck, K. 2, 29, 146, 147, 148, 149
Hawtin, M. 5, 6
Hay, C. 62
Hazel, N. 45
Heater, D. 120
Helmore, E. 31
Helsinki 81, 88
Henry Jay, B. 45
Herbert, S. 82
Herold, E. 67
Heslett, C. 40, 47
Hester, M. 1
Hill, M. 45
Hirst, P. 22
Hiscock, J. 31
HIV/AIDS 64
Holloway, W. 89
home, symbolic nature of 157
Home Office 6, 41, 129
Home Office publications: *A Coordinated Prostitution Strategy* (2006) 3, 4, 10, 30, 31–2, 33, 131; *Paying the Price* (2004) 2–3, 7, 30–1, 32, 130, 138; *A Review of Sexual Offences* (1998) 29; *Setting the Boundaries* (2000) 30; *Tackling Demand for Prostitution: A Review* (2008) 34; *UK Action Plan on Tackling Human Trafficking* (2007) 35
Howell, P. et al 24
Hubbard, P. 1, 2, 3, 6, 18n1, 23, 24, 28, 75, 78, 82, 83, 88, 93, 94, 98, 100, 104, 106, 107, 121, 125, 137, 139, 149, 151, 159
Huby, M. 45, 46
Hughes, G. 20, 21, 22, 45, 104
Hughes, R. 45, 46
Hull 134, 135
human trafficking *see* trafficking, human
Hussain, Y. 76
Hylton, C. 76
hyper-masculinity 76

ideal relationship model 26
identity: as fluid and evolving 152, 153; mistaken *see* mistaken identity; personal vs. social 157; space and place 156–7; 'spoiled' 151, 153, 155; and stigma management 152–3, 156–7
ideology 27, 36n2
Ilkkaracan, P. 58
image, street prostitution 78, 79–81
Imrie, R. 3, 7
in-depth interviews 68
indirect sex 16
individual, stigma management 155–6

indoor sex work/prostitution 3, 23, 24; and choice 59; less of a 'public nuisance,' perception of 143–5; local community benefits 96; 'quasi-legal' position 141; and recreational drugs 60; *Regina v John Barrett* 142; support for legalization 145–50; tolerating 141–50, 164–5
infections, sexually transmitted 64–5, 147
information gathering 95–6
International Committee on the Rights of Sex Workers in Europe 56
interviews 37, 38, *43*, 47, 48, 68; transcription 50–1; unrecorded 51–2
intimacy in long-term relationship, lack of 69
Ipswich murders (2006) 61–2, 84
Islamic Defenders Front, Jakarta 75, 102, 116–17
Islington Action Group, New Zealand 117

Jaccarino, M. 82
Jacobs, J. 107
Jakarta, activism in 75, 102, 116–17
Jakobsson, N. 14–15, 19, 38, 43, 54, 160
Jansson, K. 42–3, 93
Jefferson, T. 89
Jeffreys, S. 10, 11, 28, 55, 94, 147
Jenness, V. 11
Jewkes, Y. 33
John Moores University, Liverpool 138
'John Schools' (kerb-crawler re-education programmes) 132, 135
Johnson, A. 66
Johnson, A. M. 57, 66
Johnston, J. 45
Johnston, L. 13, 101, 123n1
Jones, H. 64
Jones, P. 28
Jones, T. 13, 121
Jordan, J. 66, 68, 69, 70, 71, 72

Kaminer, W. 26
Kantola, J. 25, 30, 35, 97, 151, 166
Kearns, A. 120
Kelling, G. 82
Kelly, L. 57
Kelly, V. 160
Kennedy, M. A. 135
Kentucky Street Watch Owls, California 99
kerb-crawler re-education programmes 130, 132–41; initial (1998) 39–40; scepticism 133–5

kerb-crawling 3, 62, 77, 125, 129, 161; arrests 125, 130; being mistaken for kerb crawler 89–91; construction of offence 26–7; 'costs more than you think' campaign (New Labour, 2007) 32–4; focusing on 114–15; intimidation resulting from 87–8; naming and shaming 107–9; New Labour and prostitution policy 30–1; offence of 125, 150n1; persistence requirement 27, 107, 108, 114, 125, 127, 150n1, 150n2; as policing focus 129–32; typologies 135–7; *see also* kerb-crawler re-education programmes
Kesler, K. 11, 18n4, 58
Kilvington, J. 137
Kimmel, M. S. 73
Kingston, S. 16, 30, 52, 54, 58, 124
Kinnell, H. 14, 27, 39, 62, 71, 72, 96, 126, 155
Kinsey, R. 13
Kirby, K. 159
Kitzinger, J. 46
Koskela, H. 46, 88, 89, 92
Kotsadam, A. 14–15, 19, 38, 43, 54, 160
Kulick, D. 2, 16
Kurtz, S. P. 47, 62

labour rights, sex workers 56
LaFont, S. 67
Langer, G. 67
Lapadat, J. 50
lap-dancing 2, 16, 27–8, 149
Las Vegas, Nevada 15, 38, 147, 148
Lawler, S. 142, 152
Lawrence, J. 73
Lazaridis, G. 67
Leahey, E. 45
Lee, A. K. 46
Lee, R. 37
Leeds: Community Safety audit (2003) 93; 'dumping ground' 106–7; first Anti-Social Behaviour Order issued in (2005) 126; kerb-crawler re-education programme piloted in (1998–1999) 130, 132–3; kerb-crawling campaign (2007) 33; neighbourhood protests 97; Operation Rampart 141, 142; pimps in 93–4; research conducted in 6, 38, 39–41; tolerance zones 139
Leeds Community Safety/Leeds Community Safety Partnership Boards 47
Leeds Metropolitan University, Research Centre for Violence, Abuse and Gender Relations 132
Leeson, P. T. 158
Leigh Docks, Edinburgh 139
Lewis, P. 61–2
Lim, L. L. 95
Lindsay, A. 50
Link, B. G. 153, 154, 156
Linnane, F. 24, 56, 57
liquid modernity 9
Lisbon 80
Liska, A. 93
Liverpool 97, 102; police and local government responses to community concerns 130, 137, 138; Residents Against Prostitution group 116
Loader, I. 13
local government 38, 62; civil injunctions obtained by 150n3; local authority officials 47–8, 115; and police *see* police and local government responses to community concerns
Local Government Act 1972 27, 150n3
London: kerb-crawling campaign (2007) 32; neighbourhood protests 97; street prostitution and residential concerns 79; For Your Eyes Only (lap-dance club) 27–8
loneliness, perceived motivation of client 68–9
Lonsway, K. 63
Lopez-Jones, N. 139
Lorway, R. 57
Lowman, J. 62, 121
Luken, J. N. 74

MacKinnon, C. 10
MacQueen, K. M. 5
MacTaggart, F. 31, 138, 141, 142
Mahmoud, H. 157
male employees, fear of pimps 91, 92–4
male prostitutes/sex workers 2, 57
man, client perceived as 66–7
managed zones 138
Manchester 139
Manhattan, propositioning of women in 88
Mansson, S. 136
Marina, A. B. 68
Marino, R. 64
marital status of client 72
marriage, perceptions of in 1950s 24
Marshall, G. 5
Martsin, M. 157

masculinity, and motivation for buying sex 70–1
Mason, J. 46, 51
massage parlours 16, 27, 28, 144
Matthews, R. 1, 11, 25, 27, 32, 43, 55, 56, 64, 78–9, 88, 97–8, 103–4, 106, 113–14, 116, 124, 125, 129, 131, 137, 139, 143
May, T. 47
McCabe, M. P. 69
McGuire, J. 92
McGurran, A. 61–2
McKeganey, N. 46, 64, 66, 68, 70, 71, 72, 126
McKewon, E. 113–14
McKinstry, B. 46
McLaughlin, E. 5
McLella, E. 51
McLeod, E. 68
McMillan, D. W. 5
McMullen, M. 153
McNichol, T. 89, 92, 99
McRee, N. 72, 136
McTaggart, S. 141, 142
Mead, G. H. 9
meetings (community), non-participant observation 46
Meher, D. S. 13, 14
Melrose, M. 37
"mental patient" label 154
Michael, A. (*formerly* Lord Williams of Mostyn, Deputy Home Secretary) 29
Middlesbrough 32, 130, 134
migration, vs. trafficking 58–9
Milbourne, L. 21
Miller, D. 8
Milman, B. 55
mistaken identity 85–91; being mistaken for a prostitute 86–9; being mistaken for kerb crawler 89–91; intimidation 87
Mittelmann, L. 84, 88, 108, 114
Moffat, P. 66
monogamous relationships 26
Monto, M. 16, 54, 70, 71
Monto, M.A. 72, 134, 136
Moonlite Bunny Ranch, Las Vegas 149
Moore, N. 130
'moral panic' 29, 62
moral values 76, 83
Morgan, J./Morgan Report 20
Morgan, P. 45
motivations of client, perceptions 68–76; dependency and sexual needs 70–1; excitement and fun 69–70; girlfriend experience, desire for 68–9; loneliness 68–9; masculinity 70–1; specific sexual acts, engagement in 71–6
Mower, M. 132, 134, 135
Mullan, F. 6, 41
'multi-agency' approach 20, 21, 131–2
multiple selves 153
murder of prostitutes 62; *see also* Ipswich murders (2006); violence; 'Yorkshire Ripper' murders (1980s)
Muslim background, perceptions of clients as having 75–6
myths, prostitution 63, 131

naming and shaming 75, 107–9
Nandwani, R. 66
Nationality, Immigration and Asylum Act 2002 35
naturalism 50–1
Navarro, Z. 116
Netherlands: employment rights for sex workers 57; indoor prostitution 145; prostitution as part of tourist industry 94, 164; red-light district 67; tolerance zones 137–8
Network of Sex Work Project, UK 56
Neuwirth, J. 127
Nevada (US): indoor prostitution 145; Nevada Brothel Association 149; prostitution as part of tourist industry 94; red-light district 67
Newburn, T. 13, 121
Newham Asian Women 12
New Labour 20, 21; co-ordinated prostitution strategy 31–2; 'kerb-crawling costs more than you think' campaign (2007) 32–4; *Paying the Price* (consultation paper 2004) 2–3, 7, 30–1, 32, 130; and prostitution policy 2, 29–36; *Tackling Demand for Prostitution: A Review* (2008) 34–6
Newman, O. 107
New Sociologies of Sex Work (Kingston and Sanders) 16
New Zealand 88; community action 99, 102, 108–9, 117
Nicholson, P. 40, 99
NIMBY (Not In My Back Yard) approach, and displacement 121–2
Nixon, J. 106
Nixon, K. 62
non-commercial sexual relationship, inability to form 11, 69
non-contact sexual services 28

non-participant observation of community meetings 46
normalization of sex industry 15, 29
Northampton 80, 134, 137
Nottingham 134, 138
nuisance, prostitution as 25, 83–5, 97; indoor prostitution seen as less of a 'public nuisance' 143–5
Nuttavuthisit, K. 94–5

occupational risks 61
O'Connell Davidson, J. 11, 12, 18n4, 34, 67, 73, 110, 164
O'Dell, R. 54
Oerton, S. 24, 30, 36n1, 129, 131
O'Kane, M. 46, 126
Okazaki, S. 75
oldest profession, prostitution seen as 54–7
Oldham riot (2001) 21
Old Testament, selling of sexual favours in 57
Oliver, D. 50–1
O'Neill, M. 11, 32, 33, 37, 78, 82, 90–1, 114, 124, 140
Operation Rampart, Leeds 141, 142
Others, sex workers as 104, 159
Outshoorn, J. 11, 26
Overall, C. 15, 55

Pakistani culture 73
Parsons, J. T. 55
Partington, K. 5
partners, interviews with 37
Pateman, C. 10
Paying the Price (consultation paper 2004) 2–3, 7, 30–1, 32, 130, 138
payment for commercial sex, incidence of 66–7
Peek, L. 153
Penfold, C. 62, 125
performance, identity as 152
persistence requirement 35, 36, 97; kerb-crawling 27, 107, 108, 114, 125, 127, 150n1, 150n2
Peston, J. 119
Peterborough 32
Peters, S. 66
Peterson, D. L. 46
Pfost, K. S. 46
Phelan, J. C. 153, 154, 156
Pheterson, G. 155
Phoenix, J. 11, 12, 24, 30, 36n1, 129, 131, 132
phone sex 27

Phuket, red-light district 67
physical degradation 71
Pickering, H. 68, 71, 72
pimps/pimping: ethnic background of pimps 93–4; fear of pimps 91, 92–4; 'legitimized pimping' 27; and violence 62
Pitcher, J. 1, 10, 37, 46, 54, 78, 87–8, 121, 125, 138, 139, 159
Pitts, M. K. 70
place, importance of 156–7
Plumbrige, E. 71
Plumbrige, L. 71
Plymouth 138
police 13; arrest of prostitutes in nineteenth century 64; and community action 4, 102, 107–8, 109, 118–19; inaction, responding to 116–19; informal relationships with brothel owners/independent workers 95–6; interviews 48–9; and local government *see* police and local government responses to community concerns; socio-demographics of officers 49; street sex workers, policing of 126–9; on violence against sex workers 62
Police and Criminal Evidence Act 1984 (PACE) 20
police and local government responses to community concerns 124–50; differing priorities 125–6; indoor prostitution, tolerating 141–50; kerb-crawlers as policing focus 129–32; sex workers, policing 126–9; street prostitution, policing 124–32; tolerance zones 137–41
Policing and Crime Act 2009 9–10, 35, 145, 149, 150n1, 150n2
popular culture, sexualisation from 1990s 28–9
pornography 28–9, 145
Posner, E. 74
Potterat, J. J. 60
Powers, A.M. 161
Prague: prostitution as part of tourist industry 94, 164; red-light district 67
Prasad, M. 70
Preston 138; street prostitution and residential concerns 79, 81
Pretty Woman (film) 28
Preuss, M. 81
Prideaux, S. 7
promiscuity, sexual 63
property values, effect of presence of prostitution on 40, 80–1

prostitutes, perceptions of 38, 57–66; choice and agency 58–60; 'common prostitute,' term 35; as dirty and diseased 64–5, 155, 158; divided attitudes 38; as drug-dependent 59–60; and gender 43; putting themselves in danger 60–2; rape myths 63–4; as sexual Others 104, 159; sympathy for plight 65–6; as wanting easy money 60; as women 57–8

prostitution: entertainment, viewed as 95; history 55–6, 57; illicit nature, as part of attraction 70; impact on communities 78–96; indoor, tolerating 141–50; mistaken identity 85–91; motivations for choice of work 11–12, 59–60; moving from one place to another 126, 133; myths 63; as part of tourist industry 94; perception of as oldest profession 54–7; policy *see* prostitution policy; as public nuisance 25; secretive nature 37; sensitive nature of 37; vs. sex work 16; street *see* street prostitution; tolerance of 10, 43, 137–50, 164–5; traditional forms 16; where known to exist 40–1; *see also* prostitutes, perceptions of; sex workers

prostitution policy: and community 19–36; and New Labour 2, 20, 29–36; socio-legal context of UK 22–9

Pruitt, D., 67

'public decency,' offending 24, 165

purposive sampling 47, 49

questionnaires 38

Raco, M. 3, 7
radical feminism 11, 26, 27
rape myths 63–4
Raphael, J. 47
Rayburn, N. R. 46
reconviction/re-offending rates 132, 134
recreational drugs, and prostitution 59–60, 83–4, 131
redevelopment 105, 106
red-light districts 67, 93, 97
Regina v John Barrett decision 142
Rehle, T. 16
Reimann, A. 81
relationship status of client 72
Renold, E. 45
reputation, street prostitution 78, 79–81
Research Centre for Violence, Abuse and Gender Relations, Leeds Metropolitan University 132

research of community 37–53; Afro-Caribbean residents 42, 43, 76; cold-calling technique 42, 47; description of areas under review 40, 42; difficulties 42, 51–2; ethnographic 142; fieldwork 40, 41; focus groups 43, *44*, 45, 45–6, 50–1; interviews 37, 38, *43*, 47, 48, 50–2, 68; local authority officials 47–8; local business representatives 49–52; methodological approaches/techniques 37, 38; nature of sex work research 37, 52–3; police officers 48–9; research project and aims 38; residents, accessing 41–7; sampling techniques 47, 48, 49, 51; site of research 6, 39–41; stakeholder groups 6–7

resident groups 98, 99; *see also* community action

residents, accessing 41–7; community group leaders 42; finding 'common ground' 41–2; focus groups 43, *44*, 45–6, 50–1; interviews 47, 50–1; non-participant observation of community meetings 46; socio-demographics 42–3, *44*

Residents Against Prostitution, Liverpool 116

Review of Sexual Offences, A (Home Office, 1998) 29

Rhodes, R. A. W. 3, 21
riots (2001) 21
'Risk Society' 61
Robinson, D. 40
Robson, T. 8
Rogstad, K. E. 163
Romero-Daza, N. 67
Rooney, W. 31
Rose, N. 3, 5
Ross, B. L. 99
Rostron, J. 130
Rovai, A. P. 5–6

sadomasochism 71
Safer Cities programme 20
Safer Communities: The Local Delivery of Crime Prevention through the Partnership Approach (*Morgan Report*) 20
Sagar, T. 1, 4, 10, 37–8, 93, 98, 100, 102, 104, 108, 109, 110, 118, 119, 120
Salfati, C. G. 62
Salik, S. 108
sampling techniques 47, 48, 49, 51
Sánchez-Taylor, J. 11, 67, 164

Index

Sanders, T. 1, 2, 3, 11, 13, 14, 15, 16, 23, 25, 26, 28–9, 37, 53, 58, 60, 62, 64, 67, 68, 69, 70, 72, 74, 93, 94, 100, 108, 110, 121, 126, 130, 133, 134, 135, 137, 141, 142, 155
San Francisco 135
Sanger, W. 55–6, 77n1
Scarlet Alliance (Australian sex workers' association) 56
Scarman Report (1981) 20
Schoepf, B. G. 154
Schumacher, M. 46
Schwandt, T. A. 51
Scotland 99
Scott, H. 89
Scott, J. 57
Scoular, J. 18n4, 124
Scurlock, B. 126, 139
Secret Diary of a Call Girl (TV series) 28
Segal, L. 27, 62
Seidler, V. J. 26
self 9; and geographical distance 162–4
Self, H. 24
self-responsibility 21, 128–9
Semilong Northampton Residents Group 99
semi-structured interviews 38, 47
Setting the Boundaries (Home Office, 2000) 30
Sex and Exploitation Survey (2008) 10
sex drive 23, 70, 133
sex hot-spots 102
sex industry: attitudes to 10; negative aspects 58; 'normalization' of, in media 28; and prostitution as oldest profession perception 56; research challenges 37; and sexualisation of popular culture 28–9; violence in, public perceptions of 27; *see also* clients, perceptions of; prostitutes, perceptions of; prostitution
sexual abuse 62
sexual acts, perceptions of client motivations 71–6; buying sex as a leisure activity 72–3; relationship status 72; social status 73–4
sexual deviants, clients seen as 26
sexual experimentation 70
sexual fantasies 71
sexual frustration 70
sexual gratification 71
sexual liberation movement (1960s) 26
sexually transmitted diseases, perceptions of 64–5, 147
Sexual Offences Act 1956 25
Sexual Offences Act 1985 27, 35, 125, 145, 150n1
Sexual Offences Act 2003 35, 127, 145, 150n1
sexual predator laws, US 29
sexual promiscuity 63
sexual revolution 23
sexual stimulation 71
'sex wars' 26
sex workers 2; in pre-1950s 23; in 1950s 24; arrests for soliciting 125; employment rights 56–7; nature of research 37, 52–3; policing of 126–9; prostitution vs. sex work 16; registration of 30; secretive nature of sex work 37; as victims 115, 124–5, 129, 130, 131; and violence 62, 102; zero tolerance policy against 30–1, 137; *see also* prostitution
Shapiro, D. L. 47
Shapland, J. 110
Sharp, K. 11, 68
Shaver, F. M. 37, 53
Shead, K. 93
Shearing, C. 13
Sheffield 79
Sheptycki, J. 13
Shively, M. 135
Shrage, L. 66
Shumsky, N. 107
Sibley, D. 158
Sidhu, H. 116
Silverman, M. 70, 72
Simmel, G. 8, 95
single men as clients 72
Skinner, T. 63
sleep disruption 84
Smith, J. 27, 34, 62, 73
Smith, O. 63
Smith-Miles, C. 102
Snell, J. G. 55
snowball sampling 47, 49
social class, and community action 106, 110–12
social distancing 154, 155, 157–60
social order 13–15
social status of client 73–4
socio-demographics: business representatives, local 50; community residents 42–3, *44*; local authority officials 48; police officers 49
socio-legal context of UK 19, 22–9; pre-1950s 23; reports, regulation and legislation in 1950s 24–5;

kerb-crawling, construction of offence in 1970s and 1980s 26–7; reconstructing client as threat in 1960s 26; sexualisation of popular culture from 1990s onwards 28–9; strip-club boom in 1990s 27–8; indoor sex workers 23, 24
Soho, London 118–19
Sokulsky, L. 117
soliciting 24, 125
South Africa 56
Southall, London 79
Southall Black Sisters 12
Southampton 32, 79, 130
Spanier, G. 28
spatial boundaries, street prostitution 82
Spearmint Rhino (strip club) 28
specialist services 71
speed bumps 91, 105
Spice, W. 60
'spoiled' identity 151, 153, 155
Spratt, T. 45
Springer, L. 107
Squires, J. 25, 30, 35, 97, 151, 166
stag parties 72–3, 76–7; and stigma 160–1
Stanton, S. 58
state inaction, responding to 116–19
Stedman, R. C. 156
stereotypes 15, 37, 154; female sex-worker, male client 57–8
stigma/stigma management 64, 151–66; geographical landscape and socio-spatial management 162–4; identity 152–3, 156–7; individual and community 155–6; research 37, 52; social distancing 154, 155, 157–60; stigma-neutralizing techniques 160–1; and street prostitution 78, 79–80; visibility and space 164–6; 'whore stigma' 14
stimulation, sexual 71
STIs (sexually transmitted diseases), perceptions of 64–5, 147
Stoke, community action 79
Stoker, G. E. 21
Stolte, J. F. 46
Storr, M. 126, 132, 133, 155
Strayer, J. 46
street marches 100–1
Street Offences Act 1959 24, 25, 35
street patrols 116
street prostitution: in 1950s 24; and Asian men 75; and children 85; community campaigns against 40; and crime *see* street prostitution and crime; cycle of decline 81–3; 'designing out' 103–7,

126; and drug addiction 59–60, 83–4, 131; enforcement against (1970s and 1980s) 124; and environmental debris 78, 83; fear of those involved in 91–4; impact on local communities 3, 80; local economies and entertainment 94–5; negative impacts 78–94; noise and nuisance associated with 83–5; perceived as source of the 'problem' 129; policing 124–32; positive impacts 94–6; rape myths 63–4; removal from residential streets 137; reputation and image 78, 79–81; sex workers, policing 126–9; as source of embarrassment 79; and spatial boundaries 82; spatial tolerance on street 139–41; and stigma 78, 79–80; unorganized 143; visible presence of prostitutes 85, 139; zero tolerance policy against 137
street prostitution and crime: likelihood of other crimes being committed 81–2; prevention of crime and information gathering 95–6
Street Watch (local community crime prevention initiative) 4, 37–8, 98, 101, 110, 120
strip-clubs, boom in 1990s 27–8
Suarez, E. 63
Sullivan, B. 26
Sullivan, M. L. 147
Summary Offences Act 1981 (New Zealand) 117
Surratt, H. L. 60
Sutcliffe, P. 27, 38, 39, 62, 103
Swanson, I. 99
Swedish policy 34
Swedish Prohibiting the Purchase of Sexual Services Act 1999 10
Sweet Project, *Violent Incident Report* (2007) 62
Symbolic Interactionism 9

Tackling Demand for Prostitution: A Review (2008) 34, 34–6
Tani, S. 46, 88, 89, 92
Tapaleao, V. 83, 85, 99
Tarvainen, S. 108
Taylor, M. 21
Thailand 67, 94–5, 164
Thatcher, M. 20, 27
"Third World" countries, travel to 164
Thorpe, K. 111
Tilley, S. A. 50
Tisak, M. 46

Index

tolerance of prostitution: indoor prostitution 141–50, 164–5; tolerance zones 38, 106, 137–41
Tonnies, F. 8–9
Toronto, John School diversion programme 135
trafficking, human 34, 35, 141; vs. migration 58–9
transcription of interviews/focus groups 50–1
transgendered prostitutes 2, 16, 57
transsexual prostitutes 2, 16, 57
Travis, A. 31, 138
Traynor, L. 116
Troup, J. 61–2
Tweed, J. 27
Tye, D. 161

UK Action Plan on Tackling Human Trafficking (Home Office, 2007) 35
Underwood, M. 130, 134
United States (US) 29, 99

Vagg, J. 110
Valleroy, L. A. 2, 16
Vancouver, Canada 99
Van Doorninck, M. 124, 137, 138
Vanwesenbeeck, I. 68, 71, 72
venereal disease, perceptions of 64–5
Vera, H. 73
victims, sex workers seen as 115, 124–5, 129, 130, 131
Victorian period 23, 55
vigilantism 75, 84, 93, 115, 116; and violence 101–3, 119; *see also* community action
vignettes, use of 45–6
violence: as daily hazard 62; responsibility for avoiding 60–1; in sex industry, public perceptions of 27; and vigilantism 101–3, 119
Violent Incident Report (2007), Sweet Project 62

Wagenaar, H. 138
Wahab, S. 10, 26
Wainright, M. 132
Walkowitz, J. 23, 64
Walsall, community action 79
Walsh, C. 28
Walzer, M. 8
Ward, H. 57, 66, 73
Waugh, R. 47
Weber, M. 158
Websdale, N. 29
Weeks, J. 24, 25, 36n1, 65, 166
Weitzer, R. 11–12, 16, 26, 35, 56, 59, 132
Wellman, B. 6
Wesley, J. K. 47
Westheimer, J. 5
Westmarland, N. 1
Wheeler, R. 88, 99
White, P. E. 106, 107
'whore stigma' 14
Whowell, M. 2, 57
Wickens, E. 67
Williams, K. 1, 4, 10, 38, 98, 100, 101, 108, 115, 118, 119, 120
Wilson, A. 58, 79
Wilson, J. Q. 82
Winchester, H. P. M. 106, 107
Wintour, P. 10
Without Consent (Her Majesty's Crown Prosecution Service Inspectorate report (2007) 91
Wolfenden, J. S. 24, 25, 165
Wolfendon Report (1957) 24, 25, 30
women: fear of being propositioned on the street 86–9, 91–2; prostitutes perceived as 57–8; as sexual commodities (radical feminist position) 11; Western, privileged economic status 11
Wong, M. L. 64
Wood, M. 111
Woodward, W. 34
word-for-word transcription 51
Worley, C. 5
Wortley, S. 135
Wright, S. 61–2
Wright, T. 157

Xantidis, L. 69
Xu, Y. 82

Yamin, K. 75, 117
'Yorkshire Ripper' murders (1980s) 26–7, 38, 62
Young, I. M. 5, 8
Yuval-Davis, N. 121

zero tolerance policy against sex workers 30–1, 137
Zhou, J. 95